ongress Cataloging in Publication Data

Ralph, 1900–
nd remodeling guide for home interiors.

hed in 1956 under title: Remodeling
me interiors.
gs—Remodeling.   I. Title.
8   1973   643'.7   72-13413
-015222-5

2 3 4 5 6 7 8 9 0   K P K P   7 6 5 4 3

*The editors for this book were William G. Salo, Jr., and Lydia Maiorca Driscoll,
and its production was supervised by
Teresa F. Leaden. It was set in Intertype Baskerville
by The Maple Press Company.
It was printed and bound by The Kingsport Press.*

Repairing and
Guide for Ho

PLANNING, MATERIA

J. Ralph Dalze

SECOND EDITION

Revised by **FREDERICK S. MERRITT**
Consulting Engineer

Library of C

Dalzell, James
  Repairing a

First publi
guide for ho
  1. Dwelli
TH4816.D
  ISBN 0-07

McGRAW-HILL BOOK COMPANY

New York   St. Louis   San Francisco   Düsseldorf   Johannesburg
Kuala Lumpur   London   Mexico   Montreal   New Delhi
Panama   Rio de Janeiro   Singapore   Sydney   Toronto

Contents

Preface to the Second Edition

Since the original edition, *Remodeling Guide for Home Interiors,* was prepared by the late J. Ralph Dalzell, numerous changes in homebuilding and remodeling practices have occurred. Consequently, extensive changes were required for the second edition, and much new material had to be added, while obsolete text and illustrations had to be deleted.

The most notable development since the first edition has been the increased emphasis on control of indoor environment. With materials and equipment now available, it is feasible to remodel older houses to provide high-quality lighting and air conditioning at reasonable costs. To reflect this development, two chapters have been added in the second edition to explain how such remodeling can be done.

Another notable development has been the availability of many new interior-finish materials. To explain in detail the application of all, or even many, of these in this book would be impracticable. Instead, emphasis in this edition, as in the original, has been placed on the most commonly used materials and those whose application is similar to that of a wide class of materials.

The new edition also reflects the changes that have taken place in standard sizes of materials. For example, new standard nominal sizes for lumber were introduced since the first edition was published. Also, most wall panels now come in 48-inch widths. This change alone has required that the chapter on walls be completely rewritten.

As for the first edition, many thanks are due a host of manufacturers for their help and advice in the preparation of the second edition. In addition, special acknowledgment must be made of the assistance of Ralph Torop, Chief Engineer, Forman Air Conditioning Company, New York City, who wrote the new chapter on air conditioning.

Frederick S. Merritt

Preface to the First Edition

This book was written in response to the tremendous interest in house remodeling encountered among homeowners, mechanics, and real estate people. Such interest is continuing to grow. Some of the more important reasons for its growth are set forth in the following paragraphs.

First, there are the eternal dreams of comfortable and beautiful houses planned to suit the particular needs of families. More often than not, even extensive remodeling is a great deal cheaper than new houses.

Second, there are the desires to use and to enjoy the modern and labor-saving equipment now available for kitchen and laundry activities. There are also desires to enjoy modern bathroom fixtures and a host of other devices, all of which make comfortable and modern living possible. In most cases, some remodeling is necessary before new equipment, fixtures, and devices can be used to the best advantage. For example, many old houses have ceilings which are too high in terms of modern kitchen cabinets.

Third, there are the desires to create and to enjoy new recreation rooms, additional bedrooms for growing families, kitchens with planned work centers, bathrooms which can be used by two people with privacy and at the same time, additional closets and storage spaces, and several other such innovations, which make homes much more serviceable and comfortable.

Fourth, there are the desires to modernize all interior walls, ceilings, and floors. Many new and beautiful materials are available for such purposes. There are also materials available for specific purposes such as nursery and play rooms, where fingerprints and other soil must be taken into consideration.

Finally, because of attachments and associations, many families do not want to leave old neighborhoods in order to enjoy all of the previously mentioned desires in new houses located in "garden" or "development" areas. The answer to this is remodeling.

Most of the older houses, especially those which are from 30 to 40 or more years old, are of sound construction that can be depended upon for many more years. Such houses need only interior remodeling to make them compare favorably with new houses. With such a fact in mind, this book is devoted to the simple but effective interior remodeling operations which most people are capable of doing.

Remodeling is a fascinating project for homeowners. Perhaps no other aspect of homemaking produces the pleasure and comfort made possible by the simple suggestions and procedures set forth in this book. Drab, uninteresting, inefficient and tiring old houses can be transformed into beautiful and pleasant areas where housework is greatly reduced, where there is ample space for all activities, and where modern living can be enjoyed to the fullest extent.

The remodeling suggestions and the how-to-do-it instructions set forth in this book were planned and are explained in such a manner that homeowners can do all of their remodeling work as financial budgets allow. In other words, remodeling work need not be done all at one time. The various improvements can be planned as a whole but carried out as financial ease permits.

Each of the chapters in this book is a story in itself. For example, the basement chapter is devoted to only such suggestions and instructions as pertain to the remodeling of such areas. However, it is advisable for readers to become acquainted with all of the chapters prior to the time they start to plan any particular project. In this manner, all of the important and related considerations will be understood.

This book makes a special effort to point out and explain considerations which must be applied to any remodeling project. For example, the basement chapter contains thorough explanations in connection with frequently overlooked problems and unexpected expense. Readers are urged to evaluate their remodeling plans accordingly.

In any remodeling project, large or small, careful planning must be done before the actual or manipulative work is started. Without such planning many disappointments, delays, and added expenses are likely. This book gives special emphasis to planning, and readers are urged to pay particular attention to it. Never start a remodeling project until such planning as described in this book has been carefully done.

In addition to carefully planning all remodeling projects, readers are urged to obtain preliminary cost estimates, as described in the kitchen chapter, and then to determine if such expense is worthwhile, as described in the basement chapter.

This book contains a great many remodeling suggestions which pertain to all parts of house interiors. However, readers are urged to peruse shelter magazines and manufacturers' literature all as a means of better and more effective planning. The magazines are available at news stands and the literature at lumber yards or manufacturers' show rooms. Literature can also be obtained by writing directly to manufacturers. Their names and addresses appear in magazine ads.

Each of the major remodeling, maintenance, and repair projects explained in this book are set forth in terms of typical problems and their answers. All instructions are in the how-to-do-it form which readers can use as a guide. The various procedures are explained in regular order and by means of procedures recommended by manufacturers and approved of by most city and town building codes.

The author wishes to thank a host of manufacturers for their help and advice during the time this book was being written. He also wishes to thank the many contractors and builders who contributed many and helpful manipulative procedures.

CHAPTER ONE

Woods

A good basic knowledge of the characteristics and types of woods is invaluable in connection with any form of carpentry work, especially remodeling. The selection of suitable woods has a great bearing on costs, working procedures, and ultimate results.

An expensive grade of lumber is not always necessary or best for a given project; in many instances a cheaper grade may do as well or better. In fact, some of the cheaper grades, especially if they are to be painted or otherwise hidden from view, have the stiffness and other qualities necessary to assure the most durable construction.

Wise selection of woods involves giving careful thought to the requirements of a project. Good judgment in this connection yields high returns in satisfaction. After the requirements have been determined, it is relatively easy to select proper grades of woods. For example, we may be led to believe that a wood of high strength is necessary for a given project, whereas what we actually need are good painting qualities and weather-resisting properties. Or we may think that high strength is necessary, whereas stiffness, dryness, and minimum shrinkage are actually the important points to consider.

There are many other considerations, such as workability, which we should take into consideration before making a selection of woods for a specific purpose. Therefore, the purpose of this chapter is to assist in a careful estimation of the essential requirements for different remodeling purposes, to show how the different kinds of woods meet such requirements, and to emphasize some of the principles frequently overlooked.

1

KINDS OF LUMBER

The trees commonly cut into ordinary lumber are divided into two broad groups: *hardwood* and *softwood*. Strangely enough, the term hardwood does not always refer to a tree whose wood is hard. Actually, there is no definite or exact means of determining the difference between many trees so far as softness and hardness are concerned. However, many of the so-called softwood trees have wood which is softer than several of the so-called hardwood trees. The custom has developed of calling the coniferous trees softwood, and the broad-leaved trees hardwood. Coniferous trees, generally called *evergreens,* are those with needles or scale-like leaves. Broad-leaved trees are generally called *deciduous* because they shed their leaves each autumn.

Softwoods. The lumber industry includes the following trees in the softwood group:

Cedar	Hemlock	Redwood
Cypress	Larch	Spruce
Douglas fir	Pine	

Hardwoods. The lumber industry includes the following trees in the hardwood group:

Ash	Cherry	Maple
Basswood	Chestnut	Oak
Beech	Elm	Poplar
Birch	Gum	Walnut

Availability of Lumber. The lumberyards in various sections of the country are apt to stock the kinds of lumber that are grown and cut closest to them. This practice saves on transportation expense and makes for more economical lumber prices. Therefore, it is always a good practice to visit local lumberyards to see what kinds of lumber are in stock.

HARDNESS OF LUMBER

Hardness is the property that makes a surface difficult to dent, scratch, or otherwise mar. The harder the wood, the better it resists wear and the better it can be finished or polished. However, the hardwoods are generally difficult to work with and should therefore be used only for flooring or other uses where *wearing* qualities are important.

For ordinary building purposes, carpenters like some woods because of their softness and uniformity rather than because of their hardness. Northern white pine, Douglas fir, basswood, sugar pine, redwood, and ponderosa pine are typical examples. The ease with which these woods can be sawed, planed, and nailed has made them most popular for general use, particularly where remodeling work is involved.

GRAIN OF LUMBER

The *A* part of Figure 1 indicates annual growth rings in a typical log. When such rings are narrow or close together, as in slow-growing trees, the wood is known as *close-grained*. When they are wide and farther apart, as in rapidly growing trees, the wood is known as *coarse-grained*. For example, *close grain* is used to describe such woods as birch, pine, and maple, all of which have smooth surfaces. *Coarse grain* is used to describe such woods as oak, walnut, and chestnut, all of which have slightly rough surfaces.

A log is first sawed along the lines *ab*, *bd*, *dc*, and *ca* to produce a square section such as shown in the *B* part of the illustration. The square section is finally sawed into such typical boards as shown at *C* and *D*. Small patterns of the growth rings can be seen in the boards. Depending upon the size of a log and upon the width of boards, various other growth ring patterns, known as *grain* and illustrated at *E*, *F*, and *G*, are created.

When the grain in a board forms an angle of 45 degrees or more with its side faces, as shown in board *E*, the lumber is described as *vertical grain* in softwoods and as *quartersawed* in hardwoods. When the grain in a board forms an angle of 45 degrees or less with its side faces, as shown in board *F*, the lumber is described as *flat grain* in softwoods and *plain-sawed* in hardwoods. *Mixed grain* is indicated in board *G*. Vertical-grain lumber is the strongest.

Side views of grain patterns, such as shown in the *H* part of the illustration, also indicate important characteristics. The straight-grained board is the stronger of the two and should be used for structural details which

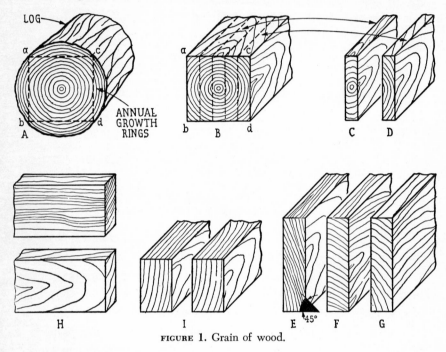

FIGURE 1. Grain of wood.

must support portions of a house. The other board could be used for panels or other facings where its irregular grain is decorative.

We should also examine lumber grain pattern at the top of lumber, as indicated at *I*. Of the two pieces shown, the straight-grained one is likely to be the stronger and more durable. The other, with its grain running off to one side, may split if used as a support.

SHRINKAGE AND SWELLING

In remodeling work, where we often place new wood alongside of or in connection with older wood, it is most important that the new wood be free of shrinkage or swelling tendencies. This is highly important from the standpoint of avoiding ceiling and wall defects, as described in Chapters 4 and 5.

Wood, like many other fibrous materials, shrinks as it dries and swells as it absorbs moisture. As a rule, however, much of the shrinkage and swelling of wood in service is unnecessary and can be avoided by using wood that has been dried to the right moisture content.

In all kinds of wood the shrinkage or swelling in the width of a flat-grained board is nearly twice that of an edge-grained board of the same width. Edge-grained wood of a kind having a high shrinkage will therefore prove as satisfactory as flat-grained stock of the kind with inherently lower shrinkage. Wood has practically no shrinkage or swelling lengthwise of the grain.

In the following, several common woods are classified according to their probable amount of shrinkage as they change from wet to dry conditions.

CONSIDERABLE SHRINKAGE

Ash	Birch	Larch
Basswood	Elm	Maple
Beech	Gum	Oak

MEDIUM SHRINKAGE

Cherry	Douglas fir	Poplar
Chestnut	Hemlock	Spruce
Cypress	Pine	Walnut

LITTLE SHRINKAGE

| Cedar | Redwood |

The foregoing classifications according to the amount of shrinkage do not tell the whole story of the shrinkage of different woods. About half the shrinkage is "taken out" of wood through air seasoning and about two-thirds by thorough kiln drying. The taking out of shrinkage in the amounts mentioned is sufficient for the ordinary uses to which wood is put in any remodeling project. Shrinkage does not always stay out when mositure is reabsorbed, but the important thing is to have it taken out prior to the time the wood is built into a house. The rate at which drying and shrinkage occur in different kinds of wood is very important in practical usage. A wood that has a relatively low total shrinkage may dry so slowly that, in actual practice, it commonly gets into use before the proper amount of shrinkage has been taken out. Pieces of some woods, such as larch, cypress, and redwood, frequently are slow to dry and therefore slow to shrink to their ultimate condition. Such pieces are apt to give a greater amount of trouble from shrinkage than the classification previously given indicates. The only remedy consists of making sure that such lumber is dry before being put to use.

How to Recognize Dry Lumber. There are several rule-of-thumb tests which we can employ as a means of recognizing dry lumber.

1. Dry lumber is apt to have small and brittle slivers on it.
2. Dry lumber produces a hollow sound when rapped with the knuckles of the hand.
3. Dry lumber weighs less than moist or wet lumber.
4. Moist or wet lumber has a sharper odor.
5. Dry lumber has more springiness.
6. Moist or wet lumber feels damp to the touch.

FREEDOM FROM WARPING

The warping of wood is closely allied with shrinkage and causes many of the same defects in ceilings and walls. Lumber that is cross-grained, such as shown at *C* in Figure 1, tends to warp, or twist out of shape, when it shrinks. Warping can be reduced to a minimum by the use of quartersawed wood.

In the following, several common woods are classified according to their tendency to warp as they change from wet to dry conditions:

CONSIDERABLE WARPING

Beech   Elm   Gum

SLIGHT WARPING

Ash	Cypress	Pine
Basswood	Douglas fir	Poplar
Birch	Hemlock	Redwood
Cedar	Larch	Spruce
Cherry	Maple	Walnut
Chestnut	Oak	

EASE OF WORKING

For some purposes the ease with which woods can be worked, so far as hand tools are concerned, is negligible. For others, and in most cases, the smoothness and facility with which they can be worked have a decided influence on the quality of finished projects. This is especially true where inexperienced mechanics are concerned.

In the following, several common woods are classified according to ease of working:

EASY TO WORK WITH

Basswood	Pine
Cedar	Poplar

DIFFICULT TO WORK WITH

Ash	Cherry	Larch
Beech	Douglas fir	Maple
Birch	Elm	Oak

MEDIUM DIFFICULT TO WORK WITH

Chestnut	Gum	Spruce
Cypress	Hemlock	Walnut
	Redwood	

PAINT HOLDING

Paint holds better on edge-grained or quartersawed wood than it does on flat-grained wood. Knots in pine do not retain paint as well as the sound knots of cedar, hemlock, or larch. Among the flat-grained boards, the bark side is more satisfactory for painting than the side which was nearer to the center of a tree. Under exposure to the weather, cedar, cypress, and the pines hold paint to excellent advantage in any climate. Hemlock can be depended upon in mild climates. Douglas fir and larch cannot hold paint as well as the woods previously mentioned.

STIFFNESS OF LUMBER

As previously mentioned, stiffness of lumber is often of more importance than what is called *breaking strength*. For example, joists made from practically any kind of lumber will safely support a floor if they are 2 by 8 or 2 by 10 inches in size, if they are spaced no more than 16 inches apart, and if bridging is installed between them. But unless the wood has ample stiffness, plaster cracking, as mentioned in Chapters 4 and 5, would surely occur.

If lumber lacks stiffness, it tends to bend or deflect when subjected to a load. For example, if floor joists do not have ample stiffness, they will bend a little each time a piece of furniture is moved across a floor they support. Such bending subjects plaster to stresses it cannot resist and it cracks as a result. Lack of stiffness in floor joists is also likely to cause vibration in a floor as it is walked on. This is another cause of plaster cracks.

The wood used for wall studs must also be stiff in order to resist tendencies of walls to bend under the weights of floors above them.

Differences in stiffness between kinds of wood may be compensated for by changing the size of such structural details as floor joists. Height and length of such details have a greater effect on their stiffness than on strength properties. A change of $\frac{1}{32}$ inch in the thickness of a standard $\frac{25}{32}$-inch board produces a change of 12 per cent in the stiffness of the board laid flat in a floor. A 2- by 10-inch joist has about one-fourth more wood in it than a 2- by 8-inch joist, but it is more than twice as stiff.

Stiffness is little affected by such defects as knots. Thus, where house remodeling work is concerned, lumber of sound but knotty grades may safely be used.

In the following, several common woods are classified according to stiffness:

HIGH STIFFNESS

Ash	Cherry	Maple
Beech	Elm	Oak
Birch	Hemlock	Pine
Douglas fir	Larch	Walnut

MEDIUM STIFFNESS

Basswood	Gum	Redwood
Cypress	Poplar	Spruce

LOW STIFFNESS

Cedar	Chestnut

FIGURE IN WOOD

The choice of woods for woodwork (trim) that are to have a natural finish (varnish or wax) is usually based upon the character of the figure or pattern of grain in the woods. Figure is due to different causes in the various woods. In woods like yellow pine and Douglas fir it results from the contrast within the growth rings; in others, such as oak and beech, it results from flakes in addition to the growth rings; in maple, walnut, and birch it results from wavy or curly grain, etc. Except where the figure in wood results from flakes, the figure is more pronounced in plain-sawed lumber than in quartersawed.

In the following, several common woods are classified according to the amount of figure they contain:

HIGHLY FIGURED

Ash	Douglas fir	Larch
Chestnut	Elm	Oak
Cypress		Pine

MODULATED FIGURE

Beech	Gum	Redwood
Birch	Hemlock	Spruce
Cherry	Maple	Walnut
	Poplar	

LITTLE FIGURE

Basswood	Cedar

HOW TO AVOID SHRINKAGE DEFECTS

When new walls, floors, and other structural details are being added to existing houses, the woods used must be exceptionally dry. Otherwise, several undesirable shrinkage defects are probable. For example, new walls and floors may shrink enough to be out of plumb or out of level so far as the old walls and floors are concerned. Also, severe plaster cracks may appear at points where old and new walls meet. Thus, the use of exceptionally dry wood is a matter of first consideration in any major remodeling project.

In general, careful observance of the following rules will help materially to prevent shrinkage defects:

1. Secure exceptionally dry lumber and keep it in that condition prior to and during remodeling operations.

2. Use paint or other protective coatings as soon as possible. Such coatings seal woods and eliminate moisture absorption.

3. Select woods having low inherent shrinkage.

4. Wherever possible, use vertical-grain or quartersawed lumber in preference to the flat-grain type.

DRESSED LUMBER

Most of the lumber used in ordinary remodeling projects is *surfaced* on both sides and both edges. Such lumber is known as *dressed* lumber because it is ready for use without reworking so far as its sides and edges are concerned.

When lumber is dressed, it is reduced from the size it was when it left the sawmill. For example, a piece 2 inches thick and 8 inches wide is known as a 2 by 8. When it is dressed, the planing (surfacing) reduces it to 1½ by 7¼ inches. However, it is still called a 2 by 8. All ordinary lumber is thus reduced somewhat in size. Such reductions should be taken into consideration when planning remodeling work.

GRADES OF LUMBER

Because any kind of lumber is apt to contain various defects and blemishes, the American Lumber Standards Committee formulated what is known as *voluntary product standards*. The purpose of setting up such standards was to ensure uniform grading throughout the country. There is now a growing practice to put indelible marks on all building lumber at the sawmill, stating the grade, kind, size, degree of seasoning (dryness), and identity of the supplier. This grade- and trade-marking program is distinctly in the interest of users.

Softwoods. There are several ways in which softwood lumber is graded. We shall discuss the most important of such ways.

AMERICAN STANDARD GRADES. Table 1 shows the various grades of lumber from the standpoints of quality and recommended uses.

STANDARD LENGTHS. Most ordinary lumber is sold in what is called standard lengths. All such lengths are multiples of 1 foot. Generally, remodeling projects should be planned to make use of standard lengths so as to avoid waste. Local lumberyards will supply information in connection with the standard lengths available.

STANDARD WIDTHS AND THICKNESSES. Various standard widths and thicknesses are available, but they vary somewhat, depending upon kinds

TABLE 1. American standard softwood yard lumber grades

	Yard lumber		*Grades*
Total products of a typical log arranged in series according to quality as determined by appearance	Select lumber	Suitable for natural finishes	B & Better (practically free from defects) C (allows a few small defects or blemishes) D (allows more defects)
	Finish items (lumber of good appearance and finishing)	Suitable for paint finishes	Superior (allows a limited number of small defects or blemishes that can be covered with paint) Prime (allows larger and more defects) E (allows more and larger defects or blemishes which do not detract from the appearance of the finish, especially when painted)
	Common lumber (lumber containing defects or blemishes which detract from the appearance of the finish but suitable for general-utility and construction purposes)	Lumber suitable for use without waste	No. 1 (sound and tight-knotted stock; size of defects and blemishes limited; may be considered watertight lumber) No. 2 (allows large and coarse defects; used for exterior exposures)
		Lumber permitting waste	No. 3 (allows larger and coarser defects than No. 2 and occasional knotholes) No. 4 (low-quality lumber admitting the coarsest defects, such as decay and holes) No. 5 (for use where appearance and strength are not basic requirements)

of lumber. Local lumberyards will supply information in connection with the widths and thicknesses available.

Hardwoods. The most desirable grades of hardwood are known as *firsts.* The next grades are known as *seconds.* Both firsts and seconds, which are generally combined, are known as *FAS.* The third-best grade is called *selects,* followed by *No. 1 common, No. 2 common, sound wormy, No. 3A common,* and *No. 3B common.*

STANDARD LENGTHS. Little standardization exists because of the scarcity and size of hardwood logs.

STANDARD WIDTHS AND THICKNESSES. No standards have been established.

Finish Lumber. Such lumber, to be used for fine cabinets and other finish items, can be purchased at most lumberyards. However, we must remember that so-called 1-inch stock will actually be less than 1 inch after dressing.

KNOTTY PINE. This specialty lumber, as used for wall surfaces, is generally available ¾ inch thick and 5½, 7½, 9½, or 11½ inches wide. The boards are known as *1 by 6, 1 by 8, 1 by 10,* and *1 by 12.*

RED CEDAR. Ordinarily, red cedar can be purchased ⅜ inch thick, 3¼ inches wide, and in random lengths. It is supplied in bundles of about 40 feet board measure. Each such bundle will cover about 30 square feet of wall area.

Floor Lumber. The wood of hardwood trees, such as oaks, birches, maples, and beeches, is graded so as to take into account the yield and size of cuttings, with one clear face, that can be sawed from the lumber. The chief grades in maple are *first, second,* and *third.* The grades in quartersawed oak are *clear, sap clear, and select.* The grades in plain-sawed oak are *clear, select,* and *No. 1.* The flaked grain of quartersawed oak is generally preferred to the figure of plain-sawed oak. The following grading rules are typical of all hardwood flooring:

Grading Rules for Maple, Beech, and Birch. The beech and birch flooring show slightly more grain pattern than maple but all three are nearly alike.

FIRST GRADE. This grade is the highest standard grade and assures the most beautiful floors. The surface is practically free from defects.

SECOND GRADE. This grade has some tight, sound knots and slight imperfections. It is especially suitable for recreation rooms where absolutely perfect floor surfaces are not required.

THIRD GRADE. This is an economical grade which contains more imperfections. It is especially suitable for cottages or dens where unusual coloring and irregularities are not serious.

BOARD LENGTHS. The better the grade of such flooring, the longer the average board length. It is cheaper to use standard lengths, as they ordinarily come in bundles, than to request all long lengths.

BOARD THICKNESSES AND WIDTHS. Several such dimensions are available. Typical thicknesses are $2\frac{5}{32}$, $5\frac{3}{32}$, $\frac{3}{8}$, $\frac{1}{2}$, and $\frac{5}{8}$ inch. Typical widths are $1\frac{1}{2}$, 2 and $2\frac{1}{4}$ inches.

The $2\frac{5}{32}$-inch thickness is most commonly used for all general purposes.

The $5\frac{3}{32}$-inch thickness is used when floors are to be subjected to extraordinary strain and wear.

The $\frac{3}{8}$-, $\frac{1}{2}$-, and $\frac{5}{8}$-inch thicknesses are satisfactory for light service and especially in remodeling projects where existing floors are to be resurfaced.

NOTE 1: See explanations relative to the use of second grade flooring in Chapter 6.

NOTE 2: There are national associations, in connection with various kinds of flooring wood, which supply all sorts of helpful information upon request.

WOOD DEFECTS

Since wood, unlike steel, is a natural product developed through many years of growth in the open air where it is exposed to varying conditions, it is likely to contain some defects. Such defects cannot be corrected. Therefore, wood should be inspected before use. Some of the commonly encountered defects are set forth in the following and illustrated in Figure 2.

Checks. See *A* part of illustration. A lengthwise separation of wood tissue between growth rings is known as *check*. Such defects should be avoided where strength, stiffness, and good appearance are required.

✘ *Knots.* See *B* part of illustration. As previously explained, knots are not serious if they are sound and confined to lumber used where it does not have to be painted or otherwise finished.

Decay. See *C* part of illustration. Decay can be recognized by the colored, soft, spongy, stringy, or crumbly condition of woods. Boards showing such symptoms should be avoided.

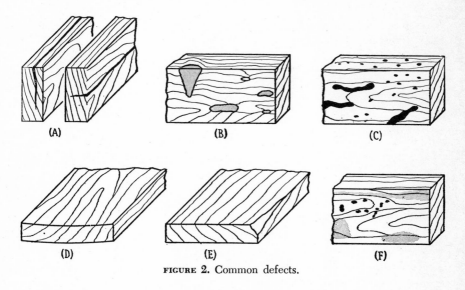

FIGURE 2. Common defects.

Warping. See *D* part of illustration. In some instances, boards develop a curve across the grain as they dry out. Slight warping can be corrected in rough structural details, but warped boards should never be used for visible details such as cabinets.

Wane. See *E* part of illustration. This is a defect on the corner or edge of a board due to lack of wood or bark. Such boards should not be used except for subfloors or in other locations where the defect will not be visible.

Pitch Discoloration. See *F* part of illustration. Owing to a moldlike fungus, discoloration sometimes appears in boards. Such a defect does not impair strength or stiffness but is objectionable for painted or natural finishes.

BOARD-FOOT CONTENT

Lumber is always sold by the board foot. A board foot consists of a unit that measures 1 by 12 inches, as shown in the *A* part of Figure 3. Both of the units shown in the *B* part also contain 1 board foot.

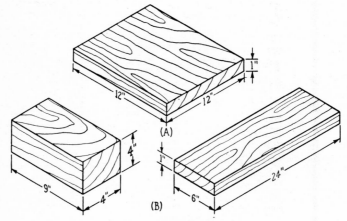

FIGURE 3. Board-foot content.

The number of board feet in lumber of any dimension can be found by means of the simple formula

$$\frac{T \times W \times L}{12} = \text{board feet}$$

where T = thickness of lumber in inches

      W = width of lumber in inches

      L = length of lumber in feet

EXAMPLE. Find the number of board feet in a 2 by 6 that is 12 feet long.

SOLUTION. Substitute numerical values for the letters in the formula.

The value of T is 2. The value of W is 6. The value of L is 12. Thus we have

$$\frac{2 \times 6 \times 12}{12} = \frac{144}{12} = 12 \text{ board feet}$$

This checks with the answer shown in Table 2.

TABLE 2. Board-foot content

Size, inches	Length, feet							
	8	10	12	14	16	18	20	22
1 × 2	$1\frac{1}{3}$	$1\frac{2}{3}$	2	$2\frac{1}{3}$	$2\frac{2}{3}$	3	$3\frac{1}{3}$	$3\frac{2}{3}$
1 × 3	2	$2\frac{1}{2}$	3	$3\frac{1}{2}$	4	$4\frac{1}{2}$	5	$5\frac{1}{2}$
1 × 4	$2\frac{2}{3}$	$3\frac{1}{3}$	4	$4\frac{2}{3}$	$5\frac{1}{3}$	6	$6\frac{2}{3}$	$7\frac{1}{3}$
1 × 5	$3\frac{1}{3}$	$4\frac{1}{6}$	5	$5\frac{5}{6}$	$6\frac{2}{3}$	$7\frac{1}{2}$	$8\frac{1}{3}$	$9\frac{1}{6}$
1 × 6	4	5	6	7	8	9	10	11
1 × 8	$5\frac{1}{3}$	$6\frac{2}{3}$	8	$9\frac{1}{3}$	$10\frac{2}{3}$	12	$13\frac{1}{3}$	$14\frac{2}{3}$
1 × 10	$6\frac{2}{3}$	$8\frac{1}{3}$	10	$11\frac{2}{3}$	$13\frac{1}{3}$	15	$16\frac{2}{3}$	$18\frac{1}{3}$
1 × 12	8	10	12	14	16	18	20	22
1 × 14	$9\frac{1}{3}$	$11\frac{2}{3}$	14	$16\frac{1}{3}$	$18\frac{2}{3}$	21	$23\frac{1}{3}$	$25\frac{2}{3}$
1 × 16	$10\frac{2}{3}$	$13\frac{1}{3}$	16	$18\frac{2}{3}$	$21\frac{1}{3}$	24	$26\frac{2}{3}$	$29\frac{1}{3}$
2 × 4	$5\frac{1}{3}$	$6\frac{2}{3}$	8	$9\frac{1}{3}$	$10\frac{2}{3}$	12	$13\frac{1}{3}$	$14\frac{2}{3}$
2 × 6	8	10	12	14	16	18	20	22
2 × 8	$10\frac{2}{3}$	$13\frac{1}{3}$	16	$18\frac{2}{3}$	$21\frac{1}{3}$	24	$26\frac{2}{3}$	$29\frac{1}{3}$
2 × 10	$13\frac{1}{3}$	$16\frac{2}{3}$	20	$23\frac{1}{3}$	$26\frac{2}{3}$	30	$33\frac{1}{3}$	$36\frac{2}{3}$
2 × 12	16	20	24	28	32	36	40	44
4 × 4	$10\frac{2}{3}$	$13\frac{1}{3}$	16	$18\frac{2}{3}$	$21\frac{1}{3}$	24	$26\frac{2}{3}$	$29\frac{1}{3}$
4 × 6	16	20	24	28	32	36	40	44
4 × 8	$21\frac{1}{3}$	$26\frac{2}{3}$	32	$37\frac{1}{3}$	$42\frac{2}{3}$	48	$53\frac{1}{3}$	$58\frac{2}{3}$
4 × 10	$26\frac{2}{3}$	$33\frac{1}{3}$	40	$46\frac{2}{3}$	$53\frac{1}{3}$	60	$66\frac{2}{3}$	$73\frac{1}{3}$
4 × 12	32	40	48	56	64	72	80	88
4 × 14	$37\frac{1}{3}$	$46\frac{2}{3}$	56	$65\frac{1}{3}$	$74\frac{2}{3}$	84	$93\frac{1}{3}$	$102\frac{2}{3}$
4 × 16	$42\frac{2}{3}$	$53\frac{1}{3}$	64	$74\frac{2}{3}$	$85\frac{1}{3}$	96	$106\frac{2}{3}$	$117\frac{1}{3}$
6 × 6	24	30	36	42	48	54	60	66
6 × 8	32	40	48	56	64	72	80	88

LUMBER FOR VARIOUS PURPOSES

In the following, several typical uses for various kinds of woods are suggested:

Exterior House Trim. The usual requirements are decay resistance, good painting and weathering characteristics, easy-working qualities, and freedom from warp.

SUGGESTED WOODS. Cedar, cypress, and redwood where decay hazard is high. Pine where decay hazard does not exist. Heartwood is preferable.

Living- and Dining-room Floors. The usual requirements are resistance to wear, attractive figure or color, minimum warp and shrinkage.

SUGGESTED WOODS. Beech, birch, maple, and oak.

Uncovered Kitchen Floors. The usual requirements are resistance to wear, fine texture, ability to withstand washing, and minimum warp and shrinkage.

SUGGESTED WOODS. Beech, birch, and maple.

Covered Kitchen Floors. Where linoleum or soft tile are to be used as surfaces, softwood plywood serves the purpose to excellent advantage.

Porch Flooring. The usual requirements are minimum decay resistance, medium wear resistance, and freedom from warping.

SUGGESTED WOODS. Cypress, Douglas fir, larch, pine, and redwood.

Rough Framing. The usual requirements are stiffness, nail-holding power, hardness, and freedom from shrinkage and warp. Dryness is the most important requirement.

SUGGESTED WOODS. Douglas fir, larch, and pine. Cypress, redwood, ash, and beech can be used when the previously mentioned kinds are not available.

Other woods, such as chestnut, elm, gum, and poplar, may be used, but they are not recommended.

Interior Trim. The usual requirements are pleasing figure, hardness, and freedom from warp.

SUGGESTED WOODS. Ash, birch, cherry, chestnut, and oak constitute the most desirable materials where natural finishes are desired.

When trim is to be painted, the following woods are suggested and listed in the order of desirability:

Hemlock	Basswood	Douglas fir
Redwood	Cypress	Gum

Roof Boards. The usual requirements are stiffness, nail-holding power, small tendency to warp, and ease of working.

SUGGESTED WOODS. Douglas fir, larch, and pine are commonly used. Cypress, ash, beech, chestnut, and hemlock may be used with somewhat less assurance of stiffness.

Window Sash. The usual requirements are moderate shrinkage, good paint-holding qualities, freedom from warping, ease of working, and screw-holding power.

SUGGESTED WOODS IN DRY LOCATIONS. Northern white pine, cypress, and redwood. Douglas fir, larch, and yellow pine can be used but with less assurance of requirements being met.

SUGGESTED WOODS IN MOIST LOCATIONS. Northern white pine. Douglas fir and larch can be used with less assurance of requirements being met.

Shelving: High-class Natural or Paint Finish. The usual requirements are stiffness, good finishing qualities, and freedom from pitch and warp.

SUGGESTED WOODS. Ash, birch, maple, oak, and walnut are suitable for natural finishes to match other interior trim. Cypress and northern white pine are suitable for paint finishes.

Shelving: Unfinished or Plain Paint Coating. The usual requirements are stiffness, ease of working, and freedom from pitch and warp.

SUGGESTED WOODS. Northern white pine, cypress, hemlock, redwood, basswood, and poplar.

Shingles. The usual requirements are high decay resistance, small tendency to curl, and freedom from splitting when nailed.

SUGGESTED WOODS. Cedar, cypress, and redwood; No. 1 shingles (all heart, edge-grain clear stock) should be used for long life and greatest ultimate economy.

Siding. The usual requirements are good painting characteristics, easy-working qualities, and freedom from warp.

SUGGESTED WOODS. Cedar, cypress, northern white pine, and redwood.

Outdoor Steps. The usual requirements are decay resistance, non-splintering, bending strength, wear resistance, and freedom from warping.

SUGGESTED WOODS. Cypress and Douglas fir. Larch and redwood are good second choices.

Subfloors. The usual requirements are high stiffness, medium shrinkage, small warp, and ease of working.

SUGGESTED WOODS. Douglas fir, larch, and pine.

Sheathing. Same as subfloors.

Concrete Forms. Same as subfloors.

Gates and Fences. The usual requirements are moderate bending, medium decay and weather resistance, high nail-holding power, and freedom from warp.

SUGGESTED WOODS. Cypress, Douglas fir, pine, redwood, and oak. Cedar, northern white pine, chestnut, and poplar can be used with almost as much assurance that all requirements will be met.

Cabinets. Same as shelving.

Furring Strips. Same as sheathing.

Sills. Same as sash.

Screen Frames. Same as sash.

SOFTWOOD PLYWOOD

In most remodeling work where panel plywood is used, Douglas fir is considered one of the best. Douglas-fir plywood is a built-up board of laminated veneers in which the grain of each piece is at right angles to the one adjacent to it. Kiln-dried veneer is united under high pressure with a bonding agent, which makes the joints as strong as the wood itself or stronger. The alternating direction of the grain with each contiguous layer of wood equalizes the strains and in this way minimizes shrinkage and warpage. It also prevents splitting.

Plywood panels, 48 inches wide and 96 inches long, are very popular in the building of houses. However, they are made in many other sizes, such as 36 inches wide and 144 inches long, and in various thicknesses. Thicknesses are from $\frac{1}{4}$ to $1\frac{1}{4}$ inches, generally in $\frac{1}{8}$-inch increments. The stock-panel width of 48 inches as well as the popular 8-foot lengths are multiples of 16 inches, which is the accepted spacing for studs and joists.

In building construction, plywoods have many uses. They are extensively used in the following types of construction:

1. Kitchen cabinets, bookcases, shelves, linen closets, utility-room cabinets, supply cases, and many other types of cabinet work
2. Interior wall paneling, partition walls, and for decorative purposes
3. Exterior wall sheathing
4. Exterior roof sheathing
5. Subflooring and underlays
6. Outside wall siding
7. Concrete formwork
8. Outside decorations, soffits, etc.

HARDWOOD PLYWOOD

Hardwood plywood is made with two types of cores—veneer core and lumber core. *Veneer-core plywood* is made of thin veneers, the face veneers running parallel to the length of the panel and the alternating plies at right angles. An odd number of plies (3, 5, 7, etc.) is used. In *lumber-core* construction, the plywood is made of narrow strips of sawn lumber with crossbands and face veneers on either side.

Veneer-core plywood has somewhat more resiliency and strength per pound than lumber-core plywood, but the latter possesses practically the same dimensional stability and is generally used for woodworking projects which call for doweled, splined, or dovetail joints, exposed edges or butt hinges.

Grading. The Hardwood Plywood Institute has adopted four grades governing the backs and faces of hardwood plywood:

GOOD GRADE (Grade 1). Used for a great variety of projects where appearance is a factor, this grade is free of obvious defects and will take a beautiful natural finish. If formed of more than one piece, it can be matched at the joints to avoid sharp contrasts in color and grain.

SOUND GRADE (Grade 2). Intended for smooth paint surfaces, this grade is free from open defects in order to provide a smooth, sound surface for the paint. It may contain defects of the kind that will be completely covered by the paint, such as mineral streaks, stain, discoloration, and patches.

UTILITY GRADE (Grade 3). A strong, serviceable material for backs, concealed constructions, and other uses where appearance is not a prime factor, this grade may contain any number of defects which do not actually weaken the material structurally. This includes knotholes up to ¾ inch in diameter, and wormholes, splits, or open joints not exceeding ³⁄₁₆ inch.

REJECT GRADE (Grade 4). This lowest grade may be used for the same purposes as utility grade inasmuch as the same defects are allowed, but the defects are permitted to be larger. For example, knotholes may be as large as 2 inches in diameter, instead of ¾ inch as in utility grade, and splits and wormholes may be ¼ inch wide if they do not exceed one-fourth of the length of the veneer. The limitations ensure that the strength and serviceability of the panel are not seriously impaired.

In addition to specifying one of these four grades, a buyer of plywood may also specify plywood by adhesion type, although it is generally enough to state whether the material is to be used for exterior or interior purposes. The three types are based on the adhesives used in joining the layers of the plywood together. Type 1 is fully waterproof, intended for outdoor and marine uses. The bond will withstand full weather exposure and will be unaffected by microorganisms. Type 2 is highly water-resistant, retaining practically all its strength when subjected to an occasional thorough wetting and drying. Type 3 is dry bond, suitable for uses not subject to water, dampness, or high humidity.

Hardwood Plywood Species. This type of plywood is produced in a full range of American hardwoods in addition to such imported hardwoods as mahogany. Six hardwood species rank above all others in plywood popularity. They are:

Gum	Mahogany	Walnut
Birch	Oak	Maple

SIZES AND THICKNESSES. Hardwood plywood is available in a great many sizes and thicknesses, but only panels in the most commonly used dimensions are customarily carried by neighborhood lumberyards. Hardwood plywood distributors, found in every good-sized city in the United States, carry a complete line of all sizes, and they will fulfill special orders as requested by the retail lumber dealer.

Panels come in widths of 2, 2½, 3, 3½, and 4 feet, and lengths of 3, 4, 5, 6, 7, and 8 feet. Standard veneer-core-plywood thicknesses range from ⅛ to $1\frac{3}{16}$ inch in 3, 5, or 7 plies. The most popular veneer-core-plywood thicknesses are ⅛, ¼, and ⅜ inch.

Lumber-core plywood is generally thicker, ½ inch and upward. Approximately six times more veneer-core plywood is sold than lumber-core.

CHOOSING PLYWOOD PANELS. One of the big advantages in working with hardwood plywood lies in the great diversity of sizes, species, grades, and prices in which the material may be obtained.

The species and grade, and consequently the price, will be governed by the nature of the project and the type of finish desired. If the user wants a paint finish, he can buy Sound Grade plywood, but if a natural wood effect is desired, he should move up to Good Grade for better results. A saving can be effected by obtaining Utility Grade for backs and concealed construction.

Economy comes into the picture again in laying out the work. By careful planning, the craftsman often can fit all the pieces of his project into one good-sized rectangle, say, 3 by 6 feet. This means that he need purchase only a single panel of that size, and that he will have a minimum of waste.

SAWING HARDWOOD PLYWOOD. Correct sawing procedure is an important factor in producing a close-fitting, well-built job. With plywood, best results are obtained by using high-speed power saws with little or no set and as much lead to the teeth as possible. If both edges of panel are to be exposed, place the panel on a plywood scrap and saw through both layers to eliminate the possibility of fuzzing. A circular saw should be 10 or more inches in diameter. A combination-blade type is the best to use. It is advisable to saw with the best side of the panel up, except when using a portable circular saw. Ordinary hand saws can also be used. Their teeth should be fine and sharp with little set.

JOINING HARDWOOD-PLYWOOD SHEETS. When working with veneer-core plywood for wall paneling and other purposes, the craftsman will have his choice of the following methods of joining:

1. V joint
2. Butt joint
3. Block-treatment joint
4. Wood-faced extruded moldings
5. Tongue-and-groove joint
6. Open recessed joint
7. Splined joint
8. Mitered joint
9. Battens of wood, plastic, or metal

The butt joint, or merely fitting two pieces together on the same stud with a flush surface, is the simplest method. Planing the edges of the two panels along the joint to form a slight "V" adds appeal. For protection against movement of the solid wood stud, which may open the joint, nail ¼-inch-thick plywood strips to the studs and apply the plywood panels to the plywood strips.

CORNER TREATMENT. Although corners may be finished without the use of moldings, they are usually preferable because they simplify the work and, in most cases, give a more professional look to the completed job. Moldings can be made in the workshop or purchased at a lumberyard in a number of different types.

For exterior corners fill in with a quarter round of the same thickness as the panels. A different effect can be obtained by using a quarter round of a slightly larger size and sanding its edges.

For interior corners, use cove molding. In order to guard against possible later damage due to movement of the studs, it is wise to employ a "floating" corner. One of the two panels which meet to form the corner should not be nailed to a stud at the corner but should be left free in order to provide a safety valve against movement.

FINISHING HARDWOOD PLYWOOD. There are many ways of finishing plywood projects. Individual preference, the type of wood, and the nature of the project will determine the kind of finish to be applied.

Paint, of course, will cover the attractive natural grain pattern of the wood, so that, generally speaking, only projects utilizing Sound Grade plywood should be painted. Good Grade plywood is usually intended for natural finishes to enhance the beauty of the grain rather than cover it.

No matter which type of finish is selected, the important first step is to prepare the wood's surface. The wood should be clean and dry, sanded smooth, and have all traces of glue removed and dents and cracks filled. Pressing with a hot iron and damp cloth will often cause small dents to disappear.

After the finishing procedure has been decided upon, completely finish a small scrap of the same plywood as was used in the project. This pre-testing procedure will give the craftsman advance knowledge of the exact results to expect so that he may make alterations if desired.

Care must be taken with natural finishes to keep them natural. The use of a light application may be pleasing—enough finish to protect the wood and give it a dull sheen, but not enough to greatly alter the tone and color.

CLEAR FINISH. Apply prime coat of clear sealer or thin coat of white shellac mixed with equal portion of denatured alcohol. When dry, fill nail holes with plastic wood dough or putty tinted the color of the wood and rub with No. 1 steel wool or No. 00 sandpaper. Apply a second coat of clear (or pigmented, if desired) sealer or varnish. Apply a third coat of dull varnish which may be buffed to a velvety sheen when dry. If the wood is open-pored, such as oak or mahogany, the only difference in the procedure is to use a white or natural filler for the second coat in order to fill the pores.

LACQUER FINISH. Apply a coat of lacquer sealer, sand lightly, and follow with several coats of clear lacquer. Buff and wax.

STAINING AND BLEACHING. Stains and bleaches are used to either lighten or darken the natural color of the wood prior to the application of a clear coating. A great variety of stains and bleaches are available and manufacturer's directions should be followed closely.

WAX. There are wax-finishing systems suitable for hardwood plywood, but the craftsman must bear in mind that paint or varnish cannot be used later because the wax enters the wood fibers and will soften paint and varnish.

ENAMELING AND PAINTING. With no grain raise, hardwood plywood provides an excellent surface for enameling or painting. The use of a filler is not required for close-grained woods such as birch and maple.

ECONOMICAL USE OF PLYWOOD

The use of plywood should be planned so as to minimize waste. Such planning can be done to advantage by drawing sketches of floors or walls to scale and then making two or more trials to see how panels of a given size can be fitted into the areas.

CHAPTER TWO

Fasteners

The stiffness of houses, whether they include all or partial wood framing, depends to an important extent on how well the various structural details, parts, and elements are fastened together. When sufficient fasteners of the correct kind and placement are used, a high degree of stiffness is assured. On the other hand, when improper and too few fasteners are used, stiffness is lacking.

Without a high degree of stiffness, houses are subject to many troublesome and costly defects, some of which are described in Chapters 4, 5, and 6. Other defects include sticking doors and windows, annoying vibrations, out-of-plumb walls, and sagging floors.

In remodeling work where structural details, parts, and elements are moved or new ones added, proper fasteners are more important than when entirely new houses are being built. Unless fasteners are used in ample quantities and according to proper sizes and placement, serious cracks and other difficulties will occur.

Even though correct fastening is so highly important, the literature of house construction and remodeling has previously contained little, if any, instruction in connection with fasteners. As a result, there is much difference of opinion as to what constitutes proper fastening, and, consequently, a large variation in practice. Such practice—usually a matter of precedent, tradition, or individual judgment—does not take into account the forces which fasteners must resist. The purpose of this chapter is to explain commonly required fasteners and to set up general specifica-

27

tions for fastening, in the hope that they will help to replace haphazard practices with sound and efficient ones.

NAIL-HOLDING POWER

In most joints of the types commonly encountered in remodeling work, one piece of material tends to slide on or along an adjacent one, owing to the weights supported or other forces which act on the joint. In some instances, the joints are not subject to analysis with respect to the forces that they must resist and, consequently, cannot be designed on an engineering basis. A good example of this has to do with the joint between the lower end of a stud and a sill. The fastening for such joints is therefore based entirely on experiments carried on by many mechanics over long periods of time. The force that fasteners are required to resist in some other types of joints can be computed and the size, quantity, and placement of fasteners accurately determined.

When joints are subject to the sliding previously mentioned, the fasteners must supply what is known as *lateral resistance*. For example, the lateral resistance of fasteners attaching sheathing to studs comes into action in resisting forces that tend to rack the wall and in carrying the weights of such materials.

The other way in which fasteners are stressed is in direct pull or withdrawal. Fasteners attaching covering materials to the lower edges of joists or rafters are stressed in direct pull by the weights of the materials. Similar stress is induced when fasteners must resist warping, vibration, and wind or earthquake tremors. When fasteners are sufficient in size, quantity, and placement to accomplish the necessary resistance, houses are stiff and the defects previously mentioned cannot occur.

Nails are important fasteners and are used to stiffen many of the structural details, parts, and elements of houses. If we assume that they are used in sufficient size, quantity, and placement, the resistance which is offered by wood to their withdrawal, under stress, is of importance. Usually, the denser and harder the wood, the greater the inherent nail-holding power.

In the following, several common woods are classified according to their nail-holding power:

HIGH HOLDING POWER

Ash	Elm	Maple
Beech	Larch	Oak
Birch		Pine

MEDIUM HOLDING POWER

Chestnut	Gum	Poplar
Cypress	Hemlock	Redwood
Douglas fir		Spruce

LOW HOLDING POWER

Basswood	Cottonwood
Cedar	Fir

The size, quantity, and placement of nails have a marked effect on the strength of a joint. Thus, more nails are required in woods of medium holding power than in woods of high holding power.

The resistance to withdrawal of nails increases almost directly with the diameter of shank; that is, if the diameter of a nail is doubled, the holding power is almost doubled, provided the nail does not split the wood when it is driven. The lateral resistance of nails is also practically doubled if their diameter is doubled.

The moisture content of the wood at the time of nailing is extremely important in terms of good nail holding. If nails are driven into wet wood, they will lose about 75 per cent of their full holding power when the wood becomes dry. Then, shrinking and warping are not resisted and the defects previously mentioned occur.

As previously stated, the splitting of wood by nails reduces their holding power. Even if the wood is split only slightly around a nail, there is considerable loss in holding power. Because of hardness and texture characteristics some woods split more in nailing than do others. The heavy, dense woods, such as maple and oak, split more in nailing than do the lightweight woods, such as basswood and spruce. Woods such as pine and Douglas fir split more than northern white pine. The most common means taken to reduce splitting is the use of smaller nails. The number of such nails must be increased, of course, to maintain the same gross holding power.

Nail Shanks. Continuous research tends to indicate that the holding power of nails depends to an appreciable amount upon their shanks. Chemical etching of shank surfaces constitutes one effort to increase holding power; the use of various coatings is another. Barbing of shanks

TABLE 1. Commonly used nails, their size, gage, and number per pound

Common	Box	Finish

Penny size	Length, inches, for common, box, and finish*	Common nails			Box and finish nails		
		Gage	Thickness, thousandths	Number per pound	Gage	Thickness, thousandths	Number per pound
2d	1	15	0.072	876	15½	0.069	1,010
3d	1¼	14	0.083	568	14½	0.078	635
4d	1½	12½	0.102	316	14	0.083	473
5d	1¾	12½	0.102	271	14	0.083	406
6d	2	11½	0.115	181	12½	0.102	236
7d	2¼	11½	0.115	161	12½	0.102	210
8d	2½	10¼	0.131	106	11½	0.115	145
9d	2¾	10¼	0.131	96	11½	0.115	132
10d	3	9	0.148	69	10½	0.127	94
12d	3¼	9	0.148	63	10½	0.127	88
16d	3½	8	0.165	49	10	0.134	71
20d	4	6	0.203	31	9	0.148	52
30d	4½	5	0.220	24	9	0.148	46
40d	5	4	0.238	18	8	0.165	35
50d	5½	3	0.259	14			
60d	6	2	0.284	11			

* Coated nails are ⅛ inch shorter.

Note: Flooring nails are similar in appearance to the finish nail but are about 1½ gage thicker for each size. They are made in sizes from 6d to 20d. Wire nails are gaged by the old standard Birmingham wire gage.

also increases holding power, especially if wet lumber must be used. Various other shank treatments, such as grooves and spirals, also tend to increase holding power. Readers may secure manufacturers' literature and study the advantages of one or another form of shank.

NAIL SIZES

The nail industry still clings to the *penny system* to indicate the length of the most commonly used nails, ranging in length from 1 to 6 inches. The symbol for penny is d. Table 1 shows several of the most commonly used nails in terms of penny and inch sizes.

RULE FOR LENGTH OF NAILS

There is a simple rule to follow when selecting nail lengths for both rough (framing) and finish (trim, cabinets, etc.) carpentry work. The rule applies to hardwoods and softwoods. Figure 1 shows the rule graphically. Suppose that pieces A and B are to be nailed together. In the case of hardwoods, the nail penetration, X, into the bottom piece should be one-half the length of the nail. For softwoods, the penetration, Y, into the bottom piece should be two-thirds the length of the nail. Thus, the thickness of the top piece determines the required nail length.

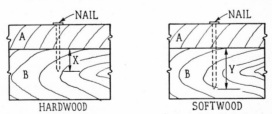

FIGURE 1. Nail penetration into hardwood and softwood.

TYPICAL NAIL DATA

Table 2 shows interesting and useful data in connection with the types of nails to use for various purposes.

TABLE 2. Typical nail data

Size and kind of material	Board measure in feet	Trade name	Nails required, lb			Length of nails	No. of nails to each bearing
			12" centers	16" centers	24" centers		
1 × 4 boards and shiplap	1,000	8d common	60	48	30	2½"	2
1 × 6 boards and shiplap	1,000	8d common	40	32	20	2½"	2
1 × 8 boards and shiplap	1,000	8d common	31	27	16	2½"	2
1 × 10 boards and shiplap	1,000	8d common	25	20	13	2½"	2
1 × 12 boards and shiplap	1,000	8d common	31	24	16	2½"	3
1 × 4 Dressed and Matched blind nailed	1,000	8d common	30	24	15	2½"	1
1 × 6 D&M blind nailed	1,000	8d common	20	16	10	2½"	1
1 × 8 D&M blind nailed and 1 face nail	1,000	8d common	31	27	16	2½"	2
1 × 10 D&M blind nailed and 1 face nail	1,000	8d common	25	20	13	2½"	2
1 × 12 D&M blind nailed and 1 face nail	1,000	8d common	21	16	11	2½"	2
2 × 4 to 2 × 16 framing	1,000	20d common	20	16	10	4"	2
		16d common	10	10	6	3½"	
		10d common	8	6	4	3"	
3 × 4 to 3 × 14 framing	1,000	60d common	30	25	15	6"	1
2 × 6 D&M flooring	1,000	20d common	35	27	18	4"	1
2 × 8 D&M flooring	1,000	20d common	27	20	14	4"	1
1 × 4 drop siding	1,000	7d siding	45	35		2¼"	2
1 × 6 drop siding	1,000	7d siding	30	25		2¼"	2
1 × 8 drop siding	1,000	7d siding	23	18		2¼"	2
½ × 4 beveled siding	1,000	6d siding	23	18		2"	1
½ × 6 bev. siding	1,000	6d siding	15	13		2"	1
½ × 8 bev. siding	1,000	6d siding	12	10		2"	1

3/4 × 10 bev. siding	1,000	7d siding	45	35		2¼″	2
3/4 × 12 bev. siding	1,000	7d siding	60	50		2¼″	3
3/4 × 4 ceiling	1,000	8d finish	18	14	9	2½″	1
½ to ⅝″ ceiling	1,000	6d finish	11	8	6	2″	1
⅞″ finish lumber	1,000	8d finish	25	12	13	2½″	2
1⅛″ finish lumber	1,000	10d finish	12	10	6	3″	2
1 × 3 flooring, softwood	1,000	8d floor brads	42	32	21	2½″	1
1 × 4 flooring, softwood	1,000	8d floor brads	32	26	16	2½″	1
1 × 6 flooring, softwood	1,000	8d floor brads	22	18	11	2½″	1
⅜ × 1½ flooring, hardwood	1,000	4d casing	13	10		1¼″	1
⅜ × 2 flooring, hardwood	1,000	4d casing	11	8		1¼″	1
13/16 × 1½ flooring, hardwood	1,000	7d casing	27	20		2¼″	1
13/16 × 2¼ flooring, hardwood	1,000	7d casing	20	14		2¼″	1

1 × 2 furring on brick walls—100 lineal ft . . 20d cut nails, requires 5¼ lb
Base per 100 lineal ft . . . . 8d finish, requires 1 lb, 16″ on centers
Sides of trim, per side of inside trim . . . . . . 4d finish
6d finish } requires about ½ lb total
8d finish

48″ wood lath, per 1,000 lath . . . . 3d fine, requires 7 lb
Metal lath, per 100 sq yd . . . . 1″ staples, require 12 lb
or metal lath, per 100 sq yd . . . . 1⅛″ No. 12 hook head nails, require 15 lb
⅜″ gypsum lath, per 100 sq yd . . 1⅛″ × 13 gage—5/16″ heads, require 10 lb
Smooth diamond points
¼″ plasterboard, per 100 sq yd . . 1″ × 13 gage—5/16″ heads, require 10 lb
Smooth diamond points
13/16″ wallboard, per 1,000 sq ft . . . . 3d flathead nail, requires 5 lb
¼″ wallboard, per 1,000 sq ft . . . . 4d flathead nail, requires 9 lb
⅜″ wallboard, per 1,000 sq ft . . . . 4d flathead nail, requires 9 lb

NAIL POINTS

Nail points are highly important and should be selected with the greatest of care. The selection depends upon the nail use. The point can influence both the holding power and the splitting resistance of the wood through which the nails are driven.

Diamond Point. Most of the commonly used nails have diamond points. The gradual taper causes nails to hold well without splitting dense woods.

Blunt-tapered Point. This type of point pierces wood fibers instead of spreading them and thus reduces splitting in hardwoods.

Long Diamond and Needle Points. Either of these points may be used when rapid driving is desired. The sharp points allow easy setting (starting), and the nails can be driven without much driving effort.

Chisel Point. This type of point helps to ease nails through exceptionally hard woods.

Duckbill Point. If nails are to be clinched, this point is recommended.

NAIL CLINCHING

In order to increase the holding power of common nails used in rough carpentry work, they should be clinched. In other words, if a portion of a nail extends out beyond the surface of wood, that portion may be bent over. As previously mentioned, nails having duckbill points can be used to advantage for this purpose.

If plain-shanked nails such as shown in Table 1 are clinched, they will have about 45 per cent greater holding power than a corresponding nonclinched nail. The clinched portion of a nail should be at least ¼ inch long. Longer clinched portions do not provide much more holding power. Clinching should be done perpendicular to the grain of wood.

NAILHEADS

The nails used in connection with all rough carpentry work should have flat heads such as shown on the common nail in Table 1. The diameter of the heads should be at least twice the diameter of the shanks. For all finish carpentry work in connection with trim and cabinets, the nailheads should be of the kind shown on the finish nail in Table 1. Some materials require nailheads of a special kind or size. In such cases manufacturers generally offer the necessary information.

GENERAL NAILING SPECIFICATIONS

The structural details shown in Figures 2 through 15 are those most commonly used in ordinary remodeling work. They will serve as a guide when planning and building additions to, or rearrangements of, existing structural details.

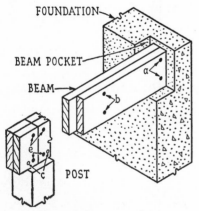

FIGURE 2. Two-piece beam.

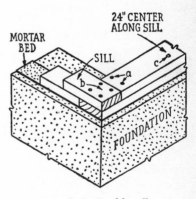

FIGURE 3. Double sill.

Figures 2 through 15 also indicate the recommended quantities and placement of nails for fastening all structural members together. The kind of wood is not taken into consideration other than to assume high and medium holding power. In the illustrations, toenailing and perpendicular nailing are indicated by small blank and solid circles, respectively. Toenailing applies when nails must be driven at a slant.

Figure 2. Two-piece Beam. Use 10d or 12d nails. Place two nails at *a*. The nails at *b* should be driven every 16 inches. At girder joints, four nails should be driven as shown at *e*. Use two toenails as shown at *c*.

Figure 3. Double Sill. Use 10d or 12d nails as shown at *a* and *b*. The *c* nails should be driven at 24-inch intervals.

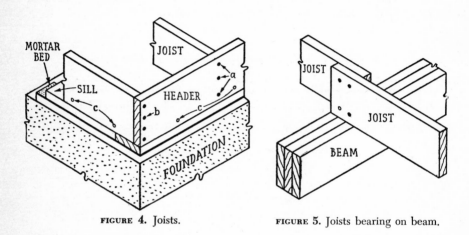

FIGURE 4. Joists.   FIGURE 5. Joists bearing on beam.

Figure 4. Joists. Drive 20d nails at *a* and *b*. Drive 10d nails for toenailing, as shown at *c*, and space them about 16 inches apart. The toenailing helps to prevent movement of the headers during times when a house is subjected to high winds or earthquakes.

Figure 5. Joists Bearing on Beam. Drive at least three 10d or 12d nails for the perpendicular fastening and at least one 10d or 12d nail for toenailing.

Figure 6. Subfloor and Sill. Boards 4 inches or less in width should be nailed using two 8d nails, and wider boards with three 8d nails at each crossing of joists and headers. Drive two 8d nails when board ends occur over joists.

The sills should be fastened by means of 16d nails spaced 16 inches apart and so that the nails go through the subflooring and into the headers.

Figure 7. Plywood Subfloor. Drive 8d nails spaced not more than 6 inches apart along all edges and 12 inches apart along intermediate members.

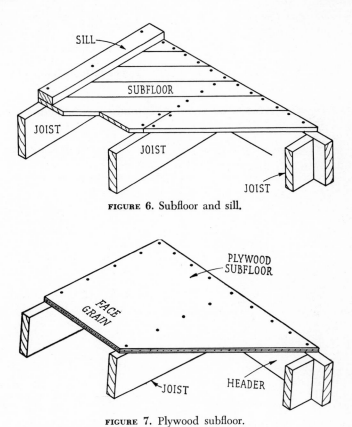

FIGURE 6. Subfloor and sill.

FIGURE 7. Plywood subfloor.

Figure 8. Studs. Drive two 8d or 10d nails on each wide face. The nails should be driven at points about 1 inch above the plate.

Figure 9. Joists Bearing on Ribband. Drive at least five 10d or 12d nails to fasten each joist to a stud.

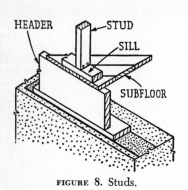

FIGURE 8. Studs.

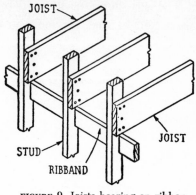

FIGURE 9. Joists bearing on ribbon.

Figure 10. Rafter Ends. Drive four 12d nails as indicated.

Figure 11. Porch Connections. Drive five 12d nails for fastening ceiling joists and rafters to the studs.

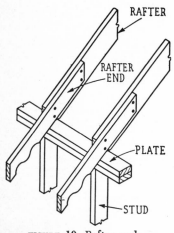

FIGURE 10. Rafter ends.

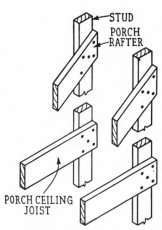

FIGURE 11. Porch connections.

Figure 12. Diagonal Wall Sheathing. Use 8d nails. For boards 8 inches or less in width, drive two nails at each end of each board, two nails through each board into studs, and three nails through each board into the corner-post assembly. For wider boards drive an additional nail at each of these points. Joints in adjacent runs of boards should be separated by at least two stud spaces. The fastening of sheathing boards is extremely important and adds greatly to the stiffness of a house.

Figure 13. Plywood Wall Sheathing. Plywood less than ½ inch thick should be nailed using 6d nails spaced 5 inches apart along edges and 10 inches apart on intermediate framing members. Plywood ½ or more inches thick should be nailed using 8d nails at the same spacings. Vertical

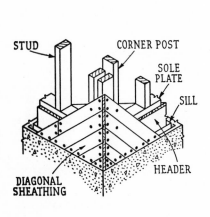

FIGURE 12. Diagonal wall sheathing.

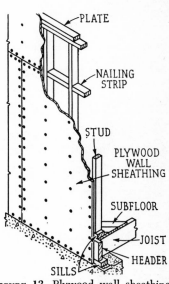

FIGURE 13. Plywood wall sheathing.

joints between plywood panels should not be on the same stud in succeeding rows of sheathing. For the horizontal joints, nailing strips should be set between the studs and nailed to them.

Figure 14. Shingles. Nail 1 inch above exposure line and ¾ inch from edge of shingles using rust-resisting nails long enough to penetrate through the roof boards. Shingles wider than 8 or 9 inches should be split and nailed as two shingles.

Figure 15. Rafter and Ceiling Joists Supported by Wall Plate. Drive four 10d nails through joist into rafter. Overlap the joists over bearing partition and drive five 10d nails. Toenail the joist and rafter to plate using two 10d nails on each side of assembly.

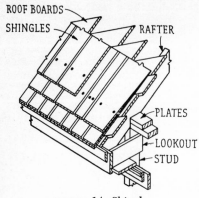

FIGURE 14. Shingles.

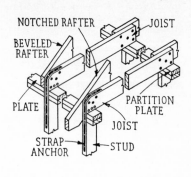

FIGURE 15. Rafter and ceiling joists supported by wall plate.

Additional security against uplift is afforded by metal straps placed as shown and nailed with four 8d nails to studs and with two 8d nails to upper edges of joists.

FASTENING DECORATIVE PLYWOOD

Nails or adhesives may be used in fastening plywoods. Often, a mechanic will want to use both nails and glue. One of the big advantages in working with plywood is that it is splitproof; thus, nails may be used close to edges, and outside fastenings or clamps may be used without fear of damage to the plywood.

For best appearance, nails should be countersunk, and the depressions filled with wood filler or plugs.

The following nailing schedule is suggested for wall paneling and other hardwood plywood projects:

Panel thickness	Nail size
¼ inch	4d finish nails (1-inch brads are used over firm backing)
⅜ inch	4d finish nails
½ inch	6d finish nails
¾ inch	6d or 8d finish nails

Several adhesives of the urea-formaldehyde type are available for use with plywood projects. They are water-resistant, easy to work with, simple to prepare, and they do not stain. In addition, liquid resin and resorcinol glue, with excellent properties, are being used widely. In all cases, the glues should be mixed according to manufacturer's instructions. The following simple instructions have proved practical for urea glues:

1. Place the amount of glue required in an enamel, iron, or glass mixing pot and add water slowly. The right consistency is reached when the glue just drips from the end of the brush. The glue remains usable for as long as it is spreadable, usually about four hours. Apply the glue with a brush.

2. Put the parts together and make sure that all joints fit properly and line up squarely. Mark the parts so that they can be identified quickly when the point of assembly is reached. Not more than 15 minutes should elapse between the time of applying the glue and the time of applying pressure to the assembled joints.

3. Apply plenty of glue to one of the two surfaces at each point of joining. Adjust hand screws and clamps to hold the work firmly together until the glue is hard. Drying takes about 16 hours, depending on the temperature and type of wood. For best curing the room temperature should be approximately 70°F.

4. Following application of the clamps, test again for alignment. Scrape off excess glue as it oozes from the joints. A helpful hint is to dust the excess glue with sawdust, which absorbs the moisture and makes the glue easier to remove. Avoid using water or a moist rag in removing the excess glue. This will only spread the glue around in a thin layer, which will show on the finished product.

5. When the glue is dry, remove the clamps and carefully remove excess glue. Sand before finishing.

FASTENING FURRING STRIPS TO MASONRY

The remodeling of basements frequently poses the problem of fastening wood furring strips to either concrete block or concrete foundations.

Concrete Block. A simple method consists of drilling holes in the block and driving wood pegs tightly into the holes. Furring strips can be nailed directly to the pegs. Star drills may be used for drilling the holes. Or, if available, electric drills with masonry bits speed up the work.

Concrete. Where solid concrete is concerned, Rawlplugs or iron expansion anchors constitute simple and sure methods of fastening furring strips to concrete.

Holes of sufficient depth and diameter to admit the plugs or anchors must first be formed with an electric drill. In the case of Rawlplugs,

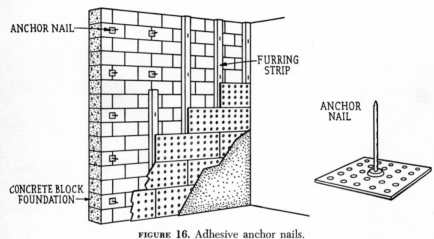

FIGURE 16. Adhesive anchor nails.

lead cores are driven into the holes. Screws can then be used to fasten furring strips to the cores at the surface of the concrete. In the case of iron expansion anchors, expansion pieces are driven into the holes and bolts used to fasten furring strips to the expansion pieces at the surface of the concrete.

In addition to the foregoing methods, the use of hardened-steel nails sometimes works out satisfactorily if they can be driven into mortar joints between concrete blocks.

Another and quite different method of fastening furring strips to masonry consists of using adhesive anchors, as indicated in Figure 16. The furring strips must be softwood, such as white pine.

To attach the anchor nails, spread enough adhesive on the anchor base with a putty knife to ensure a film of adhesive approximately 1/16 inch thick after the anchor has been firmly pressed against the masonry. Allow 48 hours for the adhesive to set. Hold furring strips against the attached anchor nails and tap lightly with a hammer. Use the resulting indentations as centers for holes to be drilled through the furring strips. Press the furring strips over the anchor nails. If the masonry is uneven, insert wood shims between the anchor nails and the furring strips. Finally, plumb the furring strips and clinch the nails.

FASTENING SILLS TO FOUNDATIONS

As shown in Figures 3, 4, and 17, single or double sills are used as a base for headers and joists. The sills are securely fastened together and the headers are toenailed to the sills. All this fastening would be of little good, so far as stiffness is concerned, unless the sills are fastened to the foundations by means of anchor bolts, as shown in Figure 17. Such bolts

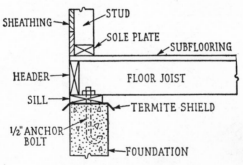

FIGURE 17. Anchor bolt for sill.

must be set in the concrete while it is still plastic and should be spaced 4′ 0″ apart.

When sills are to be supported somewhat as shown in Figure 18, powder-actuated fasteners may be employed. The fasteners are shot into place by a gunlike mechanism. This procedure saves considerable cost and time.

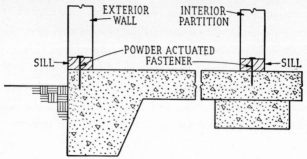

FIGURE 18. Powder-actuated fasteners for sills.

MITER STIFFENERS

When joints in frames of any kind tend to be loose, a miter stiffener, such as shown in Figure 19, can be used to advantage. The miter fits into a single saw cut making an interlocking and tight joint.

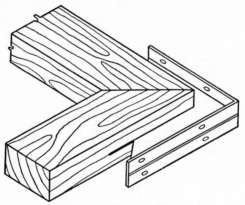

FIGURE 19. Miter stiffener.

JOIST HANGERS

In remodeling work, we are apt to encounter several situations where joists cannot be supported in the conventional manner. In such cases, steel joist hangers, such as shown in Figure 20, may be used to great advantage.

The *A* part of the illustration shows a hanger for fastening ceiling joists to beams. This hanger is especially helpful when it is impossible to put the joists on top of the beam.

The *B* part of the illustration shows how hangers may be used to fasten floor joists to beams.

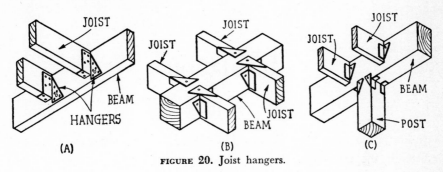

FIGURE 20. Joist hangers.

The *C* part of the illustration shows how hangers may be used to fasten new posts or columns to beams where added support is required. Also shown are somewhat different types of hangers for fastening smaller joists to beams.

CHAPTER THREE

Insulation

Authoritative tests have shown that there is a 50 per cent heat *loss* through the structural details of an *uninsulated* house during *cold* weather. In other words, *half* of the heat produced by the heating system in an uninsulated house is actually *wasted*. This means that *half* of the money spent for fuel is also wasted. In addition, such houses are subject to drafts, unequal temperatures, vapor condensation, and many other uncomfortable or unhealthy conditions.

Authoritative tests have also shown that there is a 50 per cent heat *gain* through the exposed structural details of an *uninsulated* house during *hot* weather. In other words, the interior of an uninsulated house often becomes so warm, both day and night, that it is uncomfortable to live in. If an uninsulated house is cooled by mechanical means, the required equipment is excessively expensive from the standpoints of initial cost and operating power.

In order to visualize where heat losses and gains occur in an uninsulated house, let us study Figure 1.

The *X* part of the illustration shows the percentage of heat *loss* through each of the important structural details. For example, 32.9 per cent of the total heat loss occurs through the exterior walls. In terms of the whole house, the *total* heat loss depends upon wind conditions, method of construction, and the difference between interior and exterior temperatures. But, whatever the total is, 32.9 per cent of it is lost through the exterior walls. The percentages of heat loss through other structural details are as indicated.

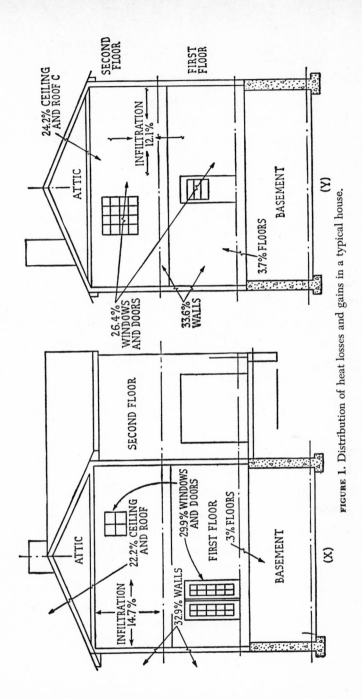

FIGURE 1. Distribution of heat losses and gains in a typical house.

The *Y* part of the illustration shows the percentage of heat *gain* through each of the important structural details. For example, 24.2 per cent of the *total* heat gain occurs because the roof and top-floor ceiling are not insulated. The *total* heat gain depends upon wind conditions, exposure to the sun, and the temperature of the exterior air. But, whatever the total is, 24.2 per cent of it comes in through the roof and top-floor ceiling.

All heat-loss and heat-gain percentages shown in Figure 1 are based upon two-story houses. The percentages are approximations and will vary, for example, with the ratio of roof area to wall area. In a one-story house, the percentage is likely to be much greater for the roof and correspondingly less for the walls. Otherwise, the values shown are reasonably typical.

Old or relatively new houses may be insulated in any one or more of several ways to give them more resistance to heat losses and gains. Such work can be done as separate projects or at the time other remodeling work is being carried on. The purpose of this chapter is to describe the kinds of insulation generally used, to explain several important aspects of its application and benefits, to suggest several effective remodeling projects, and to show how to plan and do typical installation work.

WHAT IS INSULATION?

When we start to think about insulation it is only natural that our first question should have to do with the material itself. What is it? Once we have satisfactorily answered this question, we will have something definite upon which subsequent discussions can be based.

When a material or substance possesses such special qualities that it can resist, or tend to resist, the flow of heat through its bulk, it may be called *insulation* or an *insulating material*. At this point we should understand that no known material or substance is able completely to stop the flow of heat through its bulk. So long as there is a difference in temperature between the two sides of a material, some heat will flow through its bulk.

Any solid building material will resist the flow of heat to some extent.

For example, frame and masonry walls or floors reduce the flow of heat to a slight degree. Because of its internal structure, wood is a better insulating material than any of the denser materials such as concrete or metal. However, none of the ordinary building materials, in the thicknesses generally used, are able to retard the flow of heat to any appreciable degree.

In order to qualify as an insulating material, a substance must be lightweight and contain a high percentage of air spaces or voids. Some natural substances, such as cork, fur, cotton, wool, and straw, are thus endowed and have long been used as insulating materials. However, such substances are not suitable for modern construction. Therefore, new insulating materials (substances) have had to be developed and manufactured. Such materials possess what is known as *concentrated resistance to the flow of heat*.

KINDS OF INSULATION

So far as trade names are concerned, there are many varieties of insulating materials available. However, all varieties may be grouped into six basic kinds.

Loose Fill. This kind is bulk in nature and is sold in bags. Three types are available: fibrous, powdered, and granular.

Blanket. This kind is manufactured in strips and is sold in rolls or packs. It is flexible and may be obtained in several widths and thicknesses. Two types are available: those encased in plain kraft paper, and those encased in aluminum foil.

Bat. This kind is similar to blankets except that the bats are produced in small units usually about 15 inches wide and 8 to 48 inches long.

Structural Insulating Board. Produced in large units, this kind, as the name implies, is a synthetic or manufactured insulating lumber, com monly known as *rigid boards*. It can be obtained 4 or more feet in width, 8 or more feet in length, and in ½- and 1-inch thicknesses.

Slab. Slab insulation is generally composed of small, rigid units which are 1 or more inches thick and up to 24 by 48 inches long. This insulation is especially made for use in connection with flat or nearly flat roofs.

Reflective. Reflective insulations are distinguished from all other kinds by the fact that they depend solely upon surface characteristics for their resistance to the flow of heat. While other insulations resist the flow of heat by means of air spaces and voids, this kind actually *reflects* heat. Therefore, and in order that they be effective, reflective insulations must always be so placed that their reflective surfaces face air spaces.

All the basic kinds of insulation are used in the manufacture of various and sundry products for use by the building industry. A visit to a lumberyard or to a building-material dealer's showroom will prove of great interest and help in the selection of insulation for any building purpose. Inexperienced mechanics will find that the blanket kind is easy to install and that it can be used to advantage, except as explained in connection with Figure 6.

BENEFITS OF INSULATION

Now that we have defined insulation and have reviewed the basic kinds, we can think about some of the important benefits it makes possible in any house regardless of geographic location.

At this point we should understand that insulating materials are not always *extra* or added structural costs. In many instances, they can replace or be used instead of traditional materials. For example, rigid boards can be used in place of wood sheathing and in place of traditional lathing.

The following general benefits are important considerations so far as remodeling plans are concerned:

Less Costly Heating System. Because insulating greatly reduces heat loss, new heating systems can be of small capacity and thus less costly.

Less Costly Cooling Systems. Insulation greatly reduces the amount of heat gain during hot weather. Thus, cooling equipment can be of small capacity and therefore less costly.

Fuel Savings. As indicated at the beginning of this chapter uninsulated houses waste 50 per cent of the heat supplied by heating systems. As such waste is reduced by means of insulation, fuel consumption is also reduced. Within a reasonably short time, the fuel savings pay for the insulation. After that time, the insulation constitutes a profitable investment.

Power Savings. With less heating or cooling required, fan and burner motors do not operate as long or as often.

Decorating Savings. In older houses, where wood lath were used, ceilings generally develop light and dark streaks, known as *ghost marks.* Such marks become noticeable long before a heating season is over and make frequent cleaning and redecorating necessary. Proper use of ceiling insulations prevents such undesirable conditions. In fact, well-insulated houses are much easier to keep clean and require redecorating much less often.

Protection against Vermin. Many forms of insulation, especially the loose-fill kinds, protect houses against all kinds of vermin.

Comfort. Perhaps the greatest and most appreciated benefit of insulation has to do with the living comfort it makes possible. A well-insulated house makes "climate-conditioning" a reality.

INSULATION PRINCIPLES

In order better to understand how insulation functions and the benefits it makes possible, we shall review a few simple principles, all of which are nothing more than basic laws of nature.

Heat Flow. Heat has a natural tendency to flow from a high temperature level to a low temperature level. This constitutes an unchangeable

law. In other words, if the temperature of the air within a house is 70°F
at a time when the temperature of the outdoor air is only 40°, the heat
within the house will tend to flow in the direction of the colder air. Or, if
the temperature at the interior surface of a wall is 70°, while the temperature at the exterior surface is only 40°, heat will flow from the warm to
the cold surface. The purpose of insulation is to resist such flow.

How Heat Flow Takes Place. There are three ways in which heat flow
takes place through a wall or other structural detail: conduction, convection, and radiation. All three ways of heat flow are in operation so far as
heat loss or gain is concerned.

CONDUCTION. As an example of heat flow by conduction, suppose that
we put one end of an iron bar into a fire. Before long, the other end will
become too hot to handle. The heat will have traveled from one end of
the bar to the other. In like manner, if one side of an ordinary building
material is hot or cold, heat will travel to the opposite side by conduction.
Or, if one piece of cold building material touches another piece which is
warm, heat will flow from the warm piece to the cold piece. In like manner, if cold air comes in contact with warm air, heat will flow from the
warm to the cold air.

CONVECTION. When warm air, from a radiator or other source, comes
in contact with colder air in a room, heat flow takes place, as previously
explained. Also, the warm air rises and creates a circulation. The circulation carries warm air to the cold surfaces of exterior walls (the surfaces
became cold because heat flowed to the opposite and colder surfaces),
where it loses heat to the walls by conduction. This process of heat flow
is known as *convection.*

RADIATION. Heat is radiated from the sun to the earth. In like manner,
heat is radiated from any warm object or material to a nearby colder
object or material. In other words, warm plaster radiates heat to the exterior surface materials in a wall.

How Heat Flows through a Wall. Figure 2 illustrates the manner in
which heat flows (or is transferred) to, through, and away from an
exterior wall. The source of heat in a room can be a radiator or hot-air
outlet of any kind. As indicated in the illustration, the heat flows from its

source to the interior surface of the exterior wall by means of conduction, convection, and radiation. It flows through the wall by means of conduction and radiation. From the outside surface, the flow away from the wall is by means of conduction, convection, and radiation.

During hot weather, the flow of heat is reversed.

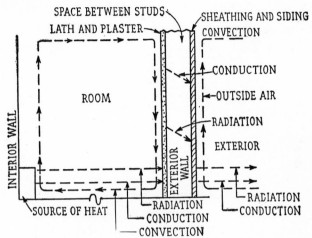

FIGURE 2. Heat transfer or flow to, through, and from a wall.

HOW INSULATION FUNCTIONS

We can safely classify most kinds of insulation into two general classes: *mass* and *reflective*. The mass class includes all kinds which have appreciable thickness or bulk, such as loose fill, blankets, bats, and rigid sheets or boards. The reflective class includes only those kinds which have little or no bulk.

When mass insulations are placed in walls or other structural details, they effectively resist the flow of heat because they have low conductivity (concentrated resistance) and because very little convection or radiation is possible. When reflective insulations are placed in walls or other structural details, they resist the flow of heat effectively because the heat is reflected back whence it came. Such insulations also retard radiation, as from plaster to exterior-surface materials, and do not have enough bulk for conduction to take place.

HOW MUCH INSULATION TO USE

The more insulation used in structural details, the more the insulation value obtained. But it is not logical, because of the law of diminishing returns, to conclude that cost savings increase with large increases in insulation. Generally, the first inch of insulation thickness is the most effective and each successive layer of the same thickness is less and less effective. For example, a single thickness of rigid insulation in a flat roof might save 200 gallons of oil per heating season per 1,000 square feet of insulated area. Adding a second layer of the same thickness might save about 80 gallons more; a third layer, only 40 gallons more. Thus, there is a point where additional thicknesses serve to little advantage but add considerable cost.

The law of diminishing returns does not apply to insulating materials which are available in only one thickness. For example, blankets, bats, and rigid sheets or boards are manufactured in certain thicknesses which, for them, is the most effective thickness to use. There must be successive thicknesses to result in diminishing returns. However, the law does apply to insulations of the reflective kinds, which can be used in one or more curtains or sheets.

CONDENSATION

The air around us always contains some moisture in the form of invisible vapor. The amount of such moisture in the air at any given time generally depends upon the temperature of the air. Under ordinary conditions, warm air is able to hold more moisture than cold air. In fact, the warmer the air, the more moisture it is able to hold. Conversely, the colder the air, the less moisture it is able to hold.

The percentage of moisture actually held, in relation to the total amount that air is able to hold, at any given temperature, is called the *relative humidity*. In other words, when warm summer air feels wet, its relative humidity is high.

The temperature at which the air is no longer able to hold all the moisture it contains is called the *dew point*. At this point of temperature, the moisture condenses out of the air. This is what happens when warm air surrounding a glass containing an ice-cold liquid is chilled by the glass to a temperature below its dew point. Moisture from the warm air condenses on the glass, which then appears to "sweat."

These facts are important because vapor moisture, in uncondensed form, can pass through most building materials—lath, plaster, wood, even masonry. And in winter, outdoor temperatures are usually far below the dew point of the warm air inside a home. Such moisture can cause many troubles within frame walls and to the siding and paint at the exterior surface of them.

It is recommended that a vapor barrier be placed in walls, top-floor ceilings, and in floors over unheated areas to prevent penetration of vapor moisture, from the warm interior, into parts of structural details where

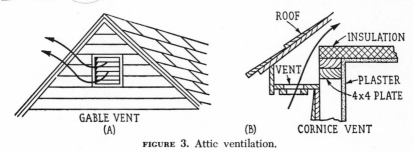

FIGURE 3. Attic ventilation.

the temperature may be below the dew point. Most kinds of mass insulations are provided with a moisture barrier on one surface. The reflective insulations, being made of metal, are natural moisture barriers.

Ventilation is another important aid to condensation control. It should be provided above insulation installed in attics. So placed, it permits the escape of vapor moisture, that in winter may find its way to the attic area. In summer, it reduces the head load on the attic insulation. All this will seem more important when we realize that an average family creates about 26 pounds of water vapor per day when bathing, doing laundry work, cooking, etc.

Attic Ventilation. When top-floor ceilings under unused attics are insulated, vents should be placed at the gables and at the cornices, as shown in the *A* and *B* parts of Figure 3. The gable vents, which are generally known as *louvers,* exhaust the air that comes in through the cornice vents. The total area of the cornice vents should be in the proportion of 1 square foot per 300 square feet of ceiling area. This proportion should be doubled for roofs having little pitch.

Where hip roofs are involved, the louvers can be cut into the roofs at points as near to their highest points as possible.

Crawl-space Ventilation. Such spaces should be ventilated by means of vents cut into the side walls. The total area of such vents should be in the proportion of 2 square feet of vent area per 100 lineal feet of enclosed wall, plus $\frac{1}{300}$ of the area enclosed by the wall.

SUGGESTED REMODELING PROJECTS

The following suggestions include only such insulating work as can be accomplished without having to tear out or otherwise disturb existing structural details. However, each and every one of the projects suggested has definite merit in terms of fuel savings and added living comforts.

Top-floor Ceilings. In cases where attic spaces are too small for use or where homeowners do not plan to create living areas in them, insulation can be placed between the joists which support the floor and ceiling, as a means of insulating the rooms below.

Ceiling insulation is of value in any climate because it reduces heat loss during the winter or cool seasons and heat gain during hot seasons. Thus the insulation will help to reduce fuel bills and make rooms much more comfortable during all seasons of the year.

INSULATING MATERIALS. Any one of the three kinds of insulation shown in Figure 4 may be used.

BLANKET OR BAT. The *A* part of the illustration shows such insulation applied between joists. Both kinds are generally placed so that their moisture barriers are in contact with the ceiling lath. For the purpose of ceiling insulation, thickness of 3 or 4 inches is sufficient. Tacks or staples can be used to fasten the nailing flanges to the joists.

LOOSE FILL. The *B* part of the illustration shows such insulation after being poured between the joists. Some form of moisture barrier should be placed in contact with the plaster.

REFLECTIVE. The *C* part of the illustration shows the insulation applied between joists. Such insulation is fragile and should not be used in top-floor ceilings unless there is a floor to protect it. Note that air spaces are

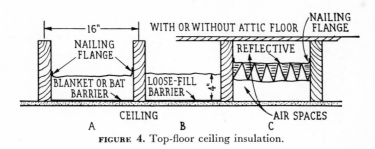

FIGURE 4. Top-floor ceiling insulation.

required both above and below it. Tacks or staples may be used to fasten the nailing flanges to the joists.

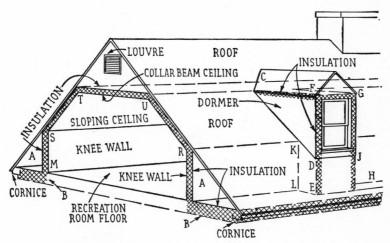

FIGURE 5. Knee-wall and roof insulation in attic space.

Attic Knee Walls and Roof. When attic spaces are being remodeled, the areas near the meeting places of roofs and floors, as shown at *A* in Figure 5, are generally too low and cramped for any good use. For this reason knee walls, also shown in the illustration, are usually constructed.

The ceilings of attic spaces are always lowered by means of collar beams. Insulation can be installed in the knee walls, the sloping ceilings, the collar-beam ceiling, and at the locations marked B.

INSULATING MATERIALS. Any one of several kinds of insulation can be used, depending upon the type of ceiling and wall-surface materials (see Chapters 4 and 5) being employed.

PLASTER. If plaster is to be applied to the walls and ceilings, a rigid insulating material 1 inch thick can be used in place of noninsulating lathing. In such cases, the areas marked B can be insulated by means of blanket, bat, or reflective insulating materials.

PLANKS, ETC. If planks, block, board, tile, or panel surfaces are to be used, the walls, ceilings, and areas marked B can be insulated by means of blanket, bat, or reflective insulating materials in much the same manner as shown in Figure 4. One-inch thick rigid panels or boards could also be used, in which case they would serve as backing for the surface materials and instead of the furring strips which would otherwise be necessary.

Dormers. In order to provide more light and better natural ventilation in remodeled attic spaces, dormers such as shown in Figure 5 are frequently constructed. Insulation is necessary in the two side walls, such as CFD; in the ceiling, such as CFG; in the front walls, such as $DJHE$; and in such areas as $KDEL$.

INSULATING MATERIALS. The same kind of insulation as used for knee walls and ceilings should be installed in the dormer details. However, where so many irregularly shaped areas are involved, the flexible blankets and bats are much easier to install.

Roofs. In many houses of recent design and construction, the attic spaces are not high enough for use except as possible storage areas. In such cases, the ceilings of rooms under the attic spaces are subject to great heat losses and gains. The heat losses are serious in terms of winter fuel bills, and the heat gains are apt to make the rooms almost unbearable, both day and night, during the summer. Insulation can be installed in either the ceilings or the roofs.

INSULATING MATERIALS. Any kind of insulation, placed in either the roofs or ceilings, would definitely help to reduce heat losses. However, a particular kind of insulation should be used as a means of avoiding the uncomfortable heat gains. This holds true only so far as roofs are concerned and when attic spaces are empty.

Empty attic spaces would be the best kind of insulation against the hot summer sun, were it not for radiation. When no insulation is used, as indicated at *A* in Figure 6, the roof absorbs great quantities of heat from the sun and radiates all of it to the ceilings of the rooms below attic

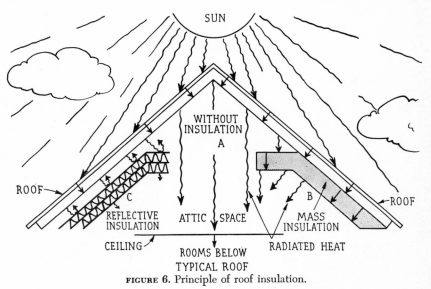

FIGURE 6. Principle of roof insulation.

spaces. Mass insulations, such as shown at *B*, may retard heat flow for a short time, but in doing so they absorb heat which is eventually radiated to the ceilings. The radiation process is apt to continue long after sunset time with the result that rooms are uncomfortably warm both day and night. Reflective insulations, such as shown at *C*, have very little mass. Thus, they cannot store much heat or emit appreciable amounts of radiation. In addition, reflective insulations tend to reflect the sun's heat away from attic spaces.

Foundations. When basements are remodeled, some form of insulation is generally required in connection with the interior surfaces of concrete or concrete-block foundations. Any one or more of several conditions may be encountered. For example, in climates where freezing temperatures occur the foundations may be cold. This would constitute a serious source of heat loss and cause the radiation of cold drafts into the living areas. In climates where a great deal of rain occurs, the surfaces of foundations may be cool and slightly damp. In other cases, foundations may sweat to the extent that water runs down their surfaces.

INSULATING MATERIALS. All of the conditions mentioned in the foregoing paragraph can be corrected or remedied by means of insulation.

Cold Surfaces. The *A* part of Figure 7 shows panels of decorative insulation applied to furring strips on a concrete-block wall. The *B, C,* and

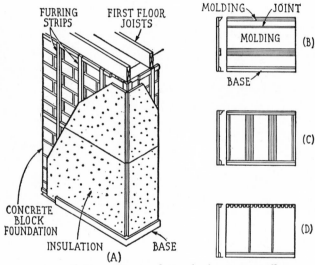

FIGURE 7. Decorative insulation for basement walls.

D parts of the illustration indicate typical patterns which can be employed. The *B* pattern may be used to create a feeling of more space in a small recreation room while the *C* and *D* patterns may be employed to make a long room appear to better advantage. The material can be secured in various colors and textures and in many sizes and thicknesses. Some brands are manufactured in neutral tones which may be painted or otherwise decorated. Colored nails to match the insulation are available.

Cool and Damp Surfaces. Masonry foundations can be insulated against cool and damp surfaces by means of reflective insulation, as shown in Figure 8. The insulation is ½ inch thick and of a width suitable for installation between 1- by 3-inch furring strips spaced 16 inches on centers. It should be fastened in place by means of laths. After the insulation has been installed, any desired surface material may be applied over the laths.

SWEATING. Sweating occurs during warm weather when the surface temperatures of foundations are below the dew-point temperatures of the air. The kind of insulation shown in Figure 7 may be used to prevent sweating.

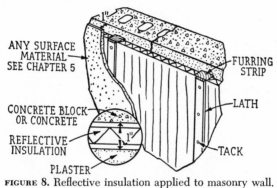

FIGURE 8. Reflective insulation applied to masonry wall.

Basement Floors. Concrete floors may be cold and damp for the same reasons explained in connection with foundations. See Figure 8 in Chapter 6.

Floor Slabs. In some unfortunate instances, concrete floor slabs for basementless houses have been placed directly on the ground, as shown in Figure 9, without insulation under them or around the foundations. In such cases, areas of the floors, such as between *A* and *B*, are apt to be especially cold. The heavy dashed line shows the path taken by low temperatures as they travel from the outside soil through the foundations and into the floors. Such conditions can be remedied by insulation.

INSULATING MATERIALS. By means of some simple excavating, 2-inch waterproof insulation can be applied to the exteriors of the foundations, as shown at *E*. Even more insulating effect can be obtained by removing only parts of the floors and installing more waterproof insulation around the interior surface of the foundations, as shown at *F*. Hot asphalt can be used to cement the insulation to the foundations.

Crawl Spaces. Unless crawl spaces are well vented, as previously explained, and unless the floors above them and the soil surface are insulated, low temperatures and dampness, especially in cold or damp climates, will flow up through the floor and cause discomfort.

INSULATING MATERIALS. Figure 10 shows a pictorial view of a typical crawl space along with the usual floor construction and other structural details. Either blanket or rigid insulation can be used between the floor

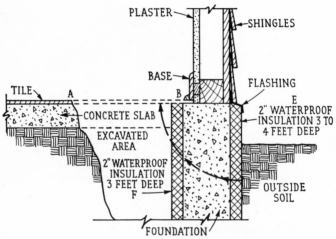

FIGURE 9. How to insulate floor slab on ground.

joists as a protection against low temperatures and dampness. As a further and also important means of protection, especially against dampness, soil surfaces can be covered using heavy, waterproof paper somewhat as shown in Figure 10. All joints between strips of the paper should be lapped 6 inches and cemented together by means of hot asphalt. The ends of the strips should be bent up 6 inches and cemented to the foundation also by means of hot asphalt.

Added Rooms. Major remodeling projects often consist of adding new rooms to existing houses. Such rooms, often similar to the room shown in Figure 11, generally have shed-type roofs and only crawl spaces under

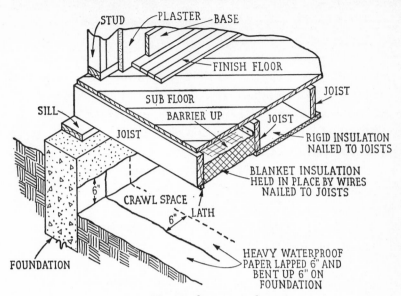

STUD PLASTER BASE

FINISH FLOOR

SUB FLOOR

BARRIER UP JOIST

JOIST

SILL

JOIST

RIGID INSULATION
NAILED TO JOISTS

BLANKET INSULATION
HELD IN PLACE BY WIRES
NAILED TO JOISTS

6"

CRAWL SPACE

6" LATH

FOUNDATION

HEAVY WATERPROOF
PAPER LAPPED 6" AND
BENT UP 6" ON
FOUNDATION

FIGURE 10. Crawl-space insulation.

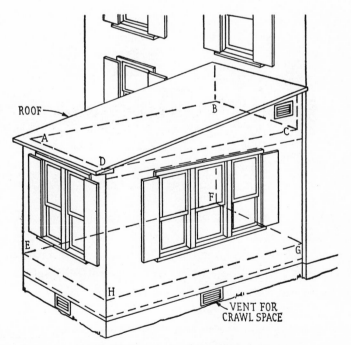

ROOF

A

B

C

D

F

E

G

H

VENT FOR
CRAWL SPACE

FIGURE 11. How to insulate added rooms.

them. The following insulation suggestions are presented in the order of their importance:

Ceilings. Ceiling areas, such as the one shown at *ABCD* in Figure 11, may be insulated using blankets, bats, rigid, loose-fill, or reflective insulation. Blankets, bats, and loose fill could be placed between ceiling joists, and rigid panels could be used in place of traditional lathing. However, because there is so little space between shed roofs and ceilings, especially in terms of heat gain, reflective insulation between roof joists is recommended.

Floors. Floor areas, as *EFGH* of Figure 11, can be insulated as shown in Figure 10, using either blankets or rigid panels.

Walls. While walls are being built, and at times immediately after the exterior wood sheathing has been applied, blanket, bat, loose-fill, or reflective insulation could be placed between studs. Figure 12 shows how

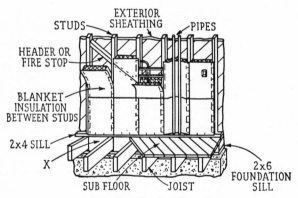

FIGURE 12. Details of wall insulation.

blankets are used in walls. (NOTE: As shown at *X*, the insulation should be placed between the 2 by 4 and 2 by 6 sills.) Rigid insulation could also be used as wall sheathing and as plaster backing.

DOUBLE GLAZING. As indicated in Figure 1, windows and doors account for almost one-third of the heat losses and more than one-fourth of the heat gains in average houses. The total window area is always much greater than the total door area. Thus, it is wise to consider any possible means of giving windows more resistance to heat flow.

INSULATING MATERIALS. There are no insulating materials, as such, that can be applied to windows. However, it is possible to install sash which have two panes of glass separated by an air space. Such sash are available in all standard sizes and can be depended upon to reduce heat flow by as much as 50 per cent. As shown in Figure 13, existing windows can be given the benefits of double glazing by means of an added pane of glass that can be removed at will.

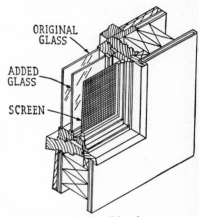

Infiltration. As indicated in Figure 1, infiltration (cracks around windows and doors) accounts for about one-seventh of the heat losses and for about one-eighth of the heat gains in average houses. The *A* part of Figure 14 shows how cold and hot air flows through such cracks. In masonry walls, cracks often occur between the window frames and the

FIGURE 13. Double glazing.

surrounding masonry units. Such cracks should be filled with caulking compound.

INSULATING MATERIALS. Heat losses and gains through the window cracks shown in the *A* part of Figure 14 can be prevented by means of the typical weatherstripping shown in the *B* part of the same illustration. In order to install such weatherstripping, the sash must be grooved as shown. Woodworking mills have the equipment for cutting the grooves. Other types of weatherstripping are also available, but they do not have the finished appearance of those shown in Figure 14.

STORM SASH. Storm sash accomplish about the same resistance to heat flow as double glazing.

Figure 15 illustrates a typical application of wood-frame storm sash to the type of windows found in most old houses. Such sash create an air space between themselves and the prime windows. The air space acts as insulation and the two panes of glass reduce heat loss by conduction. In

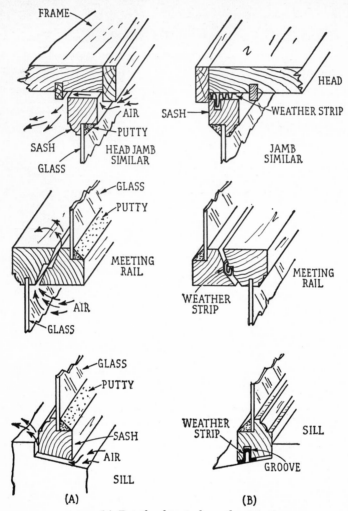

FRAME

HEAD

AIR
SASH
WEATHER STRIP
PUTTY

SASH
HEAD JAMB
SIMILAR
JAMB
SIMILAR
GLASS

GLASS
PUTTY

MEETING
RAIL

MEETING
RAIL

AIR
WEATHER
STRIP
GLASS

GLASS
PUTTY

WEATHER
STRIP
SILL

SASH

AIR
GROOVE
SILL

(A)   (B)

FIGURE 14. Details of typical weatherstripping.

addition, infiltration losses are reduced and less sweating occurs. However, in order for storm sash to be effective, they must be *tightly* fitted at such places as indicated at *B*. Unless tight fits are assured, storm sash have little value. This fact should be kept in mind.

Metal-frame storm sash are more effective than the old-style wood-frame varieties, provided that they are properly fitted.

If storm sash are employed, they should be fitted to *all* windows in houses—not confined to the sides facing prevailing winter winds.

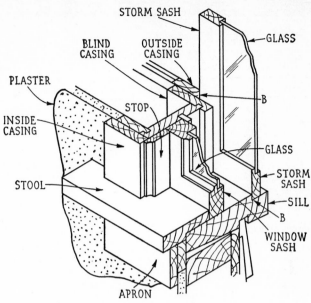

STORM SASH

BLIND CASING

OUTSIDE CASING

GLASS

PLASTER

INSIDE CASING

STOP

B

STOOL

GLASS

STORM SASH

SILL

B

WINDOW SASH

APRON

FIGURE 15. Application of storm sash.

Existing Walls. As indicated in Figure 1, walls account for more heat losses and gains than any of the other structural details in average houses. Thus, it is wise to give careful attention to ways and means of applying insulation to them. The following suggestions constitute several economical ways of providing effective insulation against excessive heat losses and gains.

Frame Walls. There are two logical ways of insulating existing frame walls. One way has to do with the application of loose-fill insulation between studs. The other way has to do with the application of rigid insulation to surfaces. Both ways avoid excessive cost.

Pneumatic Application. The application of fill insulation between studs of existing walls is somewhat difficult, owing to lack of access to such areas; but, if small areas of siding and sheathing are temporarily removed, loose-fill insulation can be blown in by means of a hose under pneumatic pressure. Such installation work must be done by professional applicators equipped with the necessary apparatus. This process works out to advantage only when no headers or fire stops, such as shown in Figure 12, are present.

The necessary vapor barriers can be provided by applying two or more coats of an efficient vapor-resistant paint, such as aluminum, to plaster surfaces, or other interior finish, prior to the time decorating work is started.

Application of Rigid Insulation. See Chapter 5.

Masonry Walls. See previous explanation in connection with Figure 7. Also see Chapter 5.

Flat Roofs. Some form of built-up roofing, consisting of waterproof paper, bitumen, and fine gravel, is generally used on flat or nearly flat roofs. In such cases, insulation can be applied in either of two ways.

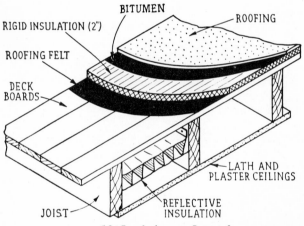

FIGURE 16. Insulation on flat roof.

INSULATING MATERIALS. As shown in Figure 16, 2-inch slab insulation may be laid on the decks of such roofs; or reflective insulation can be applied between the rafters in such a manner that air spaces above and below it are assured.

Sound Transmission. Sound actually travels through wood structural details. In other words, such materials convey sound from one location to another. For example, sounds originating in basement recreation rooms are transmitted through the floors to areas above the recreation rooms. In like manner, sounds originating in kitchens are transmitted through the walls to adjacent areas. There are several ways of controlling or reducing such sound transmission.

New Construction. If major remodeling projects include new frame walls, the studs can be staggered and blanket insulation placed between them as indicated in the *A* part of Figure 17. Note that separate studs are required for each wall surface. This arrangement of studs separates the two surfaces so that there is not a continuous material between them through which sound can be transmitted. The insulation tends to reduce the passage of sound between the studs and through the walls.

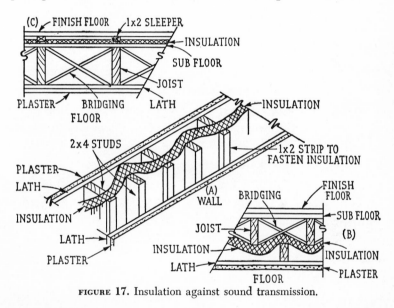

FIGURE 17. Insulation against sound transmission.

If new floors are being constructed, dual joists can be installed and blanket insulation placed between them as indicated in the *B* part of the illustration. This joist arrangement separates the ceiling and floor surfaces so that transmission of sound is greatly reduced.

Existing Floors. In cases where new hardwood finish floors are going to be laid, rigid or thin blanket insulation can be installed as indicated in the *C* part of the illustration.

Existing Walls and Ceilings. See Chapters 4 and 5.

HOW TO PLAN AND DO
TYPICAL REMODELING PROJECTS

The following projects constitute typical examples of the insulation problems most generally encountered and are set forth in keeping with approved planning and installation procedures. Only a few of the previously suggested remodeling projects are included because some of them have already been sufficiently explained and because all such work follows about the same pattern. Blanket insulation is herein used because of its popularity and simplicity.

TOP-FLOOR CEILING

This project is typical of any and all cases where top-floor ceilings, under empty attic spaces, are to be insulated against heat losses and gains.

PROBLEM 1: ANY TOP-FLOOR CEILING. For the purpose of this problem, we can assume that the attic space does not have a floor and that blankets of the double-thick variety 16 inches wide are to be used. The problem is to install the insulation between the joists.

SOLUTION. As indicated in Figure 18, a convenient length of 2 by 10 plank can be placed across the tops of the joists and used for body support during the installation work.

Unfold the blankets and cut them to approximate length by means of a saw or tin snips. Lay the strips between the joists, as shown in the picture, so that their moisture barriers are on the ceiling side.

The ends of the strips should be prepared as shown in the *A* part of Figure 19 and then sealed to the plates as indicated in the *B* part of the illustration. Heavy tacks or an automatic stapler may be used. In Figure 18 the mechanic is shown sealing a strip end to a plate.

Unfold the nailing flanges on the blankets and bend them over the top edges of the joists, as shown in Figure 18. Space the tacks or staples about 6 inches apart.

Any tears in the liners (casings) can be repaired by brushing the torn area with hot bitumen and then covering the area with a piece of the liner. Bitumen is the general term for such materials as asphalt, tar, and pitch.

FIGURE 18. Application of blanket insulation between ceiling joists.

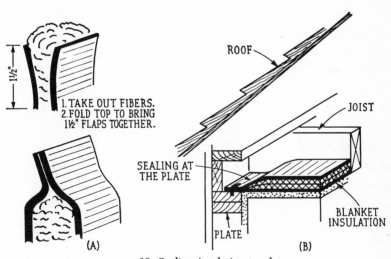

FIGURE 19. Sealing insulation to plate.

When insulating between joists, it may at some time be necessary to join two strips of blanket. This is easily accomplished by placing a 2 by 4 header between the joists and forming flanges, such as shown in the *A* part of Figure 19, at the strip ends which are tacked or stapled to the header.

In the Condensation section of this chapter we learned that when top-floor ceilings under unused attics are insulated, gable and cornice vents, such as shown in Figure 3, are necessary. Such vents are available at all lumberyards and should be installed before the advent of cold weather and the heating season. Without them, condensation in troublesome amounts is likely to occur.

KNEE WALLS

This project is typical of any and all cases where attic knee walls are to be insulated against heat losses and gains.

PROBLEM 2: KNEE WALLS IN FIGURE 5. For the purpose of this problem, we can assume that the attic space is being remodeled to create a recreation room and that the knee walls were erected to give the room a better appearance.

SOLUTION. In this solution we shall be concerned with the knee wall marked *SM* and the area under it marked *B*.

The *B* area, between the joists, should be insulated before the knee wall. Cut strips or blankets to approximate length, as shown at *X* in Figure 20, and then prepare their ends as shown in the *A* part of Figure 19. Make sure the moisture-barrier sides are down. Seal the ends of the *X* strips at points *a* and *b*, as shown in Figure 20, by means of tacks or staples. Fasten the nailing flanges to the joists.

For the knee wall, cut strips of blankets to the length shown at *Y* in Figure 20. Prepare their ends and then place them between the studs, as shown in Figure 21, so that the moisture-barrier sides face the room. Make the seals *c* and *d*, as shown in Figure 20, and fasten the nailing flanges, as shown in Figure 21. Space the tacks or staples about 6 inches apart.

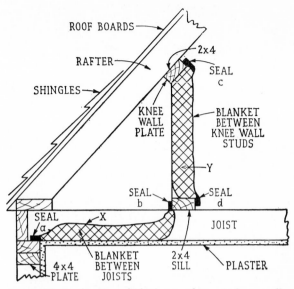

FIGURE 20. Application of blanket insulation to knee walls.

FIGURE 21. Application of blanket insulation to knee-wall studs.

COLLAR-BEAM CEILING

This project is typical of any and all cases where collar-beam ceilings are to be insulated against heat losses and gains.

PROBLEM 3: COLLAR-BEAM CEILING IN FIGURE 5. For the purpose of this problem we can make the same assumption as set forth in Problem 2, except that a collar-beam ceiling was erected as a further aid to the appearance and comfort of the recreation room.

SOLUTION. The areas marked *STUR* should be insulated using continuous strips of blankets, as indicated in Figure 22. Cut the strips of blanket to approximate length and prepare their ends. Make the seals at *e* and then draw the strips along *ST*, *TU*, and *UR* so that seals can be made at the knee-wall plate at *R*. Make sure that the moisture-barrier sides face the room.

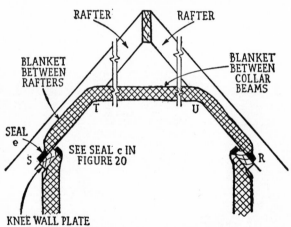

FIGURE 22. Application of blanket insulation to sloping-ceiling and collar beams.

In order to prevent any possibility of condensation in the recreation room, ample ventilation must be provided for. This can be accomplished by installing cornice vents and louvers, as shown in Figure 3 and as explained in the condensation section of this chapter. Referring to Figure 5, we can see that when the cornice vents and the louvers have been installed, air will enter the *A* areas, pass between the insulation and the roof in areas *ST* and *UR,* and enter the open space over the collar beams. From there it will be exhausted through the louvers.

CRAWL SPACES

This project is typical of any and all cases where floors above crawl spaces are to be insulated against heat losses and dampness.

PROBLEM 4: ANY CRAWL SPACE. For the purpose of this problem it can be assumed that a typical crawl space, such as shown in Figure 10, is involved. The problem is to apply insulation between the joists and to seal the surface of the soil.

SOLUTION. When new floors, such as shown in Figures 10 and 23, are being constructed, the blanket insulation can be applied in the following manner:

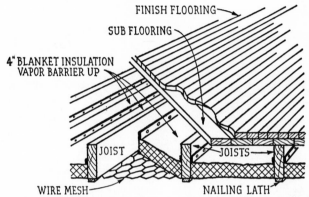

FIGURE 23. Blanket insulation between joists above a crawl space.

By means of lath, as indicated in the illustrations, fasten galvanized-wire mesh to the bottom edges of the joists. Lay the blankets on the wire so that their moisture-barrier sides are up. Use tacks or staples, spaced about 8 inches apart, to fasten the nailing flanges to the sides of the joists.

When existing floors are to be insulated, the blankets can be applied in the following manner:

Tuck the blankets up between the joists so that the moisture-barrier sides are up. Fasten wire mesh to the bottoms of the joists as previously explained.

If pipes, ducts, or other obstructions exist, shape the insulation to fit snugly around them. If necessary as a means of assuring a tight fit, cement the liners of the blankets to the obstructions by means of hot bitumen.

COMMON CONDENSATION TROUBLES

In climates where freezing winter weather occurs, many condensation troubles are apt to cause discomfort and even damage to interior trim and decorations. Generally, such troubles can be avoided or controlled by simple means. For the purpose of this discussion, we shall pose window sweating as a typical condensation trouble.

What causes window sweating? The principles of such condensation are explained in the Condensation section of this chapter. During cold

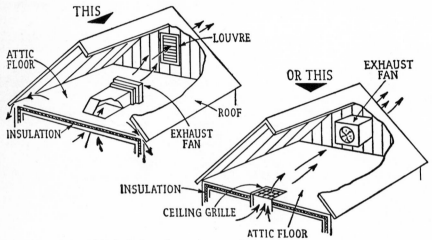

FIGURE 24. Attic fans for summer cooling and all-year ventilation.

weather, the interiors of houses are warm and the air generally has a high relative humidity. In other words, the air is warm and contains a great deal of moisture vapor. The surfaces of window glass are cold because they are in direct contact with exterior air. When the warm and humid interior air comes in contact with the cold window glass, the air is chilled below its dew point and it cannot hold as much moisture. The excess moisture is deposited on the window glass. Unless storm sash are tightly fitted, they do little to prevent such condensation.

Why is interior air humid? The excess moisture comes from cooking, bathing, the laundry where clothes are washed and dried, from occupants, from gas-fired heating equipment, from gas refrigerators, and many other sources.

How can condensation be controlled or avoided? The only remedy consists of ventilation. When cooking is in progress, kitchens should be ventilated by means of exhaust fans or open windows. The same holds true in connection with bathrooms and laundries. Enough ventilation to avoid condensation will be at the expense of some heat loss, but such losses are not serious.

Figure 24 shows typical installations of attic exhaust fans. During the winter, such fans can be used, as required, to ventilate houses—draw out humid air. Such fans also aid in the ventilation of attic spaces. During the summer months, such fans help materially to keep a house cooler, especially after sunset.

CHAPTER FOUR

Ceilings

Ceiling-surface materials often fall heir to any one or more of several natural and unfortunate defects. Natural defects are unavoidable even in the best of construction. They are caused by various changes in structural details. Unfortunate defects are caused by poor materials and by careless workmanship at the time houses are built.

Natural defects occur in the form of cracks. They are likely to appear in old houses and are actually the marks of time. Unfortunate defects, such as crumbling or roughness, are apt to appear in new houses within a year or two after construction is complete.

Defects of any kind are objectionable, because they mar or completely ruin the otherwise beautiful effects of modern decorating materials. Where defects exist, any attempt to accomplish satisfactory decorating constitutes useless expense and effort.

New structural materials, which can be used satisfactorily to repair ceilings or to give them entirely new and beautiful surfaces, are now available. The new materials are easy to apply and some of them accomplish soundproofing and insulating effects along with their highly desirable remodeling benefits. For example, previously unfinished basement and attic spaces can be transformed into attractive and usable living areas. See Chapters 7 and 9. The ceilings in such areas can be erected so that they are beautiful examples of modern materials, so that they are practically soundproof, and so that they have a high degree of insulating effect.

In this chapter we shall become acquainted with the most commonly encountered ceiling defects and learn how to judge them in terms of necessary repair or improvement. We shall also examine some typical remodeling suggestions, any one of which may be applied to any room in a house. Finally, we shall learn how to repair ceilings and how to plan and install new surface materials.

PLASTER DEFECTS

By means of the following explanations, we shall learn a great deal about the most commonly encountered ceiling defects so far as plaster on lath is involved. We shall also learn how to recognize and judge them in terms of recommended repair work and the application of new surface materials.

Cracks. As previously mentioned, cracks occur because of natural or unfortunate conditions. In some instances, both conditions are at fault.

Natural Conditions. There are several more or less natural conditions which are apt to cause plaster cracks, even though the best materials and excellent workmanship are used and exercised at the time a house is being built. In terms of practical and economical construction, such conditions cannot be avoided. They are almost sure to occur, especially as the years pass.

Lumber Shrinkage. As indicated by the typical structural details shown in Figure 1, the framing members of most houses are made entirely of wood. One wood detail supports another wood detail. All details are dependent upon each other. If something happens to one detail, one or more other details will be affected.

The best structural lumber, even when carefully kiln-dried or allowed to dry naturally over a long period of time, still contains some moisture at the time it is used to build structural details for a house. After a house has been subjected to one or more winters during which artificial heat is provided, the wood structural members lose moisture through the drying process and, at the same time, shrink in proportion to the amount of drying. Most of the shrinkage occurs across the grain. For example, the 2 by 8 joists shown in Figure 1 shrink along the 2- and 8-inch dimensions.

As shrinkage takes place in various structural members, especially in joists, plates, and sills, the supported members change positions. The plaster, being hard and brittle, cannot change its position. Therefore it cracks.

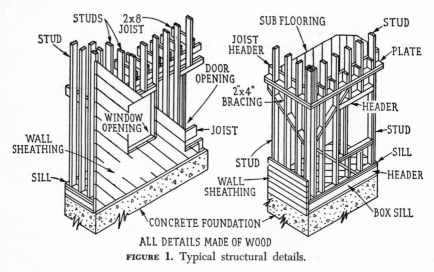

ALL DETAILS MADE OF WOOD

FIGURE 1. Typical structural details.

Settlement. Unless broad footings are provided under foundations, especially in soft soils such as clay, the foundations are apt to settle down into the soil to a variable degree. If such settlement is equal, all around a foundation, no plaster cracking is apt to happen. On the other hand, unequal settlement causes various structural members to shift positions. This invariably causes plaster cracking.

Expansion and Contraction. In climates which are subject to considerable and sudden changes in temperature, the resultant expansion and contraction in structural details causes some shifting of their positions. Such shifting is quite likely to crack nearby plaster.

Weight Shifts. Wood structural members actually bend when heavy weights or loads are applied to them. As they bend, they affect other supported members. Thus several members are apt to shift their positions. If a piano is moved from one side of a room to another side, the transfer of its weight could cause several structural members to shift their positions. Plaster cracks may be the result.

Wind Force. Severe windstorms exert a terrific pressure on one or more sides of a house. In some extreme instances, the pressure can be as much as 20 pounds per square foot. Such pressure causes various structural details to bend or to shift their positions. Plaster cracks are the inevitable result. Earthquakes also cause structural details to bend and to shift their positions. Again, plaster cracks are sure to follow.

Unfortunate Conditions. There are many more unfortunate than natural conditions which cause plaster to crack. While such conditions are deplorable, they must be recognized and understood.

POOR MATERIALS. In all too many cases, poor materials are the cause of severe and widespread plaster cracks in ceilings all through a house.

OVERSANDING. The use of too much sand in a plaster mix is a common evil often carried on as a means of reducing the amounts of more expensive cementitious materials. Such plaster is weak and is sure to crack shortly after being applied. To test for this condition, scratch the surface. If the quantity of sand used was too great, the surface will scratch deeply and the plaster is apt to crumble.

TOO LITTLE THICKNESS. Another common evil consists of applying the base coat of plaster about ¼ inch thick, whereas it should be at least ½ inch thick. In the plastering trade, this is known as *paperhanging*. Plaster cracking is almost inevitable.

IMPROPER APPLICATION. If the finish (white) coat of plaster is applied over an exceptionally dry base (brown) coat, there will be too much suction and the finish coat is apt to crack in the form of what is known as *chip cracking*. Chip cracks are short and take various directions. They form a spidery pattern all over a ceiling.

FAULTY CONSTRUCTION. The greatest cause for plaster cracking, especially in a new house, is faulty construction. Some of these causes are similar to natural conditions previously explained. However, where faulty construction exists, the cracks are larger and more frequent.

If a foundation is faulty or lacks adequate footing support, severe settlement is likely. As the settlement occurs, structural details are pulled away from their normal positions. This causes out-of-plumb conditions which crack ceiling plaster.

Poor carpentry work, probably more than any other factor, is responsible for unsightly plaster cracks. Improper bracing, poor corner construction, weak framing around windows and doors, joists too small or spaced too far apart, careless nailing, etc., all contribute to the causes for plaster cracks. Even the best job of plastering cannot stand up under such faults and the resulting strains.

GREEN LUMBER. As previously explained, even kiln-dried lumber will shrink to some extent after a year or two. However, when green lumber (see Chapter 1) is used, the resultant shrinkage is great enough to cause severe and even dangerous plaster defects.

Judging Defects. The causes of plaster cracks have a great deal to do with our judgment of them and what should be done to repair or otherwise improve the appearance of ceilings.

Cracks caused by shrinkage, settlement, faulty construction, and green lumber will eventually reach their maximum and are not likely to change thereafter. In old houses, they are at their maximums. In new houses, the maximums come after about two years. Such cracks generally run diagonally across ceilings or occur at the corners where walls and ceilings meet. They extend all the way through the plaster and are apt to be $\frac{1}{16}$ inch or more in width. They can be repaired without fear that they will reopen. Where many of them occur in a ceiling, an entirely new surface material should be used as a means of creating satisfactory appearance.

Cracks caused by expansion and contraction, weight shifts, winds, and earthquakes are generally very narrow and are likely to reoccur after being repaired. They are likely to appear near the centers of ceilings and where walls and ceilings meet. Repairing them is a gamble. Where there are enough of them to constitute an eyesore, an entirely new surface material should be used.

Defects caused by poor materials or oversanding are apt to be a combination of peeling and cracks. In other words, wherever a crack occurs some of the plaster peels off on both sides of it. Such plaster is unsound. A new and strong surface material should be applied by means of nails which are long enough to be driven through the plaster and into the ceiling joists.

When ceiling plaster is too thin, cracks will appear more or less at random or in long lines, especially along lath joints. In such cases, and as previously explained, a new and strong surface material should be applied.

As noted earlier in this discussion, cracks caused by the improper application of plaster are of short lengths and extend in all directions. Such cracks cannot be repaired. Therefore, a new surface material should be applied.

DAMAGE DUE TO WATER. A single wetting, of the kind sometimes caused by a sudden roof or water-pipe leak, is not likely to harm plaster, especially if it was in a sound condition prior to the wetting and if quick drying is possible. However, repeated wettings are apt to cause rotting and unsound conditions. To test suspected plaster, scratch it with a putty knife or other sharp tool. If the scratching causes crumbling, the plaster is beyond repair and a new surface material should be applied.

BLISTERS. If the finish coat of plaster is subjected to excessive humidity or other dampness, the formation of large blisters is likely. The blisters are caused by a particular type of lime which contains a high percentage of unhydrated magnesium. The humidity or dampness causes the magnesium to expand and the blisters are thus formed. If the blisters occur over a large area, satisfactory repair work is impossible and a new surface material should be applied.

FROZEN PLASTER. If plaster is applied during a time when it is subjected to a freezing temperature, it is apt to be permanently damaged. Unfortunately, the results of such damage are not always visible at the time the freezing takes place. Months or years may pass before the finish coat starts to peel. In such a case, no repair work is possible. A strong new surface material should be applied by means of nails which are long enough to be driven through the plaster and into the ceiling joists.

DRYOUTS. This condition is apt to occur when plastering is done during hot summer weather or when a dry wind is blowing. The wind enters through window and door openings and evaporates water from the new plaster. Unless corrected immediately, dryouts form rough areas which cannot be successfully painted or otherwise decorated except with ceiling paper. A new surface material should be applied.

OVERLY RETARDED PLASTER. Sometimes plaster contains too much of an ingredient known as a retarder. When this happens, the plaster becomes soft and powdery after it is applied. To correct such a condition, plasterers spray the plaster with alum and water or zinc sulfate and water. Lumps of the retarder often form on the surface of the plaster. If they are not removed, they will burn through the finish coat and any paint or other decorations applied to the ceiling. There is no easy or satisfactory method of repair. Therefore, a new surface material should be applied.

GYPSUMBOARD DEFECTS

In a great many modern houses, various forms of gypsum wallboard are used as ceiling surfaces instead of the traditional plaster. When properly installed, such ceilings are excellent and can be decorated the same as plaster. By means of the following explanations, we shall learn something about the most commonly encountered ceiling defects. We shall also learn how to recognize and judge them in terms of recommended repair work and the application of new surface materials.

Poor Joists. Most of the gypsumboards can be joined, one to another, in such a manner that the joints are not visible after painting or other decorating is completed. However, if the joints are carelessly made, using improper materials, they are apt to buckle a little, open up, or in other ways become unsatisfactory in appearance. If the condition is not severe, repair work can be done. Otherwise, a new surface material should be applied.

Cracks. Sometimes because of extreme settlement, shrinkage, or excessive shifting of structural details, gypsumboards may crack. Because of the surface materials such boards are made of, crack repairing seldom proves successful. A new surface material should be applied.

Damage Due to Water. Excessive wetting is quite likely to make most plasterboards unsatisfactory. Sometimes their surface materials peel. In other instances, they warp or buckle. When any such defects are present, repair work is difficult and seldom satisfactory. A new surface material should be applied.

Nail Holes. Gypsumboards are generally fastened to ceiling joists by means of nails. The nailheads should be driven just below the surface and the resulting dents filled with a mortar supplied by manufacturers. Now and then, because of careless workmanship, such patches can be seen under decorations. Here again, repair work is seldom satisfactory. A new surface material should be applied.

SUGGESTED REMODELING PROJECTS

Whether a house is large or small, comparatively new or old, the ceilings can be restored to their first or even greater beauty. This promise holds true regardless of how badly cracked or otherwise marred the ceilings may have become. Years of extensive research among building-material manufacturers, plus a great deal of experience, have developed scientific and practical materials and methods for creating beautiful ceilings. The costs are low and the methods have been simplified. Any of the following suggestions can be applied to ceilings under any and all conditions:

Repairing Cracked Plaster. In cases where cracks are not large, not extensive, not in prominent locations, and not likely to reoccur, repair work is the easiest and most economical improvement method. For example, suppose that we are concerned with a medium-sized crack along one side of a room where the wall and ceiling meet. Further suppose that we have observed the crack and are convinced that it is of shrinkage origin and therefore not likely to reoccur. Such a crack can be repaired with little difficulty and in such a manner as to make the ceiling look like new.

New Surfaces over Sound Plaster. There are many cases where ceiling plaster is sound—holds tightly to the lathing—but where cracks, of one kind or another, make the plaster unsightly and not suited to modern painting or other decorations. Also, we may want to give one or more rooms the benefit of soundproofing or cut down the amount of sound transmitted to rooms above. Finally, we may want to enjoy the beauty that only new ceiling-surface materials provide.

SURFACE MATERIALS. There are many types and kinds of new surface materials available. A visit to a lumberyard or to a building-material dealer's showroom will prove to be interesting and helpful when deciding which materials we may want to use. The following materials are typical:

ACOUSTICAL TILE. Both soundproofing and insulating qualities are included in this tile. When it is applied to a ceiling, the following benefits are assured:

1. The room will be much more quiet.

2. Less sound will be transmitted to rooms above.

3. The amount of heat loss and heat gain through the ceiling will be appreciably reduced.

As shown in Figure 2, this tile can be cemented to existing plaster.

KINDS. The kind illustrated in Figure 2 is known as *perforated* tile. Note that the surface contains many small holes. A *plain* tile without holes is also available.

SIZES. Most manufacturers produce such tile in 12- by 12-, 12- by 24-, 16- by 16-, and 16- by 32-inch sizes and in thicknesses which range from ½ to 1 inch.

COLORS. Both kinds of this tile can be secured in a wide range of colors. Or, as indicated in Figure 3, both kinds can be painted.

FASTENING. As shown in Figure 4, the tile can be fastened to existing plaster by means of cement. It can also be nailed to furring strips. Instead of furring strips, long, Z-shaped, metal clip strips can be used to support the tile without nails.

PATTERNS. By use of the tile sizes previously mentioned, any of the typical ceiling patterns shown in Figure 5 may be obtained. Generally, the 12- by 12- or 12- by 16-inch sizes are used on small ceilings and the 12- by 24- or 16- by 32-inch sizes on large ceilings.

TILE EDGES. Acoustical tile are provided with tongued-and-grooved edges of the type shown in Figures 8 and 9. Narrow and extra-wide flanges are also available. The extra-wide flanges are desirable when the tile is fastened by means of nails.

FIGURE 2. Typical perforated acoustical ceiling tile for application on old plaster.

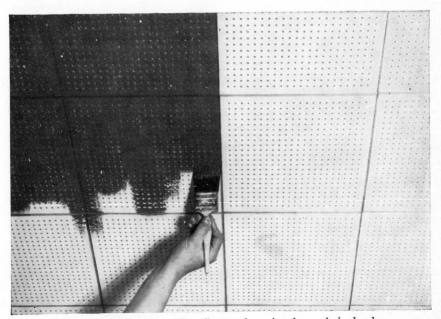

FIGURE 3. Acoustical ceiling tile may be painted any desired color.

FIGURE 4. Over old plaster, acoustical tile may be cemented into place.

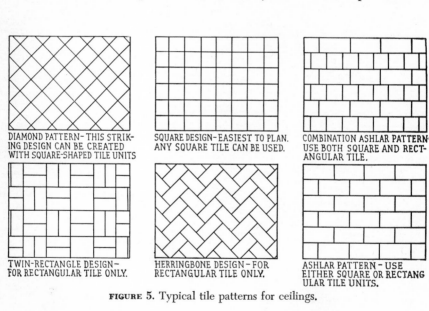

DIAMOND PATTERN— THIS STRIK-
ING DESIGN CAN BE CREATED
WITH SQUARE-SHAPED TILE UNITS

SQUARE DESIGN—EASIEST TO PLAN.
ANY SQUARE TILE CAN BE USED.

COMBINATION ASHLAR PATTERN·
USE BOTH SQUARE AND RECT-
ANGULAR TILE.

TWIN-RECTANGLE DESIGN—
FOR RECTANGULAR TILE ONLY.

HERRINGBONE DESIGN—FOR
RECTANGULAR TILE ONLY.

ASHLAR PATTERN — USE
EITHER SQUARE OR RECTANG
ULAR TILE UNITS.

FIGURE 5. Typical tile patterns for ceilings.

PREFINISHED CEILING TILE. Other kinds of tile, which can be applied to existing plaster, are available in a wide range of colors. Some of them have factory-finished surfaces and other qualities which include square edges, high light reflection, high insulating value, and waterproof texture. However, such tile do not reduce noise in a room.

New Surfaces over Unsound Plaster. When plaster is not sound, furring strips should be used (see Figure 6). The furring strips should be nailed to the ceiling, using nails which are long enough to go through the plaster and lath and into the joists. This procedure creates a firm base for tile and holds the plaster firmly in place.

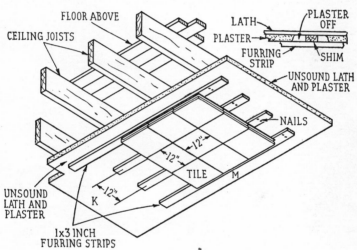

FIGURE 6. Acoustical tile being applied over unsound plaster.

SURFACE MATERIALS. Same as mentioned in connection with New Surfaces over Sound Plaster.

ACOUSTICAL TILE. Same as mentioned in connection with New Surfaces over Sound Plaster, except that the tile must be fastened to furring strips.

KINDS, SIZES, COLORS, AND PATTERNS. Same as mentioned in connection with New Surfaces over Sound Plaster.

FASTENING FURRING STRIPS. As previously mentioned and as shown in Figure 6, the furring strips must be nailed over the plaster so that the nails penetrate into the joists. The nails should be at least 3 inches long.

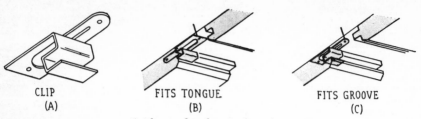

CLIP
(A)

FITS TONGUE
(B)

FITS GROOVE
(C)

FIGURE 7. Clip used to fasten tile to furring strip.

FIGURE 8. How clips are nailed to furring strips.

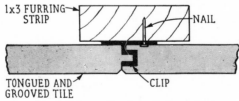

1x3 FURRING STRIP

NAIL

TONGUED AND GROOVED TILE

CLIP

FIGURE 9. Section view showing how clip is nailed to furring strip and how tile fits into clip.

FASTENING TILE. There are three methods of fastening tile to the furring strips. Any one of them may be employed.

CLIPS. The use of clips constitutes a sure way of fastening the tile and at the same time allows a floating surface which compensates for irregularities in the level of the plaster and furring strips. The *A* part of Figure 7 shows a typical clip. The *B* and *C* parts of the same illustration show how the clip fits the tongues and grooves at the edges of the tile. Figure 8 indicates how the clips are nailed to furring strips as a ceiling project is in progress. Figure 9 is a section view that illustrates how clips are fastened to furring strips and how the tile fits into the clips. Figure 10 indicates the recommended number of clips for the different sizes of tile. Note that the furring strips should be spaced on 8-inch centers where 16-inch tile are involved.

STAPLES AND NAILS. Either staples or nails can also be used for fastening tile to furring strips. Figure 11 shows the use of wide-flange tile and how staples or nails can be employed. Staples and nails should be rust-proof and no longer than $\frac{9}{16}$ inch. The recommended number of staples or nails per tile is set forth in Figure 12.

ALTERNATIVE METHOD. Instead of furring strips, long, Z-shaped, metal clip strips can be nailed over the plaster to support the tiles without nails or staples.

PREFINISHED CEILING TILE. Same as explained under New Surfaces over Sound Plaster, except that the tile must be nailed to furring strips.

New Surfaces over Gypsumboard. When gypsumboard ceilings contain one or more defects as previously explained, the same general plan as set forth under New Surfaces over Unsound Plaster can be used. The old gypsumboard must be securely renailed before furring strips are applied.

New Surfaces on Joists. When basement and attic spaces are being remodeled as a means of providing additional living space in a house, it is probable that unfinished ceiling surfaces will be involved and that new surface materials will have to be applied directly to ceiling joists or rafters. In other cases, old lath and plaster may be in such poor condition that they must be entirely removed. In still other cases, sound-proofing and insulation may be desired.

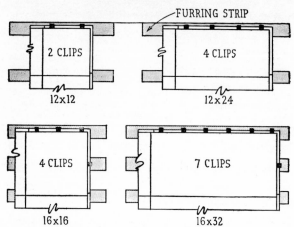

FIGURE 10. Recommended number of clips for the different sizes of tile.

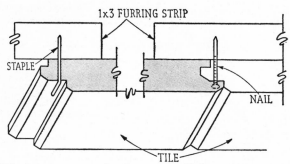

FIGURE 11. Tile having extra-wide flanges should be used when they are to be fastened with staples or nails.

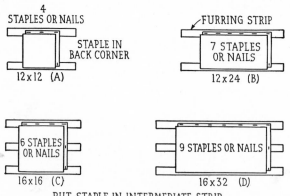

PUT STAPLE IN INTERMEDIATE STRIP
FIGURE 12. Recommended number of staples or nails per tile.

SURFACE MATERIALS. Same as explained under New Surfaces over Unsound Plaster.

INSULATION. In order greatly to reduce the transmission of sound from a basement recreation room to the rooms above it, blanket-type wool insulation (see Chapter 3) can be stuffed between the ceiling joists prior to the time furring strips are applied (see Figure 13). The benefits thus obtained are worth the added cost of the insulation. Attic spaces can be insulated as set forth in Chapter 3.

FIGURE 13. Blanket insulation being applied between joists in a basement ceiling.

ACOUSTICAL TILE. Same as mentioned in connection with New Surfaces over Sound Plaster, except that the tile must be fastened to furring strips.

KINDS, SIZES, COLORS, AND PATTERNS. Same as mentioned in connection with New Surfaces over Sound Plaster.

FASTENING FURRING STRIPS AND TILE. Same as mentioned in connection with New Surfaces over Unsound Plaster. Instead of furring strips, however, long, Z-shaped, metal clip strips can be nailed to the under side of joists or rafters to support the tiles.

GYPSUMBOARD. This type of surface material is manufactured in large sheets whose dimensions are multiples of 16 inches so that the sheets can be applied to joists or rafters which are spaced 16 inches on centers. All joints and nail dents can be finished so that they are not visible under paint or other decorating materials. This material is particularly well suited to attic remodeling.

KINDS. The various manufacturers of this material employ their own trade names to identify their products. *Sheetrock* is one example. Generally, the material is manufactured in ¼-, ⅜-, ½-, and ⅝-inch thicknesses. The two surfaces are composed of heavy cardboard, and the core is made from gypsum or an insulating substance. Some manufacturers offer decorative textures that are factory-prefinished.

SIZES. Most manufacturers produce gypsumboard in 4-foot widths and in various lengths, all of which are multiples of 16.

FASTENING. Gypsumboard is fastened with nails or adhesives and nails. Some manufacturers suggest special kinds and sizes of nails. In general, nail penetration into studs or furring strips should be ⅞ inch for smooth-shank nails and ¾ inch for annular-ringed nails. The nails should be placed at least ⅜ inch from the edges of boards and spaced no more than 7 inches apart.

EDGES. For remodeling work, where painted surfaces are required, the plasterboard should have tapered edges so that the joints can be reinforced and filled according to manufacturers' directions.

NEW LOWERED CEILINGS. As discussed in Chapter 9, thousands of old houses, while being structurally sound and valuable, were built in keeping with living and utility standards of a past era. Such houses can be remodeled, following any one or more of several possible plans, to make them comply with modern living requirements and tastes. For example, the ceilings in old houses are often from 10 to 12 or more feet above the floors. Based on our present-day ideas of beauty, comfort, and utility, such ceiling heights increase decorating costs, add to heating and cooling expense, and do not blend with such equipment as kitchen cabinets or other new and desirable items of modern living. High ceilings can be lowered and new surfaces applied, all at reasonable cost.

To lower a ceiling it is only necessary to add new and generally light-weight framing which can be suspended from the old ceiling and attached to the walls. Then, any of the new surface materials previously discussed can be applied. The results, especially in kitchens and in utility rooms, are exceptionally worthwhile.

LUMINOUS CEILINGS. A lowered ceiling can be combined with electric lighting to achieve a decorative effect plus high-quality, uniform lighting throughout a room. This is done by installing long fluorescent lamps under the old ceiling and placing translucent plastic panels under the lamps. The panels may be supported by aluminum inverted tees and angles.

MAKING CEILINGS SEEM HIGHER. There may be cases where ceilings are too low rather than too high. In such cases, the rather oppressive feeling conveyed by a low ceiling can be overcome by introducing vertical lines into wall decorating schemes. Borders and other horizontal trim should be eliminated.

HOW TO PLAN AND DO TYPICAL REMODELING PROJECTS

As repeatedly stressed all through this book, any and all remodeling projects should be carefully planned and laid out prior to the time materials are purchased and the actual work is started. Careful planning will prevent undue expense and avoid unnecessary labor and other difficulties. Any well-planned project will progress much faster and yield the desired results. The following typical ceiling projects are presented in such a manner as to exhibit proper planning and to provide helpful how-to-do-it instructions:

REPAIRING PLASTER CRACKS

In previous discussions we have learned that some types of plaster cracks are due to natural shrinkage and settlement and that once such conditions have reached their maximums, after a house is about two years old, the cracks can be repaired with reasonable assurance that they will not reoccur. We also learned that other types of plaster cracks occur because of unfortunate conditions which are apt to be repeated and that there is no assurance that such cracks will not reoccur after being repaired. Thus the first planning procedure consists of studying cracks—watching them—in an effort to determine their cause and to decide if we want to chance reoccurrence possibilities.

Large Cracks. If a large crack, ⅟₁₆ to ¼ inch in width, seems to be stable and not likely to reoccur, the following procedure is recommended:

PREPARATION. For cracks which are from ⅟₁₆ to ¼ inch wide, and where the plaster on either side of the cracks is sound and not loose, use a chisel or sharp screwdriver to remove all bits of loose plaster and to create an inverted V, as shown in the *A* part of Figure 14. Dig out the inverted V to the lathing.

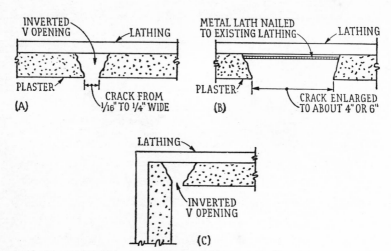

FIGURE 14. How to prepare plaster cracks for repair.

PATCHING MATERIAL. Use any plaster-patching material such as obtainable at hardware stores or from building-material dealers.

PATCHING. The first step in the patching process is to wet the interior of the crack and the exposed lath two or three times about an hour before applying the patching material. A paint brush can be used to make sure the water reaches all areas of the crack.

Mix the patching material as per the directions on its container. Add just enough water to make the material plastic and easy to spread. Use a putty knife to force the material into the crack and to ⅟₁₆ inch of the surface of the surrounding plaster.

Allow the patch to dry for at least 24 hours. Then mix fresh patching material and completely fill the crack. This procedure avoids any chance of a slightly concave surface on the patch due to shrinkage. Smooth the surface of the patch flush with the edges of the surrounding plaster and remove any excess patching material.

When the patching material has thoroughly dried, after two or three days, apply a liberal coat of shellac or other sealer to it.

If a crack is more than ¼ inch wide and if there seems to be some possibility that it will reoccur, the following procedure is recommended:

PREPARATION. Use a chisel and a hammer to deliberately increase the width of the crack to 4 or 6 inches, as shown in the *B* part of Figure 14. Create the inverted V as previously explained. Next, nail a piece of metal lath securely to the existing lathing. Drive the nails at an angle.

PATCHING MATERIAL. For a patch of such width and where metal lath is involved, it is best to use a regular brown coat plaster mix to fill most of the crack and a regular white coat mix for the surface. Both materials are available at lumberyards.

PATCHING. Using the brown coat mix, fill the crack just enough to cover the metal lath. Allow this to dry for a day or two. Then, using the same mix, fill the crack to within ¹⁄₁₆ inch of the surface of the surrounding old plaster. Allow this part of the patch two days for drying. Finally, use the white coat mix to finish the patch flush with the old plaster.

Allow the white coat to dry for two weeks, and then apply a liberal coat of shellac or other sealer to the general area of the patch.

Corner Cracks. When cracks are at the line where a ceiling and wall meet, dig out an inverted V, as shown in the *C* part of Figure 14, and apply patching material as explained in connection with cracks from ¹⁄₁₆ to ¼ inch wide. Seal as previously recommended.

Small Cracks. If cracks are less than ¹⁄₁₆ inch wide, the following procedure is recommended:

PREPARATION. Clean out all visible dirt or bits of plaster by means of a stiff brush.

PATCHING MATERIAL. Same as recommended for ¹⁄₁₆-inch cracks.

PATCHING. Wet the cracks about an hour before applying patching. Apply the patching material by means of a putty knife. Force the material into the cracks and trim the surface flush with the surface of surrounding plaster. Seal as previously recommended.

Conclusion. Where cracks are numerous and when they are likely to reoccur, repairing is seldom worthwhile, especially if painted decorations are desired.

NEW SURFACES OVER SOUND PLASTER

The following project is typical of any and all cases where ceiling tile is to be applied over old but sound plaster. The project is presented in terms of a typical problem and its solution.

PROBLEM 1. KITCHEN CEILING. For the purpose of this problem we shall assume that Plates I through VI, which are at the back of this book, show the plans for an *old* house. We can further assume that the kitchen-ceiling plaster, while still sound, contains a great many small cracks which are sure to reoccur and which create a poor appearance. The problem is to remodel the ceiling so that its appearance will be in keeping with new cabinets and other equipment we plan to install.

SOLUTION. First, it can be assumed that we would like to apply acoustical tile directly to the old plaster. Such tile will create a new and beautiful appearance, reduce noise in the kitchen, and add some insulating effect to the ceiling. The insulating effect will be worthwhile because the ceiling is under attic space which is cold during winter and hot during summer.

PLANNING. The first planning item consists of checking the ceiling to see if it is level enough for the application of tile. The checking can be done with a long and straight piece of 1 by 3 or 2 by 4. Hold this straightedge at various locations against the ceiling. If the surface of the plaster touches the straightedge at all points along the length, the ceiling is level or flat enough for tile. We can assume that it is and that cemented tiling is therefore possible.

The next item of planning has to do with the size and pattern of tile. Since the kitchen is only 10′ 0″ by 11′ 6″, the small or 12- by 12-inch tile size will create the best appearance. And, because the room is almost square, the square design shown in Figure 5, without a border, is in keeping with good taste.

LAYOUT. What is commonly called layout work is actually part of the planning. In this solution, the purpose of layout is to locate the center point of the ceiling and to determine by sketch trials the best position for the first piece of tile.

The X part of Figure 15 shows what constitutes the center point of the ceiling. The dashed line is located by four dimensions: G and H near one end of the room and J and M near the opposite end. The center point is located by two dimensions, such as N and P, near each side of the room. Locating the center point of a room in this manner compensates for any minor irregularities in the dimensions of the room.

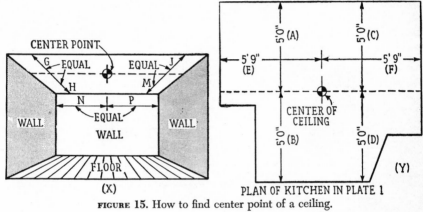

FIGURE 15. How to find center point of a ceiling.

The Y part of Figure 15 is an outline of the kitchen shown in Plate I and illustrates how the foregoing procedure, explained in connection with the X part of the illustration, is put to actual use. Dimensions A and B, along with dimensions C and D, locate the dashed line. Such a line can be made on a ceiling by means of a chalk string. To establish the center point of the ceiling, dimensions E and F should be exactly the same.

Once the center point of a ceiling has been established and marked, the next logical step is to plan the tile positions or layout. The best procedure is to plan the exact position of the first piece of tile to be applied. Then, all other pieces will follow the established pattern.

The W part of Figure 16 shows four center points at A, B, C, and D. The letter L indicates the center points and the letter K indicates the first pieces of tile. The first piece of tile may be applied in any one of the four positions shown relative to the center point. However, we cannot be sure which position to use in this solution until we draw a few sketches accurately to scale.

NOTE: When the sketches are drawn accurately to scale, they represent the actual ceiling. This may be visualized if we imagine that the sketches indicate what we would see if we looked up at the ceiling. Once the sketches are complete, we can use chalk or a chalk string to create lines on the ceiling which are similar to the lines on the sketches. Thus, the

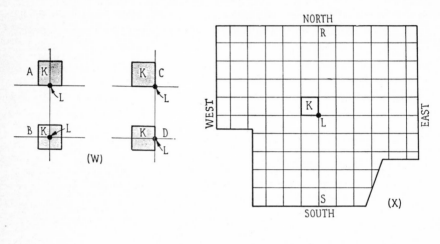

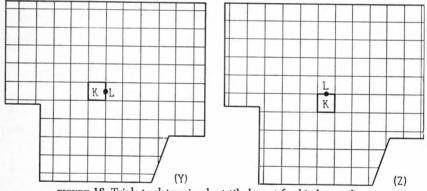

FIGURE 16. Trials to determine best tile layout for kitchen ceiling.

sketches constitute the means by which layout can be planned. This fact will be emphasized in the following explanations:

The X part of Figure 16 shows the outline of the kitchen, the center point L, a trial position for the first piece of tile K, and how all other pieces of tile will appear if we imagine that we are looking up at the ceiling. This arrangement is good, owing to the fact that the north and south borders consist of full pieces of tile and because the west and east borders will not require much tile cutting. The sketches shown in the Y and Z parts of Figure 16, where the first pieces of tile are shown in different positions, are not good because of the irregular borders. Therefore, the arrangement shown in the X part of the illustration should be employed, NOTE: Accurately scaled sketches should always be drawn as part of the layout work in connection with tile surfaces.

The tile should be unpacked so that all pieces can adjust themselves to temperature and humidity conditions. Finally, and as indicated in the X part of Figure 16, nail a straightedge next to line RS. The first row of tile should be applied using the straightedge as a guide.

APPLICATION OF TILE. All manufacturers of ceiling tile make specific recommendations in connection with the adhesive (cement) to use with their tile. Generally, such adhesive has the consistency of putty and can be handled by means of a putty knife. NOTE: All wallpaper or calcimine must be removed from the ceiling before applying tile.

As shown in Figure 4, four dabs of the adhesive should be placed on each piece of tile. In the illustration, the dark spots on the ceiling indicate the approximate positions of the four dabs on the tile. Each dab of adhesive should be about the size of a walnut. The amount of adhesive may be increased or decreased to compensate for low or high places in the ceiling.

In Figure 17 the straightedge and the first row of tile are shown in proper positions. Tile 1 is the same as tile K in X part of Figure 16.

Start with tile 1. Apply the four dabs of adhesive. Then, as indicated in Figure 2, press the tile against the ceiling. The grooved side of the tile must touch the straightedge. Apply uniform pressure and a slight weaving motion. As shown in the illustration, one corner of the tile must touch the corner point L. Be sure that the grooved edge is snug against the straightedge.

Next, apply tile 2. Be sure that the surface of this piece is at the same level as the level of tile 1, so that the tongued-and-grooved joints can interlock properly. If tile 2 has been pressed too much, remove it and add a little more adhesive at all four points.

In like manner, apply tiles 3, 4, 5, 6, 7, 8, 9, and 10 in the order indicated. Tiles 8 and 10 must be about $\frac{1}{16}$ inch away from the walls to allow for expansion. If necessary, these pieces can be sawed to make them fit.

When the first row of tile has been applied, remove the straightedge and apply the second row. All other rows are applied in the same manner. Be sure that all joints and bevels match. The slightest variation would cause undesirable appearance.

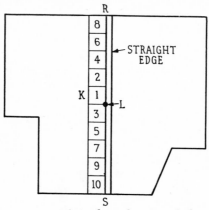

FIGURE 17. Applying first row of tile.

Finally, nail a cove molding all around the wall next to the tile.

PAINTING. The manufacturers of acoustical tile recommend paints which have oil, rubber, or water bases. Such paints will not decrease the sound absorption of the tile. Paint small areas at a time and follow joint lines to avoid undesirable laps in the paint.

NEW SURFACES OVER UNSOUND PLASTER

The following project is typical of any and all cases where tile is to be applied over unsound plaster. The project is presented in terms of a typical problem and its solution.

PROBLEM 2. KITCHEN CEILING. We can assume that the ceiling plaster in the kitchen specified for Problem 1 is badly cracked, impossible to decorate, and probably unsound. The problem is to remodel it and for the same reason set forth in Problem 1.

SOLUTION. First, it can be assumed that we have decided to use acoustical tile and for the same reason as outlined in Problem 1.

PLANNING. The first step consists of checking the old plaster. This can be done by pressing it with our hands. Considerable looseness is indicative of an unsound condition. We shall assume the unsound condition. Therefore, 1- by 3-inch furring strips must be nailed to the joists, as explained in connection with Figure 6. The distance between furring-strip center lines must be the same as the width of the tile.

We shall again assume the use of 12- by 12-inch tile and the square design explained in the solution to Problem 1. We shall also assume that the tile is to be fastened to the furring strips by means of nails.

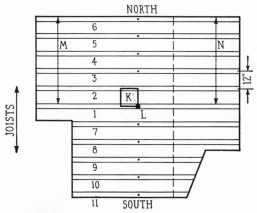

FIGURE 18. Layout of furring strips.

LAYOUT. The center point of the ceiling can be found as explained in the solution to Problem 1.

In order to plan the layout of furring strips, we must draw the outline of the kitchen to scale. Figure 18 shows the required drawing. Furring strip 1 should be directly over the center point L and at right angles to the joists. The tile positions can be planned as explained in the solution to Problem 1. The first piece of tile should be applied in the position indicated by the illustration.

APPLICATION OF FURRING STRIPS. Place furring strip 1 so that its center line is directly over the center point L. Drive one nail near the center of the furring strip to hold it in place. Then adjust it until dimensions M and N are the same. This procedure makes sure that the furring strip is square with the room. Use two nails at each joist location. The joist locations can be determined by tapping the plaster with a hammer. The hammer taps sound solid at joist locations. Fasten furring strips 2, 3, 4, 5, 6, 7, 8, 9, and 10. Make sure that their center lines are exactly 12 inches apart. If spots of plaster fall, use shims as indicated in Figure 6. Furring strips 6 and 11 should be snug against the wall, even if the distances between 6 and 5 and 11 and 10 are not exactly 12 inches.

Check the level of the furring strips by pressing a straightedge up against them. See dashed line in Figure 18. If one or more of them do not touch the straightedge, drive shims between them and the plaster.

APPLICATION OF STARTER STRIP. In order to apply the first row of tile in a straight line, a starter strip is required. See Figure 19. It should be nailed along the center line of furring strip 1. Starter strips can be obtained where the tile is purchased.

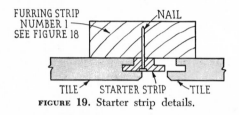

FURRING STRIP NUMBER 1 SEE FIGURE 18 — NAIL

TILE STARTER STRIP TILE

FIGURE 19. Starter strip details.

APPLICATION OF TILE. Place the first piece of tile (see K in Figure 18) so that its groove engages the tongue of the starter strip. See Figure 19. Make sure that the corner of the tile touches the furring strip above the point L. See Figure 18. As recommended in the A part of Figure 12, use four nails. Apply the first row of tile as indicated in the A part of Figure 20. Install the second row so that the flanges lead in the opposite direction. After two rows have been applied, adjacent rows should be applied beginning at the ends of the already applied rows and across the ceiling. This procedure allows nailing at the corner of each tile. It is important to line up the joints, so that they are straight, before nailing since adjustment of tile is difficult once the nails have been driven. This is shown graphically in the B part of Figure 20. A $\frac{1}{16}$-inch expansion space must be provided between the tile and the walls.

Finally, nail a cove in place as explained in the solution to Problem 1.

PAINTING. Same as explained in solution to Problem 1.

NOTE. Some mechanics and homeowners prefer to use plasterboard instead of furring strips when unsound plaster is involved. In such cases, the plasterboard should be applied to the ceiling by means of nails which

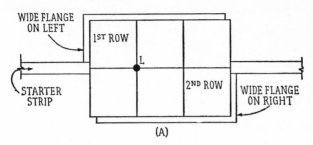

WIDE FLANGE ON LEFT

1ST ROW

L

STARTER STRIP

2ND ROW

WIDE FLANGE ON RIGHT

(A)

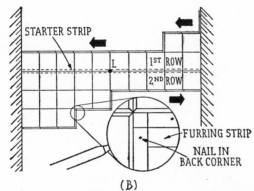

STARTER STRIP

L

1ST ROW

2ND ROW

FURRING STRIP

NAIL IN BACK CORNER

(B)

FIGURE 20. Tile application to furring strips.

are long enough to go through the plasterboard and plaster and penetrate firmly into the joists. The tile is planned, laid out, and applied as explained in the solution to Problem 1.

NEW SURFACES WITHOUT PLASTER

The following project is typical of any and all cases where ceiling tile is to be applied directly to ceiling joists or rafters. The project is presented in terms of a typical problem and its solution.

PROBLEM 3. BASEMENT CEILING. For the purpose of this problem, we can assume that part of the basement space shown in Plate II is to be transformed into a recreation room. The problem is to create a beautiful ceiling which will soundproof the area and reduce the transmission of sound to the first-floor rooms above.

SOLUTION. First, it can be assumed that we have decided to apply acoustical ceiling tile as surface material, and wool blankets between the joists as insulation to prevent sound transmission.

PLANNING. The first step of the planning consists of selecting the insulation. We shall assume the use of the blanket type (see Chapter 3). The blankets can be stuffed between the joists and fastened to the bottom edges of them by means of laths and nailing flanges.

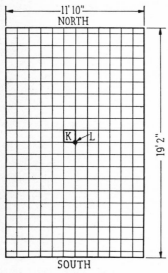

FIGURE 21. Tile layout for recreation-room ceiling.

The next item of planning has to do with the size and pattern of tile. As indicated in Plate II, and as suggested in Chapter 7, one possible plan for the recreation room could be 19′ 2″ long and 11′ 10″ wide. Ordinarily, we would plan to use either 12- by 24- or 16- by 32-inch tile for an area of such size. However, in this solution we shall assume the use of 12- by 12-inch tile in order to take advantage of explanations given in previous problem solutions. We shall also assume the square pattern and that the tile will be fastened by means of nails.

Plate II indicates that the ceiling joists above the recreation room are supported by means of an I-beam. We can assume that the joists are set between the flanges of the beam so that the beam does not extend below the bottoms of the joists.

LAYOUT. In this problem the layout must be planned in a different manner, owing to the fact that the ceiling is not plastered and there is therefore no surface on which we can mark the center point of the room. The following procedure will be helpful to inexperienced installers:

Use the concrete floor instead of the ceiling as a surface on which to indicate the center point of the room. A plumb bob can be used to transfer the center point to the ceiling when the first furring strip is being applied.

Here again it is necessary to draw a sketch accurately to scale. Figure 21 shows the type of sketch required when planning the tile layout. The center point of the room is indicated at L. The position of the first piece

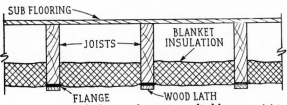

FIGURE 22. How blanket insulation is applied between joists.

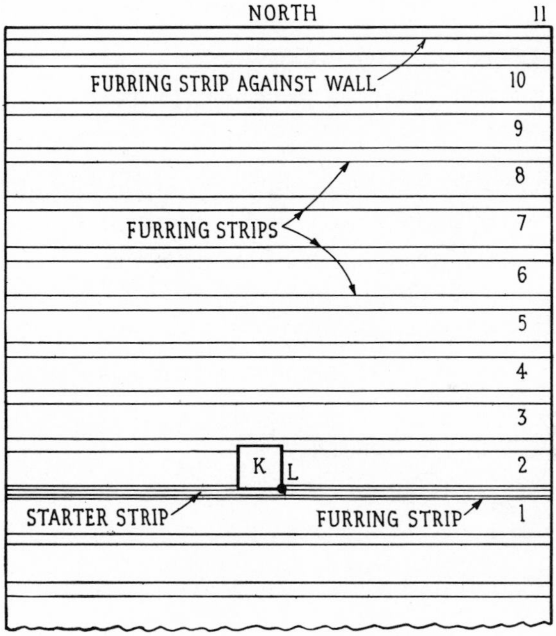

NORTH   11

FURRING STRIP AGAINST WALL   10

                                                        9

                                                        8

FURRING STRIPS   7

                                                        6

                                                        5

                                                        4

                                                        3

                          K L   2

STARTER STRIP   FURRING STRIP   1

FIGURE 23. Layout of furring strips.

of tile K was determined following the same trial procedure as was explained in the solution to Problem 1.

Application of Insulation. Figure 13 shows how the blanket insulation should be stuffed between the joists. The tool shown in the picture is an automatic stapler used to fasten the insulation.

Figure 22 shows how wood laths are used to fasten the blanket nailing flanges to the bottom edges of the joists.

Application of Furring Strips. Figure 23 shows the furring strips for one half of the recreation-room ceiling. They are nailed over the wood laths shown in Figures 8 and 22. Place furring strip 1 so that its center line is directly over the center point *L* indicated in Figure 23. Adjust this furring strip as explained in the solution to Problem 2. Next fasten furring strips 2, 3, 4, 5, 6, 7, 8, 9, and 10 so that their center lines are all exactly 12 inches apart. Strip 11 must be snug against the wall. Test the level of the strips as explained in the solution to Problem 2.

Application of Starter Strip. Apply the starter strip as shown in Figure 23 using the procedure set forth in the solution to Problem 2.

Application of Tile. The tile is applied as explained in the solution to Problem 2. Sawing and trimming will have to be done where the tile meets all four walls of the room. See Figure 21. When fastening trimmed tile at the north and south walls, the sides of the tile against the walls should be nailed to the furring strips by means of 1½-inch nails driven from the face of the tile. The cove molding will hide the nail heads.

Painting. See solution to Problem 2.

SLOPING ATTIC CEILINGS

When attic spaces (see Chapter 9) are remodeled to create living areas, part of the ceilings in such areas generally slope. In other words, ceiling-surface materials must be applied to the bottom edges of the rafters. Various kinds of tile may be applied to such ceilings in much the same manner as it is applied to horizontal ceilings.

Figure 24 illustrates the application of acoustical tile to a sloping ceiling. Note that wood laths are not used to fasten the blanket insulation to the rafters. However, the usual furring strips are required. Note, too, that a border composed of 12- by 24-inch plain tile is part of the design. The walls may be surfaced as explained in Chapter 5.

Except for the omission of wood laths, the planning, layout, and application procedures for a ceiling of this type are the same as explained in the solution to Problem 3.

FIGURE 24. Tile being applied to sloping attic ceiling.

LOWERED CEILING

The following project is typical of any and all cases where ceilings are to be lowered:

PROBLEM 4. KITCHEN CEILING. For the purpose of this problem, we can assume that the ceiling height of the kitchen indicated in Plate I is 12′ 0″. The problem is to plan and erect a new ceiling which will be 8′ 0″ above the floor.

SOLUTION. Figure 25 will be helpful in visualizing the required framing for the lowered ceiling. The walls, the original ceiling, and the floor are named. The 2 by 4 pieces at E should be fastened to the walls by nails which are long enough to go through the lath and plaster and into the studs. The 2 by 4 ceiling joists should be nailed to the E pieces.

The X part of Figure 26 may be visualized as though we were directly above the new framing and were looking straight down at it. All framing members are composed of 2 by 4 pieces. The pieces marked E correspond to those marked E in Figure 25. Eleven joists are required.

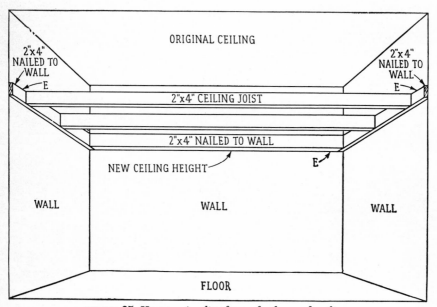

ORIGINAL CEILING

2"x4" NAILED TO WALL
E

2"x4" NAILED TO WALL
E

2"x4" CEILING JOIST

2"x4" NAILED TO WALL

NEW CEILING HEIGHT

E

WALL

WALL

WALL

FLOOR

FIGURE 25. How to visualize frame for lowered ceiling.

Installation of E Pieces. First, cut a 2 by 4 to a length of 11′ 6″. This is for the MN wall shown in the X part of Figure 26. See dimensions in Plate I. Measure a distance of 8′ 0″ up from the floor and draw a line on the MN wall. Use a carpenter's level to make sure this line is horizontal. Place the MN 2 by 4 so that its bottom edge coincides with the line. The long side of the 2 by 4 should be flat against the wall. Drive one nail at each end of the 2 by 4. Use 3½-inch nails and make sure that they enter studs in the wall. Test the level again. Then drive at least one nail at each stud location.

Fasten the 2 by 4 pieces on walls TS, PR, WR, SW, NR, RT, and

PM in the order named. Make sure that each piece is horizontal and that bottom edges are exactly 8′ 0″ above the floor.

Installation of 2 by 4 Joists. The joists should be 12 inches on centers. Use a measuring tape to determine the exact length required for each. They should fit snugly against the *E* pieces. Toenail them to the *E* pieces. Use 2½-inch nails.

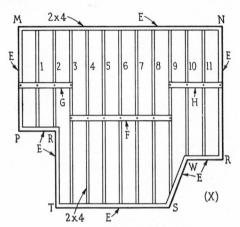

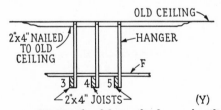

FIGURE 26. Details of frame for lowered ceiling.

In order to stiffen the framing, install 1- by 4-inch pieces as shown at *G, F,* and *H*. Nail these stiffeners securely to the joists.

Joists 3, 4, 5, 6, 7, 8, and 9 are long and should therefore be provided with some support from the original ceiling. The *Y* part of Figure 26 shows how such support can be accomplished.

Nail a 2 by 4 to the ceiling, above the position of stiffener *F*. Make sure that the nails penetrate into the joists of the original ceiling. The 2 by 2 hangers should be nailed to the ceiling 2 by 4 and to the 2 by 4 joists.

Application of Furring Strips. The furring strips must be nailed to the joists and at right angles to them. The procedure is the same as explained in the solutions to Problems 2 and 3.

Application of Tile. This is the same as explained in the solution to Problem 3.

Luminous Ceiling. Installation of a luminous ceiling is similar, except for the placement of lighting fixtures. Depending on the size of a room, the fluorescent lamps may be up to 4 feet long. In a long room, the lamps may be set in a line with short spacing between them. Transversely, the spacing between lines of lamps may be 4 or 5 feet. The closer the spacing, the more uniform will be the lighting.

Framing below the lamps is much like that for tile installation. For the *E* pieces in Figure 25, however, aluminum angles with 1-inch legs are attached to the wall. Instead of wood joists and furring strips, a grid of aluminum inverted tees with 1-inch flanges is seated on the angles. Additional support for the grid is provided by hangers attached to 2 by 4's nailed to the original ceiling. Finally, panels of translucent plastic are seated in the grid on the flanges of the tees.

LADDERS AND SCAFFOLD PLANKS

Where ceiling work is concerned, the use of both ladders and scaffold planks is recommended as a means of providing more convenience and greater safety. If only a ladder is used, it will have to be frequently moved. This slows the work and makes for unhandy and tiring working conditions.

Types of Ladders Recommended. For most ceiling work, household safety stepladders may be used. They should include full-rodded steps and double top irons, 5- or 6-foot heights serve the purpose.

Safety Hints. When working on a ladder without scaffolds, always face the ladder when ascending or descending. Make sure the ladder is fully spread and locked with all four legs resting on the floor. Never stand on the top of a ladder or try to reach more than 2 feet to either side.

CHAPTER FIVE

Walls

Good taste in home decoration is evidenced by many items which combine to make a harmonious whole. The choice of colors, the pictures, and the furnishings all contribute to the general effect. But, more than any other item, attractive and defect-free walls are the foundation of successful interior decoration.

Nearly every old house has at least one room that is a source of constant disappointment and embarrassment because of unsightly defects in wall surface materials. As explained in Chapter 4, such defects can be classified as *natural* and *unfortunate*.

Natural defects generally occur above or around window and door openings, in the form of thin cracks which resemble spiderwebs. Unfortunate defects are apt to occur more or less at random, in the form of large cracks which are jagged and deep.

Unsightly walls can be repaired or remodeled to create greatly improved appearance or entirely new and beautiful surfaces. This chapter proposes to suggest typical repairing and remodeling projects and to explain how such work can be planned and accomplished.

PLASTER AND GYPSUMBOARD DEFECTS

The defects most generally found in ceiling-surface materials are explained in Chapter 4. The same explanations apply to the defects most generally found in wall-surface materials. However, the defects in wall-surface materials are usually more pronounced and are therefore more unsightly.

JUDGING WALL DEFECTS

Before deciding whether to repair or to remodel wall surfaces, we should consider the types of defects involved and exercise some judgment in connection with reoccurrence possibilities.

Natural defects, such as spider-web cracks above or around window and door openings, generally reach their maximum extent by the time houses are two or three years old. After that time, such defects can be repaired without much chance that they will reoccur. Wallpaper or any of the fabric wall coverings can be applied over the repaired areas.

Unfortunate defects, such as large and jagged cracks, are unstable and likely to reoccur. Thus, their repair constitutes a gamble even if one of the previously mentioned fabric wall coverings are applied over the repaired areas.

Extensive repair work is never completely satisfactory unless wall surfaces are covered with paper or fabric decorating materials.

In general, except where *natural* defects are confined to small areas and where a paper or fabric covering is to be applied, the repair of wall defects is not feasible owing to the fact that they are much more noticeable than similar defects in ceilings and because the best of repair work is seldom satisfactory.

SUGGESTED REMODELING PROJECTS

Whether a house is old or relatively new, the walls in it can be restored to their original or even more desirable beauty. This promise holds true regardless of how badly cracked or otherwise marred the walls may have become. After many years of extensive research and a great deal of experience, building-material manufacturers have created new, beautiful, and enduring wall-surface materials. The costs are low and the installation procedures have been simplified. Any of the following suggestions can be applied to walls under any and all conditions.

Repairing Cracked Plaster. In cases where the cracks are above or around window and door openings, or at a corner where two walls meet, repair work constitutes the easiest and most economical improvement method.

MATERIALS. Any regular plaster-patching mix, such as sold by hardware and paint stores, can be used. Various patching "pencils" are also available for use in connection with hairline cracks.

Repairing Holes in Plaster. In houses which have been occupied at various times by several different families, and in some cases where only one family has been involved, the plaster or plasterboard may have been injured in many locations by hangers, nails, or screws used to hang mirrors, pictures, shelves, etc. Such injuries are generally in the form of holes. They can be repaired in such a manner as to leave no trace of them.

MATERIAL. Any plaster-patching mix.

Plastic Wall Coatings. Several such coatings, under various trade names, are available at paint and hardware stores. In most cases, the coatings look like thick paint and may be applied by means of a paint brush. In theory, the coatings fill cracks and other irregularities and at the same time create new surfaces which will not crack even when used in connection with unstable defects. The new surfaces are washable.

MATERIAL. The coatings may be obtained in cans ready for application. Several colors are available.

Fabric Wall Coverings. Several such coverings, under various trade names, are available. They are applied like wallpaper. In theory, the coverings will not crack or even tear when used in connection with unstable defects. The new surfaces are washable.

MATERIAL. The coverings can be obtained in rolls and are applied by means of a paste. Generally, several patterns and colors are available.

New Surfaces over Sound Plaster. As previously mentioned, nearly every old house is likely to have one or more wall surfaces which are not suitable for modern decoration. Sometimes the defects do not affect the soundness of the plaster. In such cases, the problem is to select new surface materials which can be applied *over* the plaster. Any one of the following materials can be depended upon to provide new and enduring beauty.

FIGURE 1. Installation of plywood panel over sound plasterboard. (*Courtesy Georgia-Pacific*)

SURFACE MATERIALS. Many types and kinds of new surface materials are available. A visit to a lumber yard or to a building-material dealer's showroom will prove to be interesting and helpful in deciding which materials to use for various rooms.

Plywood Panels. Chapter 1 contains a great deal of information about plywood, none of which is repeated here. What is discussed in the following relates to plywood paneling made especially for wall surfaces:

KINDS. Two general kinds are available. One kind is manufactured with a decorative factory finish. Another kind must be finished before or after application. Figure 1 shows a plywood panel being installed over sound gypsum wallboard.

SIZES. Panels are 4 feet wide and usually 8 feet long. Usual thicknesses when only a decorative surface is desired are ⅜ and ¼ inch. For application directly to studs, or for use as a wall surface in a basement, ¾-inch-thick plywood is generally used.

FIGURE 2. Remodeled kitchen showing use of panels on walls. (*Courtesy Georgia-Pacific*)

COLORS. Panel colors are determined by the kind of wood selected.

PATTERNS. The pattern of plywood panels, like their colors, is determined by the kind of wood selected. They can be obtained in mahogany, birch, knotty pine, walnut, elm, oak, and many other woods, all of which have their own particular patterns. Figure 2 shows a kitchen paneled with a cinnamon birch facing. Figure 3 shows a bedroom with ceilings as well as walls faced with walnut finish. And Figure 4 shows a dining area with walls given a pecan finish. In all cases shown, the panels are striated to give the appearance of boards, but nonstriated panels also are available.

FASTENING. Panels can be fastened with adhesives, nails, or screws. When nails or screws are used, they should be driven into studs or into furring strips nailed to studs.

EDGES. Plywood panels are manufactured with square edges. Various kinds of joints, however, can be obtained by means of beveling, rabbeting, or formation of tongues and grooves.

FIGURE 3. Remodeled bedroom with panels applied to walls and ceiling. (*Courtesy Georgia-Pacific*)

Hardboard Panels. Hardboard panels are made of wood fibers or other organic fibers, refined or partly refined, and felted under pressure into a panel. Other materials may be added during manufacture to improve quality or add desired characteristics. Figure 5 illustrates the use of such panels in remodeling a bathroom. They are installed in much the same way as plywood panels.

KINDS. Two kinds of hardboard are available, standard, or Type 1, and tempered or treated, called Type 2.

Type 1 is hardboard substantially as it comes from the press, except for drying and trimming to size. It is available in two classes. Class 1 is a standard hardboard with about 30 per cent less strength than Type

2 hardboard. Class 2 is a standard hardboard with lower density and less strength than Class 1.

Type 2 is hardboard that has been tempered or treated to improve stiffness, strength, and water resistance. In tempering, the manufacturer adds a drying material and uses heat to stabilize the resulting product.

FIGURE 4. Typical application of grooved panels to a dining area. (*Courtesy Georgia-Pacific*)

SIZES. Panels are 4 feet wide and usually 7 to 10 feet long, in 1-foot increments. Usual thickness is about ¼ inch. When deep grooving is desired for decorative effect, thicker panels are used.

COLORS. Panels come with a smooth surface that can be painted or with factory-applied colored finishes. The latter may be a single color or a combination of colors.

PATTERNS. A great variety of patterns are available, including tile, embossed, striated, prefinished, and perforated.

Tile patterns are formed by grooving Type 2 hardboard on one face.

Embossed patterns, pressed into one face of either type of hardboard, may produce different effects, such as basket-weave, or may simulate leather or wood grain.

FIGURE 5. Typical panels used in remodeling a bathroom.

Striated patterns, formed by pressing or machining one surface of hardboard, produce an effect similar to combed wood.

Prefinished panels are Type 1 or Type 2 hardboard with a factory-applied decorative coating, often simulating wood-grain finishes. They also may come with an additional, outer, transparent plastic coating to protect the factory-finished surface against abrasion and make it easy to clean.

Perforated panels are discussed later.

FASTENING. Panels can be fastened with nails, screws, or adhesives. Nails or screws should be driven into studs or into furring strips nailed to studs. The nails along the edges should be applied last. Various types of molding also are available for fastening purposes.

EDGES. Hardboard panels are manufactured with square edges.

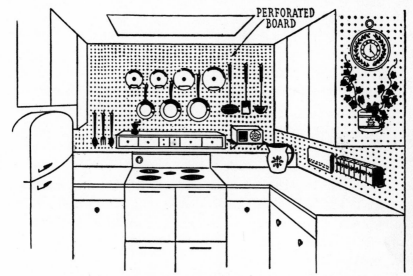

FIGURE 6. Typical installation of perforated hardboard in a kitchen.

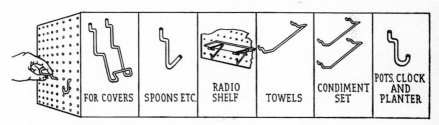

FIGURE 7. Typical hanging fixtures for use in kitchen.

Perforated Panels. Perforated panels are a type of wall-surface material that is useful as well as decorative. The perforations are generally ³⁄₁₆ inch in diameter and are spaced 1 inch apart throughout the panels.

Figure 6 shows a typical application of such panels to the walls of a kitchen. Note that all sorts of objects may be hung in any desired positions by means of the hangers illustrated in Figure 7. A great variety of such hangers is available. They lock on the panels or lift off without the use of tools of any kind.

The panels offer a unique opportunity for personality expression with an almost endless variety of potential arrangement of pictures and wall decorations. In children's rooms, recreation rooms, garages, living rooms, and workshops the panels may serve a multitude of uses.

Because many of their characteristics are similar to wood, the panels will tend to change slightly in dimension when exposed to fluctuations in humidity conditions.

The panels can be fastened directly to studs, furring strips, joists, or other framing members spaced not more than 16 inches on centers, or over a solid backing of wood, plasterboard, or plaster. Leave at least a ⅜-inch space between panel and wall.

SIZES. Several sizes are available in thicknesses of ⅛ and ¼-inch. In most cases, panel sizes can be selected to fit specific wall areas with little or no waste. The ⅛-inch thickness is used where the load on the hangers is not great. The ¼-inch thickness is a heavy-duty panel which should be used in places where the load on the hangers is exceptionally high.

COLORS. Tan and brown.

PATTERNS. Smooth or leatherlike.

FASTENING. Nails, screws, or glue.

EDGES. Square.

Gypsumboard Panels. Closely resembling plaster in many ways, gypsumboard consists of a gypsum core sandwiched between tough paper or other sheet material. Some panels come with a surface layer of plastic or aluminum foil on one face.

Gypsum is made from a special type of rock containing water in chemical combination. Manufacturers remove most of this water with high heat to obtain a product called *plaster of paris.* This product is used to make plaster, gypsum lath, and gypsumboard.

Gypsumboard is made by mixing plaster of paris with water and additives and spreading the mix between sheets of paper. The minerals recrystallize to form gypsum rock in the core, which, as a result, has excellent fire resistance.

KINDS. Different kinds of gypsumboard panels with different names may be used for walls and ceilings, although one type actually is called "wallboard." Also, several kinds of gypsum wallboard are available, generally differing in types of facing materials used.

Regular gypsum wallboard has gray liner paper on the back. On facing side and edges, this wallboard has a smooth paper covering, usually cream colored, that can accept paint.

Insulating gypsum wallboard has bright-finished aluminum foil bonded to gray liner paper on the back. The foil provides a vapor barrier and reflective insulation.

Prefinished gypsum wallboard has a decorative plastic or paper sheet bonded on the front face. No additional decorative treatment is necessary.

Gypsum backing board has gray liner paper on all surfaces and edges. It is intended for use as a base layer where several plies of gypsumboard are required for extra fire resistance, sound insulation, and strength.

Insulating backing board has bright-finished aluminum foil bonded to the back face. The foil serves the same functions as it does in insulating wallboard.

Gypsum coreboard is a special type of backing board intended for use as a base in space-saving, self-supporting walls erected without framing or in demountable walls. Coreboard may be a solid, 1-inch-thick backing board or two factory-laminated, ½-inch-thick layers of backing board.

Type X gypsumboard differs from the preceding types of board in that fire resistance of the core has been improved by addition of glass-fiber reinforcement and other materials. Type X may be wallboard, backing board, predecorated panel, or other types.

Water-resistant gypsum backing board has a water-resistant gypsum core and water-repellent facings. It is intended for use as a base for application of wall tile in bathrooms and other wet areas.

SIZES. Standard sizes for wallboard are 48 inches wide and 8, 10, 12, and sometimes 14 feet long. Coreboard usually comes 24 inches wide and 8 to 12 feet long. Backing board may be 24 or 48 inches wide and 8 feet long, although some manufacturers also make 12-foot-long panels.

Backing board generally is ⅜, ½, or ⅝ inch thick. Wallboard may be ¼, ⅜, ½, or ⅝ inch thick. The thinnest panels are intended for use as a low-cost covering for rehabilitation of old wall and ceiling surfaces. The ⅜-inch panels are used principally as the outer face in two-layer wall systems or as a better covering in repair and remodeling work. The ½-inch panels are used in single-layer wall and ceiling systems in new construction. The thickest panels are recommended for single-layer walls and ceilings where increased resistance to fire and noise transmission is desired. Coreboard, as mentioned previously, comes 1 inch thick.

COLORS. Desired colors can be obtained on regular wallboard with paint. The surface, however, should be sealed or primed before paint is applied. An emulsion sealer blocks the pores and reduces suction and texture differences between paper facing and joint compound. A good primer provides uniform texture and conceals color and surface variations. Some coatings make possible sealing and priming in one application. High-quality latex paints often have good sealing and priming properties and require no special preparation of the wallboard.

Colors also can be obtained with paper, fabric, or plastic wall coverings. Sealers should be used under these coverings so that they can be removed in the future without marring the wallboard surface and so that an adequate base will be left for redecorating.

In addition, colors can be obtained on prefinished wallboard. Because colors may vary slightly from lot to lot, all the panels used in a room should be from the same lot. If this is not possible, the joint between two different lots should be in a corner.

PATTERNS. A wide variety of patterns are available with coatings, coverings, and prefinished wallboards. Deep textures, for example, can be obtained with special paints and sprays. Designs with coverings range from repetitive patterns to complete murals. And prefinished wallboards offer a similar wide range, including simulated wood-grain finishes and textile effects in plastic.

FASTENING. Gypsumboard can be fastened to studs or furring strips with nails or screws. The base layer in multilayer construction, however, can be attached with clips or staples. Adhesives can be used to bond single-ply gypsumboard to framing, furring, masonry, or concrete, or to laminate a face ply to a base layer. Nails often are used in addition to adhesives, though.

Special nails, staples, screws, and adhesives are required for fastening gypsum wallboard. Nails should be driven with a crown-headed hammer until somewhat countersunk. A uniform depression, or dimple, not more than $\frac{1}{32}$ inch deep, should be formed around the nail head, without breaking the face paper or crushing the gypsum core. Ordinary nails are not designed for this purpose and should not be used. Screws for attaching gypsumboard to wood or steel framing should have cupped Phillips heads designed for use with a drywall power screwdriver. If properly driven, the specially contoured head leaves a uniform depression free of ragged edges and fuzz.

The depressions at fastener heads are later filled in with joint compound when the joints are taped. Additional coats of compound are applied over the fasteners when similar coats are applied to the joints.

Adhesives for wallboard are classified as stud, laminating, contact, and modified contact types. Stud adhesives are specially prepared for fastening single-ply wallboard to steel or wood framing. Laminating adhesives are designed to bond gypsumboards to each other and to suitable concrete and masonry surfaces. Contact adhesives, which offer the advantage of immediate bond, are intended for laminating gypsumboards to each other and for bonding wallboard to metal studs. Modified contact adhesives, which may take up to $\frac{1}{2}$ hour to grip firmly, may be used for attaching wallboard to all kinds of supporting construction.

EDGES. Standard edges on gypsumboard used for walls and ceilings are rounded, beveled, tapered, square, or combinations.

With regular gypsum wallboard, joints between panels and at interior corners are covered with paper tape after the panels have been fastened in place. Exposed edges and exterior corners are capped with metal or plastic beads. Joint compound is then applied to conceal fasteners, tape, and beads and to give the panel a smooth, unbroken surface, before decorative treatment is applied.

With prefinished wallboard, joints are sometimes covered with special moldings or battens or concealed with decorative material. Sometimes, however, joints are left exposed—for example, to obtain a plank effect.

Tiles. A tile is a small and thin, generally flat, surfacing material for walls, floors, and ceilings, sometimes flexible, but too stiff to be rolled.

It may be made of any of a wide variety of materials, including stone, clay, metal, plastic, asphalt, linoleum, concrete, glass, rubber, and cork. Walls, floors, and ceilings faced with tiles inherently have distinctive patterns because of the lines formed by the joints between the units.

Tiles with impervious faces often are used in bathrooms, kitchens, and other wet areas because they are water-resistant and easy to clean. Cork and special tiles generally are selected because of acoustical and decorative properties.

KINDS. Since tiles may be made of a wide variety of materials, many different types are available. Selection of any one type depends mainly on decorating objectives and availability. Only a few kinds are discussed in the following. The discussion, however, is generally applicable to the other types.

Ceramic tile is made by heating to a high temperature clay or a mixture of clay and other materials. The product is hard and dense. Glazing fuses ceramic materials to the face of a tile, to make it smooth, hard, and impervious. Unglazed tiles, however, often are preferred for floors because they are less slippery.

Metal tile may be formed from strip steel, stainless steel, aluminum, copper, brass, or other metals. Any of these metals may be given a decorative and protective finish.

Plastic tile may be made of vinyl, polystyrene, or other plastic, with additions of fillers and pigments.

Matching trim and accessories usually are available with most types of tile. Trim includes caps, bases, coves, and corners, which are necessary for edging a tile area or for making a transition between intersecting surfaces. Accessories include such bathroom items as soap dish, paper holder, tumbler and toothbrush holder, and towel bars.

SIZES. Tiles generally are square, rectangular, or hexagonal. They range in size from a tiny mosaic with sides about $\frac{3}{8}$ inch long to squares with 12-inch sides. Thickness ranges from about 0.015 inch for metal tiles and about $\frac{1}{16}$ inch for some plastic tiles to $\frac{3}{8}$ inch or more for ceramic tiles. Over-all thickness for a ceramic tile facing depends on the method of attachment, whether the tiles are set in a mortar bed or bonded with adhesive.

COLORS. Some types of tile, such as cork, aluminum, copper, brass, and stainless steel, may be used with a natural finish. If desired, however, metal tile may be obtained with factory-applied colored coatings. Ceramic tiles are made with a very wide range of colored facings. Plastic tiles usually come with color extending through the thickness of the tiles.

PATTERNS. Pattern is obtained in two ways with tile. One is the effect achieved with the joints between tiles. The joints may be made obscure, as in a mural, for example, or they may be accentuated, for example, with contrasting joint material. The second way is to texture the face of the tile. This type of pattern may be simple, such as mottling of colors or striations molded into the face, or complex sculptures, with designs in low or high relief.

FASTENING. Tiles must be set on a rigid backing. Generally, the easiest method is to bond the tiles to the backing with an adhesive. Manufacturer's recommendations for type of adhesive and method of application should be followed closely. Ceramic tile also may be attached with conventional portland-cement mortar, latex-portland-cement mortar, or a special dry-set mortar.

EDGES. Tiles usually come with square or rounded edges. Square edges permit joints to be filled flush with grout or other joint compound. With rounded edges, tops of joints may be recessed below the face of the tile. Some tiles have lugs on two adjacent edges to facilitate uniform spacing of the tiles.

New Surfaces without Plaster. When basement and attic spaces are being remodeled, as a means of providing recreation areas and bedrooms, it is likely that wall-surface materials are not present and that new surface materials must be applied to masonry foundations or to rough framing. In other cases, old lath and plaster may be in such bad condition that they must be removed.

SURFACE MATERIALS. All of the previously described panel materials can be applied to foundations or to rough framing by means of furring strips. Therefore, their descriptions are not repeated here. Tile can be preassembled on a rigid backing and treated as a panel or set in a mortar bed.

New Surfaces over Poor Backing. When existing plaster or wall panels are in very bad condition, the entire defective area should be removed and replaced. If only small areas are involved and can readily be bridged by new surfacing, or if the defects are mainly scratches or small dents, new surfaces can be applied directly over the existing walls.

SURFACE MATERIALS. If existing materials are removed, the replacement can be treated in the same way as described for "New Surfaces without Plaster." If covering materials can be used, panels or tile can be applied as described for "New Surfaces over Sound Plaster." When however, unsound areas must be bridged, panels should be thicker than those acceptable with sound plaster, and tile should be set in a mortar bed reinforced with metal lath or wire mesh nailed to studs.

HOW TO PLAN AND DO TYPICAL REMODELING PROJECTS

As repeatedly mentioned in connection with all of the projects explained in this book, remodeling work should be carefully planned and laid out prior to the time materials are purchased and actual work is started. Such procedure will prevent material waste, cut down the amount of labor, and assure much better final results. The following wall projects are presented in such a manner as to exhibit proper planning and to provide helpful how-to-do-it instructions:

REPAIRING PLASTER CRACKS

As previously mentioned, wall cracks are much more objectionable than similar cracks in ceilings. This is because the wall cracks are at a level where they are more likely to be seen. Another important consideration relates to the fact that wall cracks are apt to reoccur. Thus, the repair of them constitutes a gamble in terms of appearance and decorating expense. With this fact in mind, such repair work should be done with the greatest possible care.

Large Cracks. When cracks are more than ⅛ inch wide, regardless of their probable cause, they should be enlarged and some reinforcement installed before the patching material is applied.

PREPARATION. The dashed lines in the X part of Figure 8 indicate the original position of a large crack. In order that reinforcement can be installed and the benefits of keyed patching assured, the crack should be enlarged, in the form of an inverted V, so that its opening is at least 4 inches wide and so that it extends to the face of the lathing. This part of the work can be accomplished using a chisel and a hammer, being careful not to strike heavy blows. Use a stiff brush to clean all plaster dust out of the enlarged crack.

PATCHING. Thin metal lath can be used for reinforcement. Short pieces of it can be cut to the lineal shape of the enlarged crack and to a width

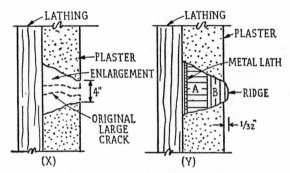

FIGURE 8. Repair of large wall cracks.

that will make a snug fit against the face of the original lathing, all as shown in the Y part of Figure 8. Use 1-inch brads, spaced about 2 inches apart, to nail the reinforcement securely in place.

For a patch of such width and where metal lath is involved, it is best to use a regular plaster mix for the patching shown in the A part and a regular white coat mix for the B part. Use a brush to wet thoroughly the interior of the crack prior to the time patching is started. Then, using regular plaster, fill the A part of the crack. Force the new plaster against the metal lath and make sure that it is in firm contact with the sides of the crack. Where wall cracks are concerned, the A part of the patch should constitute about two-thirds the depth of the crack. Allow this part of the patch to dry for a day or two and then apply the white coat in enough quantity to create a $\frac{1}{32}$-inch ridge, as shown in the illustration. The ridge allows possible white-coat shrinkage without fear that its final surface will be lower than the surface of the original plaster. After a day or two, what is left of the ridge can be sandpapered down so that it is flush with the original plaster.

When the white coat is thoroughly dry, after about two weeks, apply a liberal coat of shellac, or some other sealer, to the patch.

Small Cracks. Where cracks are only about $\frac{1}{16}$ inch wide, the patching procedure set forth in Chapter 4, in connection with cracks $\frac{1}{16}$ to $\frac{1}{4}$ inch wide, may be employed.

HAIRLINE CRACKS. Where very small cracks of hairline width are involved, any of the patching pencils available at hardware and paint stores may be used to fill them. Follow directions which accompany such pencils.

CRACKS IN THIN PLASTER

It is hoped that not many readers will be confronted with what was previously (see Chapter 4) described as *paperhanging*. Large cracks in thin plaster cannot be repaired. In such cases, the only alternative is to apply furring strips as a base for panels.

REPAIRING HOLES IN PLASTER

In newer houses, lathing is likely to be in the form of a gypsumboard that has heavy paper surfaces and a gypsum core. In old houses, lathing is likely to be in the form of small wood strips. Holes in plaster vary from those made by nails or screws to those made in connection with toggle bolts and other fasteners.

Small Holes. If holes are no more than $\frac{1}{16}$ inch in diameter, their repair is quite simple.

PATCHING. Use a nail to dig out all loose plaster, dirt, or dust. Wet the hole and then force the patching mix into it. Leave a small ridge. After a day or two, the ridge can be sandpapered flush with the surrounding plaster and sealed by means of shellac or other sealers.

Large Holes. If holes are ¼ inch or larger in diameter, their repair demands somewhat more work and care.

PREPARATION. If the lathing is gypsumboard, use an ice pick or awl to enlarge the hole near the surface of the lathing. This is the same inverted-V principle previously explained. Clean out all plaster particles, dust, and dirt.

PATCHING. Wet the interior of the hole. Then mix the plaster-patching material into a stiff but plastic state. Force the mix into the hole by means of a small trowel or an old pencil. Enough of the mix should be used to create the anchor shown in the *X* part of Figure 9. To prevent

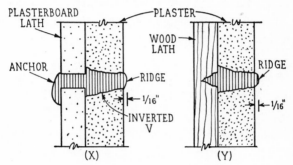

FIGURE 9. Repairing holes in plaster.

surface shrinkage, leave a little ridge at the surface of the old plaster. When the ridge is sandpapered flush and a sealer has been applied, the patch will not be noticeable under paint.

If a large hole extends through plaster and wood lath, the same procedure is recommended.

If the holes do not extend through the lathing, the procedure indicated in the *Y* part of Figure 9 is recommended. In such cases, the lathing serves as the anchor.

NEW SURFACES OVER SOUND PLASTER

The following projects are typical of all cases where panel coverings are to be applied over old but sound plaster. The projects are presented in terms of typical problems and their solutions:

PROBLEM 1. BEDROOM WALLS. For the purpose of this problem, we can assume that Plates I through VI, which are at the back of this book, show the plans for an *old* house. We can further assume that bedroom 3 is to be converted into a nursery in which soilproof walls are required. The problem is to apply panel surfacing to the walls.

SOLUTION. It can be assumed that plywood panels, such as shown in Figure 1, are to be used. Edges are offset tongue and groove.

PLANNING. When contemplating the use of such panels, the first step consists of checking the walls for level. This can be done by holding a long and straight 1 by 3 or 2 by 4 piece at various locations along the walls. If the surface of the plaster touches the straightedge at all points along its length, and at all locations, the walls are level enough for panels to be applied without furring strips. Level conditions can be assumed.

In order to assure the best and lasting results, we shall use both fastening clips and adhesive. Both of these items are available where the panels are purchased.

LAYOUT. With panels with accentuated joints, the purpose of layout is to plan their exact locations on the walls so as to create the best appearance. It is not often that wall dimensions are such that whole panels can be used without some cutting. In most cases, two of the panels for each wall must be made narrower. In this solution, we shall do the layout work for a typical wall in bedroom 3.

In order to do the layout work accurately and to the best of advantage, we shall draw a sketch of the wall next to the living room. Our sketch must be drawn to scale.

The X part of Figure 10 illustrates the best type of sketch for inexperienced mechanics to draw. In the sketch, $ABCD$ represents the wall. The center point of the wall is shown at L. The vertical line EF represents a joint between two panels.

Each panel is 48 inches wide. Lines LM and ST represent joints. These lines are drawn 48 inches apart. Thus, panels 1 and 2 can be full width, while panels 3 and 4 must be cut to about 10-inch widths. This balances the wall and creates the best appearance.

APPLICATION OF PANELS. Panel 3, as shown in the X part of Figure 10, should be applied first. In order to be sure that it is plumb, even

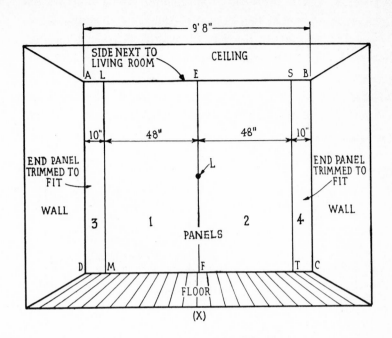

(X)

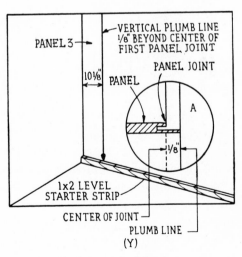

(Y)

FIGURE 10. Panel layout.

if the corner *AD* of the room is not plumb, mark a plumb line from the ceiling as shown in the *Y* part of the same illustration. However, we must add ⅛ inch to the 10-inch width of panel 3 for the reason shown at *A*. The plumb line constitutes a guide for application of the first panel.

Typical clips and how they are used to fasten panels are shown in the *A* part of Figure 11. They should be spaced about 16 inches apart

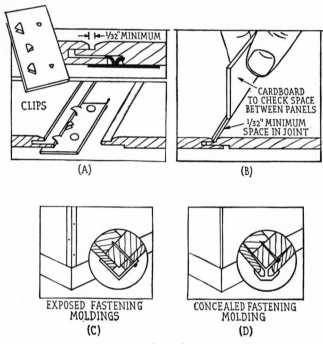

FIGURE 11. Applying first two panels.

and nailed by means of lath nails. In order to allow for expansion between panels, a ⅟₃₂-inch space must be provided. It can be measured as shown in the *B* part of the illustration.

The panels should not touch the floor when applied to the wall. Thus, a temporary 1- by 2-inch level starter strip, as shown in Figure 12, should be nailed to the wall above the floor. The panels should rest on this strip during application.

Cut panel 3 to length and to the exact width of 10½ inches. Saw the panel with the finished surface up. If the corner *AD*, as shown in the X parts of Figures 10 and 12, is not plumb, the edge of the panel must be cut to fit and so that its groove edge coincides with the plumb line.

Apply adhesive to the rear face of panel 3 and press it into proper position, as indicated in the X part of Figure 12. Quickly attach and nail the clips. Apply adhesive to panel 1 and insert its tongue into the groove of panel 3. See Y part of Figure 12. Press panels firmly together but do not force them. See the A part of Figure 11 for proper spacing. All other panels are applied in the same manner except the last one (number 4 in the X part of Figure 10) which is only cemented into place.

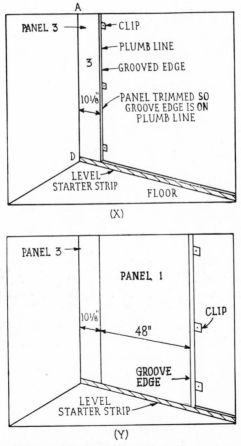

FIGURE 12. Typical clips and panel spacing.

The layout work and installation of panels for other walls is carried on in the same manner. Around windows and doors, the panels should be cut so as to fit snugly against the wood trim.

The *C* and *D* parts of Figure 11 show typical metal corner moldings and how they are installed.

When all panels have been applied, the starter strips can be removed. Figure 13 shows how a piece of scrap panel should be used back of the base and where the nails should be driven.

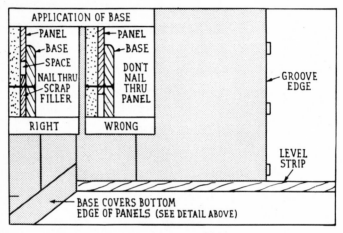

FIGURE 13. How to apply base.

Cove or other types of moldings can be nailed to the corners where walls and ceiling meet. This will give a finished appearance to the remodeled walls.

PROBLEM 2. BEDROOM WALLS. For the purpose of this problem, we can assume that bedroom 2, as shown in Plate II, is to be remodeled to serve the dual purpose of a den and sewing room. We can further assume that the existing wall decoration consists of several layers of wallpaper and that in one large area the plaster has been damaged. The problem is to remove the old wallpaper, to repair the damaged area, and to apply plywood panels with a tile-like pattern and basket-weave texture to the walls.

PLANNING. The room has three windows all of which are located at one corner. This situation will require some careful planning in order to place the basket-weave design in such a manner that panels around the ceiling, windows, and floor will appear well balanced. We shall use both adhesive and fastening clips.

LAYOUT. As explained in the solution to Problem 1, the purpose of layout is to plan the exact locations of all panels prior to the time application of them is started. This is highly important because the room dimensions and the window locations are not likely to be such that whole panels can be used for all areas. In this solution, we shall do the layout work for one typical wall in bedroom 2.

In order to do the layout work accurately, we shall draw some sketches of the rear wall.

The X part of Figure 14 illustrates the best type of sketch for inexperienced mechanics to draw. In the sketch, $ABCD$ represents the wall. The center point is shown at L. The window openings are shown in terms of the edges which the panels will contact. Panels are 4 by 8 feet.

Each tile is 16 inches square. Starting at the center point, we can lay out panels 1 through 4 in such a manner that end tiles at vertical corners are of equal width and constitute a balanced border. The 8′ 0″ ceiling height makes six rows of whole tiles possible. However, this layout has two flaws. First, it is not a good policy to place the bottom edges of the first row of tiles at the floor level. Second, the vertical joint between panel 1 and panels 3 and 4, as indicated at M, does not have a balanced appearance.

The Y part of the illustration shows a better layout. The first row of tiles has been moved so that their bottom edges are several inches above the floor level. This is in keeping with the recommendation shown in Figure 13. The joint between panel 1 and panels 3 and 4 now coincides with the edge of the window trim. One end tile is a little wider than the other, but the difference will not be noticeable in the window corner.

Panels should be arranged so that the basket-weave pattern continues in adjoining panels.

REMOVING OLD WALLPAPER. Ordinarily, old paper can be soaked with warm water and then scraped off using a wide-blade putty knife. Washing soda may be added if clear water does not loosen the paper.

REPAIRING DAMAGED AREA. The damaged plaster can be removed entirely and in such a manner that the edges of the remaining plaster,

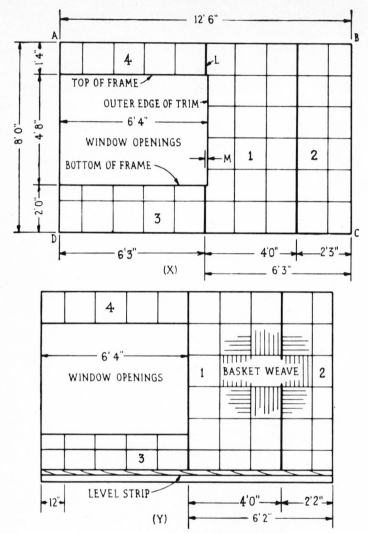

FIGURE 14. Layout of rear wall of bedroom 2.

around the damaged area, are straight and square. A piece of gypsum-board can be nailed to the lathing to take the place of the removed plaster.

APPLICATION OF PANEL. Nail the starter strip to the wall, making sure that it is level regardless of the level of the floor.

Start the installation with panel 3 and be sure that the groove edges, as shown in Figure 15, are toward the area to be covered. If necessary, as shown in the *Y* part of Figure 14, cut the first panel to size. Trim off the tongue edge. Remember that panels should be sawed with the finished surface up. As indicated, install the first panel in the left-hand corner and others beyond it toward the right-hand side, keeping the groove edges of each panel on the top and to the right-hand side. Apply adhesive to the back of each panel, and nail clips as illustrated in Figure 15. Clip application and joint spacing are as illustrated in the *A* and

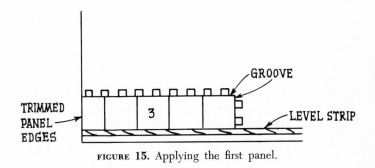

FIGURE 15. Applying the first panel.

B parts of Figure 11. Other application procedures are the same as explained in the solution to Problem 1.

NEW SURFACES OVER FOUNDATIONS

The following project is typical of all cases where decorative wallboard is to be applied to the surfaces of concrete-block foundations. The project is presented in terms of a typical problem and its solution.

PROBLEM 3. BASEMENT RECREATION ROOM. For the purpose of this problem, we can assume that the basement space shown in Plate II is to be remodeled to provide a recreation area. The problem is to apply wallboard to the surface of the concrete-block foundation. The surface of the foundation is often damp.

SOLUTION. It can be assumed that the west end of the basement, between the pilaster and the chimney, is the area involved. The space is 19′ 2″ long and 11′ 10″ wide.

PLANNING. As indicated in Chapter 7, the east wall of the area will be framed, using 2 by 4 studs. Because the foundation is sometimes damp, the wallboard should be protected by applying a thick coat of white portland-cement paint or other waterproofing directly to the block. The application can be done with a brush. As an added protection against the transmission of moisture to the wallboard, asphalt-saturated and coated paper should be tacked to the face of the furring. Lap the paper 6 inches at joints. As a further protection, a ¼-inch air space should be left above and below the wallboard. This will allow a circulation of air behind it and help to keep the space between it and the foundation dry.

LAYOUT. In this problem the layout consists of planning the most economical size of wallboard to use and then to plan the furring strips. Just as an example of how such layout is done, we shall be concerned with only the west wall where the pilaster is located. As usual, we must draw a sketch, accurately to scale, which will represent the west wall. Figure 16 shows such a sketch.

The area *ABCD* represents the west wall. The wall areas on either side of the pilaster are 8' 11" long and 7' 6" high. Wallboard panels 4 feet wide and 10 feet long can be used without too much waste. The *G* and *H* areas are 4' 0" wide and 8' 11" long. Thus, only 13 inches of wallboard is wasted. The *E* and *F* areas are only 3' 6" wide; hence 6 inches of wallboard will have to be wasted. However, this is a satisfactory layout, and it provides a horizontal joint 4' 0" above the floor. This is a good design where such a long room is involved.

Figure 17 shows the details of furring strips around the pilaster and of the interior and exterior joints, such as at *X* and *Y*.

Figure 18 shows the details of the vertical and horizontal furring strips. The horizontal strip at *P* must be under the joint indicated in Figure 16.

APPLICATION OF FURRING STRIPS. The furring strips shown in Figure 18 constitute the minimum number recommended. A sturdier wallboard installation would result if double that number were used. Before applying the furring, paint the wall with a waterproofing compound, as previously mentioned.

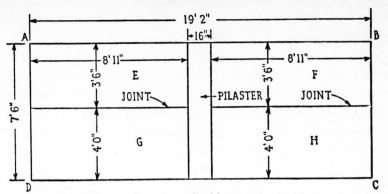

FIGURE 16. Layout for west wall of basement recreation room.

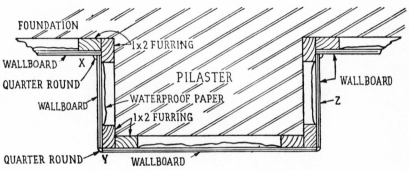

FIGURE 17. Details of furring around pilaster.

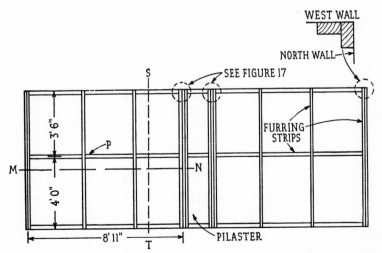

FIGURE 18. Details of furring strips for west wall of basement recreation room.

Apply the vertical pieces first, and then fill in the horizontal pieces, as shown by the details in Figures 17 and 18.

The strips can sometimes be fastened to the block by means of special concrete nails which are available at hardware stores. If such nails do not hold the strips firmly in place, an electric drill can be used to drill holes for wooden plugs or toggle bolts. In most cases, the wooden-plug procedure shown in Figure 19 works out satisfactorily. Enough plugs should be used to hold the strips securely in place. Use a straight-edge and a carpenter's level, at such locations as noted by the dashed lines *MN* and *ST* in Figure 18, to plumb all furring strips. Drive shims as may be required to bring them up to the required level.

APPLICATION OF MOISTUREPROOFING. Apply waterproof paper over the furring strips as indicated in Figure 17.

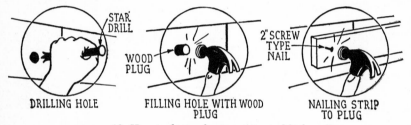

DRILLING HOLE   FILLING HOLE WITH WOOD PLUG   NAILING STRIP TO PLUG

FIGURE 19. How to fasten furring strips to block wall.

APPLICATION OF WALLBOARD. The back of the wallboard can be given a sealer coat of paint as a final precaution against moisture. Apply adhesive to the furring strips. Drive nails spaced about 6 inches apart on the outer edges of each panel and 12 inches apart at the intermediate furring strips. For details, see the following discussion of "Gypsumboard Glued to Studs."

WALL-SURFACE MATERIALS ON FRAMING

When surface materials are to be applied directly to wall or partition framing, the recommended application procedures are the same as explained in the solutions to Problems 1 and 2, except that panels are nailed or glued at each stud. If studs are not straight and spaced exactly 16 inches on centers, horizontal 1 by 3-inch furring strips should be

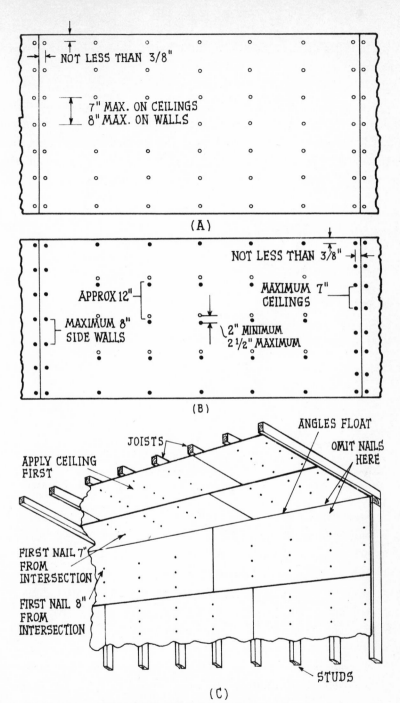

FIGURE 20. Nail spacing for fastening gypsum wallboard to studs.

nailed to the studs for attachment of the panels. The following details are typical:

Gypsumboard Nailed to Studs. Wallboard can be attached by a single-nailing or a double-nailing method. Double nailing can produce tighter board-to-stud contact and fewer loose boards. Single nails should be spaced 7 inches apart on ceilings and 8 inches apart on walls along

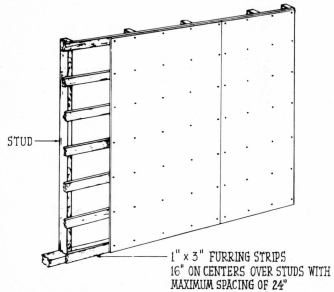

STUD

1" x 3" FURRING STRIPS 16" ON CENTERS OVER STUDS WITH MAXIMUM SPACING OF 24"

FIGURE 21. Nailing of gypsum wallboard to furring strips attached to studs.

studs, as shown in the *A* part of Figure 20. In double nailing, a first set of nails should be driven 12 inches apart in the interior portion of the panel. Then, a second set should be driven 2 inches from each of the nails in the first set, as indicated in the *B* part of Figure 20. Because the board is squeezed more tightly against the framing after the second set of nails have been driven, the first set should now be given an extra blow to reseat those nails firmly. Spacing of perimeter nails should be the same as for single nailing.

In general, perimeter nails should be driven at least ⅜ inch away from panel edges and ends, as shown in the *A* and *B* parts of Figure 20. Where ceiling and wall panels intersect, however, perimeter nails

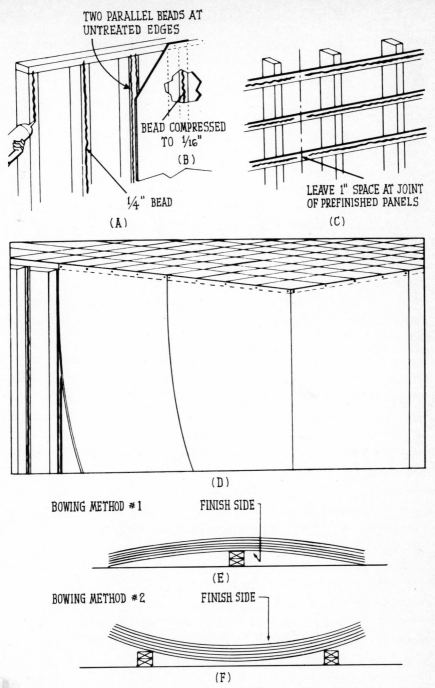

TWO PARALLEL BEADS AT
UNTREATED EDGES

BEAD COMPRESSED
TO ¹⁄₁₆"
(B)

¼" BEAD

(A)

LEAVE 1" SPACE AT JOINT
OF PREFINISHED PANELS

(C)

(D)

BOWING METHOD #1   FINISH SIDE

(E)

BOWING METHOD #2   FINISH SIDE

(F)

FIGURE 22. Attachment of prefinished panels with adhesive and nails.

should be omitted. As indicated in the *C* part of Figure 20, the first row of nails should be 7 inches from the intersection in ceiling panels and 8 inches away in wall panels.

The construction with furring strips shown in Figure 21 should be followed where studs are warped, unevenly spaced, or poorly aligned. Shim out the furring strips where necessary to form a solid, even nailing surface for panels.

Gypsumboard Glued to Studs. Wallboard may be attached with an adhesive to studs that are straight, spaced 16 inches on centers, and with edges in the same plane. Nails usually are used to supplement the adhesive, but are required only along the perimeter. A tight bond results that yields a stronger, stiffer assembly with fewer fastener defects.

Adhesive should be applied to each stud with a caulking gun in accordance with manufacturer's recommendations. A bead $\frac{1}{4}$ inch in diameter, laid in a straight line or zigzag, as shown in the *A* part of Figure 22, should be applied to the stud faces in the interior of each panel. A zigzag bead should be used where two adjacent panels are attached to the same stud if the joint is to be treated. Where the joint between prefinished panels is to be left untreated, however, two parallel beads of adhesive should be applied, one near each edge of the stud. This decreases the possibility of adhesive oozing through the joint onto the prefinished surfaces. When the wallboard is pressed into place, the adhesive is expected to spread to a width of about 1 inch and a thickness of about $\frac{1}{16}$ inch (see the *B* part of Figure 22).

Where studs do not meet the requirements given above, furring strips should be nailed to them, as shown in Figure 21. Application of adhesive is similar to that for studs (see the *C* part of Figure 22).

When applied to the adhesive-coated studs, each panel should be bowed or precurved over its full length, as indicated in the *D* part of Figure 22. Bowing applies pressure against the adhesive and framing at the center of the panel when nails are driven at top and bottom. Bowing may be accomplished by stacking the panels as shown in the *E* or *F* part of Figure 22 for one or more days. Nail each panel first at the ceiling line with $1\frac{1}{4}$-inch wallboard nails spaced 6 to 8 inches apart. Then, nail the panel in a similar manner at the floor line.

CHAPTER SIX

Floors

The advantages of well-laid and beautiful floors are familiar to everyone. Good floors are easy to keep clean. They are comfortable to walk on. They constitute important and pleasing aspects of decorating schemes. On the other hand, defective floors catch dust and dirt. They are unsightly. They are also severe and lasting sources of annoyance and keen disappointment.

Like many other details of houses, floors are subject to many natural and unfortunate defects. Natural defects are unavoidable. The unfortunate varieties are the results of poor materials or of careless workmanship at the time houses were built.

Natural defects, such as small cracks between boards or shrinkage, are likely to appear in old houses and are actually the marks of time. Unfortunate defects, such as large cracks between boards and dished surfaces, often appear in new houses.

Unsightly or defective floors may be repaired or remodeled to create greatly improved appearance or entirely new surfaces. Many new materials are available for such purposes.

The new materials are easy to use and apply. Some of them provide soundproofing and insulating effects in addition to highly desirable beauty.

For example, when attic spaces are being remodeled to provide new recreation or bedroom areas, the new floors may include soundproofing qualities which prevent the transmission of objectionable noises or sounds to other areas at lower levels. Or, when basement spaces are being remodeled to create new recreation areas, the new floors may include some of the soft qualities of a rug-plus-insulation protection against dampness and chill from the soil underneath the floors.

Previously unfinished spaces, such as basements and attics, may be transformed into living areas as explained in Chapters 7 and 8.

The purpose of this chapter is to explain the important fundamentals of floor defects, to discuss typical repair and remodeling projects, and to show how such projects are planned and accomplished.

FLOOR DEFECTS

By means of the following explanations we shall learn the fundamentals of floor defects, how to recognize such defects, and how to judge them in terms of recommended repair and remodeling work.

Cracks in Wood Floors. When cracks appear in wood floors, the faults generally stem from natural or unfortunate conditions and, in some cases, from a combination of both.

NATURAL CONDITIONS. There are several natural conditions which are apt to cause cracks, even though the best of materials and excellent workmanship are used and exercised at the time houses are being built. Such cracks are not disgraceful. They are almost sure to occur as the years pass.

LUMBER SHRINKAGE. The best of flooring lumber, even when carefully kiln-dried or allowed to dry naturally until its moisture content is low, may eventually shrink across the grain. In the *A* part of Figure 1, the double-headed arrow at *X* points across the grain of a typical floor board. When only a small amount of such shrinkage occurs, thin cracks between boards are sometimes visible. Such cracks may appear in isolated locations or they may be quite general.

As explained in Chapter 4, the structural details of houses may shrink and cause some shifting of their positions. If such shifting occurs to any appreciable extent, floor boards may be pulled apart so that cracks appear between them. Or, the boards may be pushed together with enough force to cause them to buckle and form humps in floors.

WETTING. When floors are not well protected by means of varnish or other sealers, frequent wetting may cause the boards to swell beyond their normal widths. In a case of this kind, the boards press against one another. This is apt to cause crushed fibers along their edges. After subsequent drying and shrinkage, there are cracks between the boards, owing to the fact that the crushed fibers do not recover their original shapes.

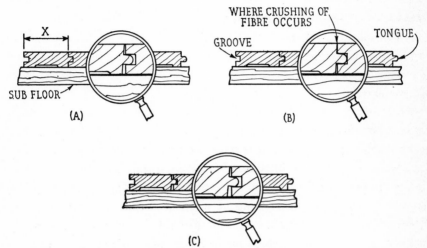

FIGURE 1. How compression set makes cracks. A, flooring when laid; B, the same flooring after it has absorbed moisture as a result of damp conditions in unfinished house; C, the same flooring after subsequent drying. The inverted-V-shaped joint is permanently deformed and there is a wide crack.

SETTLEMENT. As explained in Chapter 4, settlement often causes shifts in the positions of structural details. When such shifting occurs, floor cracks are likely to occur.

UNFORTUNATE CONDITIONS. Unfortunate conditions are always caused by inferior flooring lumber or by careless carpentry work. Such conditions are beyond logical excuse. Yet, they must be recognized and understood.

EXCESS MOISTURE. When cracks develop in new floors, within a year or two after the floors are laid, the fault can generally be traced to excess moisture in the flooring stock.

Well-informed manufacturers of flooring lumber make every effort to dry flooring stock properly and to keep it dry in their warerooms prior to sale and shipment. However, there are other cases where careless handling and unethical sales of wet stock take place. When wet (green) floor lumber is used, large cracks between boards and most unsightly appearances are sure to occur.

Properly seasoned (dried) lumber can absorb dangerous amounts of moisture if it is stored prior to use in a house where plaster and masonry walls or floors are not dry. Or, if especially humid conditions exist in houses, either before or immediately after floors are laid, the boards will absorb moisture. Whatever the reasons for moisture absorption, cracks are sure to occur. The only remedy consists of keeping lumber dry until completed floors can be sealed by means of shellac, varnish or other finish materials.

COMPRESSION SET. If several days of damp weather occur immediately after a floor is laid (see *A* part of Figure 1) and before the finish, such as varnish, shellac, or other sealers have been applied, the moisture content of the floor is likely to increase greatly. Such moisture can cause floor boards to press against one another as they swell. Heavy pressure of this sort generally results in crushing of wood fiber near the joints between boards. Technically known as *compression set* (see *B* part of Figure 1), this crushing is another common cause for cracks between boards. A relatively narrow margin of each board has to take the brunt of the compression. After boards have once been compressed, they seldom recover. See *C* part of Figure 1.

CROOKED STOCK. Another cause of cracks between floor boards, also aggravated by moisture changes, is the use of crooked boards; that is, boards that have bent edgewise. If a crook is so pronounced that much pressure must be applied to drive a board into place, three cracks are sure to appear, sooner or later—one at each end of the board on one side and another along the middle part of the board on the opposite side.

DISHED BOARDS. Many old houses have softwood floors in which the boards are 3 or more inches wide. Unless such flooring is very well protected by means of paint or varnish, frequent wetting or humid conditions may cause the edges of the boards to warp or curl in such a manner that their centers will be lower than their edges. This condition is unsightly and unsanitary.

DIRTY FLOORS. The best of floors will soon lose most of their original beauty unless they are kept clean and otherwise taken care of as outlined in a subsequent part of this chapter. Dirt ruins finishes! Once this happens, the boards absorb moisture, and cracks appear.

FLOOR SQUEAKS. In most instances, floor squeaks develop because too few nails were originally driven in each of the floor boards. To be effective, the nails should be spaced no more than 10 inches apart. Screw-type nails have more holding power than the plain-shanked varieties and are therefore better suited for application to floors.

JUDGING DEFECTS. The *causes* of floor cracks should have considerable influence on our judgment of what to do so far as repairs and remodeling are concerned.

Natural cracks in the floors of old houses are likely to be at their maximum widths and are not apt to increase in number or extent. If they are not too unsightly, they can be repaired without fear that they will reopen.

Unfortunate cracks are apt to be unstable and cannot be repaired with any assurance that they will not reoccur. Such cracks practically ruin the appearance of floors and they are not sanitary. The only satisfactory remedies consist of wall-to-wall carpeting or the application of new surface materials.

Cracks in Concrete Floors. There are a few natural reasons why cracks appear in concrete floors. However, most such cracks are due to unfortunate conditions.

NATURAL CONDITIONS. The following conditions are classified as *natural* reasons why concrete floors develop cracks. Here, the term *natural* is used to indicate items which are not the fault of poor materials or careless workmanship.

WASHOUTS. Sometimes the soil under concrete floors is partly washed away. In such cases, parts of the floors are left without support, and cracks occur because plain concrete has very little tensile strength.

FOUNDATION SETTLEMENT. If foundations and footings settle, the resulting movement is apt to cause strains which the small tensile strength of plain concrete cannot cope with. Cracks are the result.

FREEZING. If the soil under concrete floors should freeze, the resultant expansion would cause cracks in the concrete.

HEAVY BLOWS. Because plain concrete has so little tensile strength, severe blows from a heavy instrument, or the dropping of a heavy object on it, could cause cracks.

UNFORTUNATE CONDITIONS. All of the unfortunate causes of cracks in concrete floors can be traced to poor proportioning of ingredients, improper mixing, too little thickness, or downright carelessness by mechanics.

PROPORTIONING AND MIXING. Concrete is one of the best and most durable of building materials when correct proportions of portland cement, sand, crushed rock or gravel, and water are used and when mixing is carried on properly. It is only when too little cement, dirty sand, cheap crushed rock or gravel, and too much water are used, together with careless mixing, that concrete floors are subject to undue cracks and poor appearance.

TOO LITTLE THICKNESS. Any concrete floor should have a total thickness, including base and topping, of at least 4 inches. Where thinner floors are placed, even with the best of concrete, cracks are apt to occur.

CARELESSNESS. If mechanics fail to observe the foregoing specifications, allow mixes to reach initial set before being placed, forget to compact the placed concrete, add water after mixing is complete, allow the concrete to freeze, neglect proper curing, etc., the resulting floors will fall heir to cracks, lack of waterproof qualities, and unsightly appearances.

DUSTING. If the surfaces of concrete floors are always "dusty," in spite of frequent sweeping or washing, the fault can be traced to excessive steel troweling at the time the floors were placed. Dusting is also the result of using dry cement to hasten the setting of newly placed floors.

PEELING. Sometimes the surfaces of concrete floors have a tendency to peel or flake off, in spots, leaving unsightly holes or depressions. This happens when topping is placed on bases that are too dry. It also happens if mechanics fail to apply a thin grout coat (cement and water) to bases before topping is placed.

DIRTY FLOORS. The best of concrete is somewhat porous, especially when topping is not used in connection with floors. Grease, dirt, and spilled liquids will penetrate into the pores of concrete unless quickly or frequently removed. Once such penetration has taken place, the stains are impossible to remove.

WET FLOORS. When basement concrete floors are wet most of the time, the cause can be traced to poor concrete or to the fact that a static head of water is present under such floors.

Judging Defects. Natural defects, especially in old houses, are quite likely to be at their maximum. In cases where only a few small cracks are involved, repair work may be carried on without fear that the cracks will reoccur. Where many large cracks are involved, repair work is not feasible. In such cases, a new surface material should be applied.

Unfortunate defects cannot be repaired with any assurance that they will not reoccur. Any repair work constitutes a gamble and there is little chance that repaired floors will be anything but eyesores. In such cases, new surface materials should be planned.

SUGGESTED REMODELING PROJECTS

As mentioned in the first paragraph of this chapter, floors constitute an important aspect of the decorating schemes employed for interiors of houses. In fact, remodeling or modernization plans are not complete unless or until careful attention has been given to existing and proposed new floors. Therefore, the following suggestions are presented as a means of showing some of the projects and materials we can work with to create beautiful and modern floors in many areas of our homes:

Repairing Cracks in Wood Floors. In older houses where natural cracks between boards are not wider than $\frac{1}{16}$ inch, it is safe to fill them and then do some refinishing work. The results are generally satisfactory in terms of beauty and economy. Cracks originally caused by compression set or crooked boards can also be repaired if we are sure they are at their maximum and if they are not wider than $\frac{1}{16}$ inch. The repair of wider cracks, especially where they are likely to reoccur, is a gamble not likely to produce satisfactory or lasting results.

MATERIALS. For the repair of narrow floor cracks only fine sawdust and shellac are required.

Repairing Large Cracks. As previously mentioned, the repair of large cracks, $\frac{1}{8}$ inch or more in width, is a gamble which is not likely to produce satisfactory or lasting results. However, such repair work can be tried before resorting to the more expensive alternative of an entirely new floor. The repair procedure consists of inserting slivers of wood into the cracks.

MATERIALS. Slivers of wood, fine sawdust, and shellac.

Correcting Floor Squeaks. Floors can be tightened by means of nails driven from the surface of the boards into the joists. The nailheads can be driven below the wood surface and the dents filled.

MATERIALS. It is advisable to use special flooring nails of the screw type. Such nails have much greater holding power than ordinary plain-shanked types.

Replacing Damaged Boards. It sometimes happens that one or more boards in a floor become damaged or are otherwise unsightly. Such boards can be replaced by means of a simple procedure. Unless the whole floor is refinished, the new boards are likely to be prominent.

MATERIALS. Only new boards, of the same kind and color as the existing boards, and a few nails of the screw type are required.

New Flooring in Place of Old. If an existing hardwood floor contains so many natural or unfortunate defects that it is beyond repair, it can be torn out and replaced by a new hardwood floor. However, such a procedure is quite expensive and not recommended unless an old house is to be practically rebuilt. The necessary hammering could easily dislodge otherwise sound plaster on ceilings under the floors and cause other difficulties. As a worthy alternative, we can resurface such floors with soft tile. The process is not difficult, it creates new and beautiful surfaces, and the cost is low.

MATERIALS. Many kinds of soft tile are available including plastic, asphalt, cork, and rubber. A visit to any lumberyard or to a building-material dealer's showroom will prove to be interesting and helpful.

SIZES AND COLORS. A great variety of sizes and colors are available. Selection can be based on room sizes and color schemes desired.

FASTENING. Most soft tile are applied or fastened by means of adhesives which manufacturers recommend and supply. However, some of the plastic tile may be applied without the use of adhesives or other fasteners.

PATTERNS. Manufacturers and dealers will supply suggestions which can be used in planning tile patterns for any room.

Repairing Cracks in Concrete Floors. When cracks in concrete floors are not more than 1 inch wide, and when the floors are dry and in otherwise good condition, repair work can be depended upon to produce satisfactory surfaces for paint or stain.

MATERIALS. Mortar of portland cement and clean sand. Various prepared compounds are also available at hardware stores.

Soft Recreation-room Floor over Concrete. If an existing concrete floor in a basement recreation room is sound, level, and fairly dry, a luxurious new surface can be applied. It will feel soft when walked on, and as previously explained, will provide insulation against dampness and chill.

MATERIALS. Rigid insulation board or panels 1 inch thick provide the softness and insulating effects. Thin hardboard is required so that table and chair legs will not dent the insulation. Any kind of soft tile or carpeting can be used for the surface.

Parquet Squares or Blocks over Concrete. If an existing concrete floor is sound, level, and always bone-dry, hardwood parquet squares or blocks can be cemented directly to it. They are easy to lay and the cost is reasonable. They can be finished the same as any other hardwood floor.

MATERIALS. The squares are manufactured from oak, maple, birch, and beech woods. They have tongued-and-grooved edges.

SIZES. The squares are available in sizes ranging from 8 by 8 to 12 by 12 inches square and $2\frac{5}{32}$, $3\frac{3}{32}$, and $\frac{5}{16}$ inch thick.

FASTENING. The squares are fastened to the concrete floor by means of adhesives which the manufacturers recommend and supply.

PATTERNS. There are a great variety of patterns available from the various manufacturers. The pattern shown in Figure 2 is the most popular.

Plank Floors for Remodeled Attic Areas. Colonial-type hardwood plank flooring constitutes an ideal floor surface for bedrooms in remodeled attics. It can be applied over any type of wood subflooring, along with insulation to reduce the transmission of sound to rooms at a lower level.

MATERIALS. Figure 3 shows a section of typical plank flooring in which the edges of the boards are square and therefore create flush joints. If shallow V-joints are desired, boards with beveled edges should be used.

FIGURE 2. Typical parquet squares.

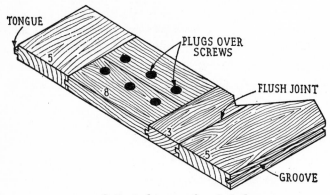

FIGURE 3. Typical pattern for plank floor.

Such flooring must be carefully handled and stored in a dry, well-ventilated place prior to laying. It should not be laid unless or until the interior temperature is at least 70°F.

KINDS. Oak and Maple.

SIZES. The planks are manufactured in random lengths. Widths range from 3 to 8 inches and thicknesses from $^{25}\!/_{32}$ to $^5\!/_{16}$ inch.

FASTENING. Nails and screws.

PATTERN. As indicated in Figure 3, boards of various widths can be employed to create patterns. The numerals in Figure 3 indicate board widths in inches.

Floor-sag Correction. There are many instances, especially in very old houses, where floor joists have suffered permanent deflection. There are other instances where the joists bend under the weight of people or furniture. In either case, the remedy consists of installing one or more screw-type columns as a means of pushing the joists up to a level position and keeping them there.

MATERIALS. Screw-type columns can be obtained in various sizes.

Tile over Plywood in New Attic Rooms. In cases where attic spaces do not have flooring, plywood may be used to excellent advantage. Any of the soft tiles may be applied to it.

MATERIALS. Any good grade of ¾-inch thick softwood plywood. See *tile* in previous explanation.

Tile over Wood Floors in Bad Condition. In very old houses there are many instances where softwood floors are badly dished, worn, and unsanitary. Such floors may be remodeled by means of plywood and soft tile or carpeting.

MATERIALS. Same as previously explained.

New Board-type Hardwood Floors over Concrete. The traditional or board-type hardwood flooring may be applied over concrete floors. There is a simple and easy way to do it. Wood sleepers can be fastened to the concrete by the methods explained in Chapter 2. The hardwood flooring can be nailed to the sleepers. If hot asphalt is mopped on the concrete before the sleepers are installed, the floor will be dampproof.

New Masonry Surfaces for Concrete Floors. There are several kinds of masonry materials which can be applied in thin coats over old concrete floors to create new and desirable surfaces.

MATERIALS. Special concrete is made using sand and an epoxy.

The mixture produces a hard, smooth surface, which is easily applied. Perlite concrete uses a special type of aggregate to produce a coating which has a high degree of insulating ability, as well as a desirable surface.

Refinishing Existing Hardwood Floors. By means of electric sanding machines, hardwood floors which are in sound condition may be given a brand-new surface for refinishing. The final result is equal in quality to a new floor.

New Hardwood Floor over Softwood. In a case where all of the floors in an old house were originally laid using softwood, a new and modern hardwood flooring can be applied directly over the old flooring.

MATERIALS. For this purpose, oak and maple boards from 1 to $1\frac{1}{2}$ inches wide and $\frac{3}{8}$ inch thick can be used.

HOW TO PLAN AND DO TYPICAL REMODELING PROJECTS

Following our usual and recommended procedures, we shall study several typical remodeling projects from the planning and installation standpoints. The procedures herein set forth are explained in terms of inexperienced mechanics. No inference is implied that possible other methods would not be as effective.

REPAIRING SMALL CRACKS IN WOOD FLOORS

In previous discussions we learned that small cracks are apt to occur between the boards in wood floors. We concluded that such cracks are at their maximum widths after houses are two years old and that repair work is feasible.

The *A* part of Figure 4 shows a section view of typical hardwood flooring over wood subflooring. The joint between the two boards is tight and flush. The *B* part of the illustration indicates a crack between tongued-and-grooved boards. The *C* part shows a crack between shiplap boards. Shiplap boards are not employed for modern floors, but they may be encountered in old houses. In the illustration, the cracks are exaggerated for visualization purposes.

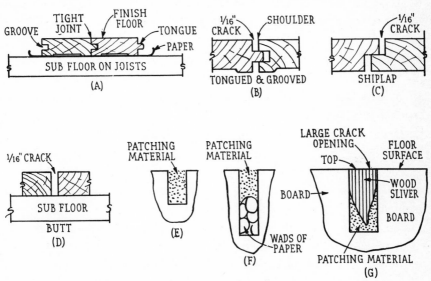

FIGURE 4. Typical cracks and repair.

Preparation. First, use a stiff brush or a small knife blade to clean out the cracks as much as possible. (Care should be exercised not to cut or mar the shoulders. See *B* part of illustration. If the shoulders are cut, crack repair is much more difficult.) Then, wipe the surface of the boards, near the cracks, with a damp cloth to remove particles of dust or dirt. If the floor is in need of a thorough cleaning, such work should be done prior to the repair work. The floor should be dry and the room temperature warm. If repair work is done during extremely cold weather or when the floor is cold, later expansion might squeeze out the patching material.

Patching Materials. If possible, fine sawdust from the same kind of wood as the floor should be obtained by sawing pieces of such a board. A more laborious process, consisting of sandpapering such a board, provides superior dust for the purpose. A small amount of ordinary, fresh shellac is necessary. If the surface of the floor is considerably darker than the sawdust, a little stain can be mixed with the sawdust and shellac until the mixture matches the color of the surface.

PATCHING. Add shellac to small amounts of sawdust until the mixture is plastic and easy to spread. Where tongued-and-grooved and shiplap joints are concerned, use a small putty knife to force the patching mixture into the cracks until, as shown in the *E* part of the illustration, the crack is full. Pull the putty knife along the cracks to make the surface of the patching material flush with the shoulders of the boards. Allow to dry for at least two hours. If the surface of the floor has a natural finish, the patches may be lightly sandpapered using No. 00 sandpaper. When all patching is complete, the floor can be varnished and waxed or just waxed.

The *D* part of Figure 4 indicates a crack between square-edged boards and a butt joint. The patching process is the same as previously explained, except that very small wads of paper, such as facial tissue, should be shoved into the cracks so as to fill them partially, as indicated in the *F* part of the illustration, prior to the time the patching material is applied. The wads of paper are especially useful if such flooring does not have a subflooring under it.

REPAIRING LARGE CRACKS
IN WOOD FLOORS

As previously explained, unfortunate and large cracks between floor boards are apt to be unstable. In other words, they are likely to become larger or to open and close with the seasons. Any attempts to repair them constitute rank gambles because the patching materials are apt to be squeezed out at a later time. However, when such gambles are recognized, the following procedures may be tried:

Preparation. Same as in connection with small cracks.

Patching Materials. A mixture of sawdust and shellac, used alone, is not apt to stay in large cracks long enough to merit the time and effort involved. Therefore, slivers of the same kind of wood as the floor boards should be made by means of a knife. Make such slivers so that they have tops, as shown in the G part of Figure 4, which are flat and level.

PATCHING. Where tongued-and-grooved or shiplap boards are concerned, force a little of the sawdust-and-shellac mixture down to the bottom of the cracks, as shown in the G part of the illustration. Then apply shellac to the slivers and shove them into the cracks, also as shown at G. Where butt joints are concerned, use the wads of paper as previously explained, prior to the patching procedures. Pull a putty knife along the cracks to make sure that the tops of the slivers are flush with the shoulders of the boards and to remove excess shellac and sawdust. A cloth soaked with alcohol can be used to clean off any hardened shellac or sawdust mixture. After two hours, the patches may be lightly sandpapered. If the patches are lighter colored than the floor surface, use a little stain to color them as may be necessary.

CORRECTING FLOOR SQUEAKS

When too few plain-shanked nails are used in laying floors, any one of the natural and unfortunate conditions previously mentioned could exert enough force to pull the boards loose. In fact, ordinary expansion and contraction is apt to, and often does, loosen the nails. Once the nails are the least bit loose, ordinary walking on the floor will further loosen them. Soon thereafter, squeaking is bound to occur.

The W part of Figure 5 indicates how most hardwood floors are constructed. The subflooring should be nailed in a diagonal position to the joists. The finish floor boards should be nailed to the subfloor so that they are 90 degrees to the joists. To correct squeaking, the procedure is as follows:

Preparation. Walk around a floor until all areas where squeaking occurs are located. Mark the areas by means of chalk lines. Next, locate the joist positions. This can be done by tapping the floor with a hammer and noting where the tapping sounds solid. When one joist position has been located, we know that all others are probably at 16-inch intervals.

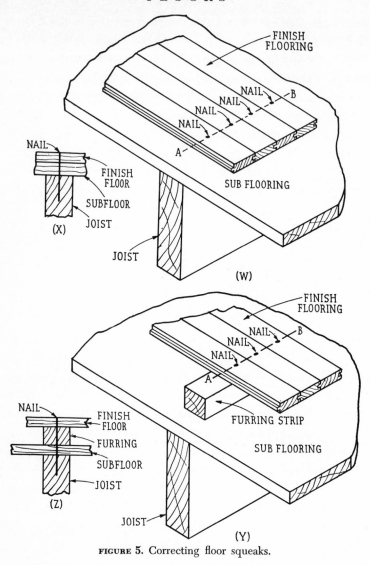

FIGURE 5. Correcting floor squeaks.

Materials. Only nails and some plastic wood are required. The nails should be of the screw type with finishing nailheads. Their length should be at least 2½ inches so that they can go through the finish and subflooring and be firmly embedded in the joists, as shown in the *X* part of the illustration. The plastic wood can be stained to match the floor surface.

NAILING. The dashed line *AB*, in the *W* part of the illustration, indicates a position directly over the joist. Drive one nail through each of the boards in the squeaking area at each joist location. If the nails tend to bend as they are driven, bore a small hole into the boards prior to nailing. The hole should have a smaller diameter than the nails. Use a nail set to drive the heads of the nails slightly below the surface of the boards. Fill the dents above the nailheads with the plastic wood, making sure that the plastic wood is flush with the floor surface.

It is wise to nail the boards, in any squeak area, to at least two joists.

The *Y* part of Figure 5 shows another and less common way in which hardwood floors are constructed. The subflooring should be nailed to the joists. Above each joist furring strips are nailed to the subfloor. The finish floor should be nailed to the furring strips and be at 90 degrees to the joists.

The squeak-correcting procedure is the same as previously explained, except that longer nails must be used. As shown in the *Z* part of the illustration, the nails should go through the finish floor boards, the furring, the subflooring, and well into the joists. It is wise to assume that the furring is at least 1½ inches thick. Therefore, the nails should be at least 3½ inches long.

REPLACING DAMAGED FLOOR BOARDS

If one or more finish floor boards have been damaged, or are unsightly in appearance, new boards can be inserted into the floor as per the following procedures:

Preparation. Let us suppose that we are looking down at a small area of a floor such as shown in the *W* part of Figure 6. Let us further suppose that the dashed-line rectangle, *ABCD,* indicates a damaged place in the floor. Boards *b, c,* and *d* are involved.

Parts of the three boards involved have to be removed so that new parts can be inserted.

First, draw a line on the floor, such as *f* in the *X* part of the illustration, which coincides with the joints marked *m* and *n* in the *W* part of the illustration. In like manner, draw a line on the floor, such as shown at *g*, which coincides with the joint marked *p*. The boards within the area

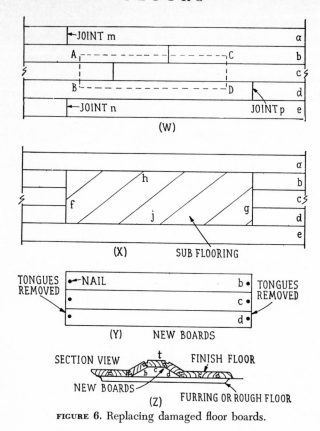

FIGURE 6. Replacing damaged floor boards.

bounded by lines *f*, *h*, *g*, and *j*, as shown in the *X* part of the illustration, must be removed.

Removing Boards. Use a sharp chisel to cut boards *b*, *c*, and *d* along lines *f* and *g*. Make the cuts at least ¼ inch deep. Then use the chisel to splinter board *c* enough to remove it. Boards *b* and *d* can be removed in much the same manner, being careful not to splinter the boards beyond lines *f* and *g*. When the three boards have been removed, the subflooring will be visible as indicated in the *X* part of the illustration.

Placing New Boards. Cut three new boards, as shown in the *Y* part of the illustration, to the exact length of line *h* in the *X* part of the illustration, so as to make a snug fit. Remove the tongues from the *ends* of the new boards.

Put the new boards in place, as indicated in the Z part of the illustration, so that the side tongues partly engage the grooves. Then stand on the middle board, t, to press the new boards into position.

Nail the ends of the boards as indicated by the dots in the Y part of the illustration. The nails should be 1½ inches long. If the new boards seem loose, add one or more nails along their lengths, as may be required.

Drive the nails slightly below the surface of the boards and fill dents with plastic wood. Stain the new boards to match the floor and finish with varnish or shellac.

If we should find that a floor has furring strips, as shown in the Y part of Figure 5, the cutting lines f and g, as shown in the X part of Figure 6, must be drawn directly over the center lines of the furring. It may be necessary to draw and cut several such lines in order to locate the furring strips. Otherwise, the procedures for inserting new boards are the same as previously explained.

SOFT TILE OVER OLD WOOD FLOOR

The following project is typical of any and all cases where plastic (no adhesive) tile is to be applied directly to old wood floors. The project is presented in terms of a typical problem and its solution:

PROBLEM 1. KITCHEN FLOOR. For the purpose of this problem, we can assume that Plates I through VI, which are at the back of this book, show the plans for an *old* house. We can further assume that the kitchen floor contains a great many cracks and is undesirable in terms of other remodeling plans. The problem is to apply a plastic tile that needs no adhesive.

SOLUTION. First, it can be assumed that the plastic tile is 9½ inches square. Such tile, in any color, will make a beautiful floor and one which will be easy to keep clean.

PLANNING. The first step consists of checking the old floor to make sure that all boards are tightly nailed. If additional nailing is required, use screw-type nails which are 2½ inches long and drive their heads slightly below the surface. It is best if the nails can be driven into joists. If the boards are dished, the edges should be scraped or sanded down until they are flush with other parts of the boards. Apply a generous coat of shellac or other sealer to the wood floor. This will seal the surface so that no moisture can come through the boards.

LAYOUT. The *A* part of Figure 7 shows a scaled sketch of the kitchen indicated in Plate I. In this sketch, we assumed that the first full piece

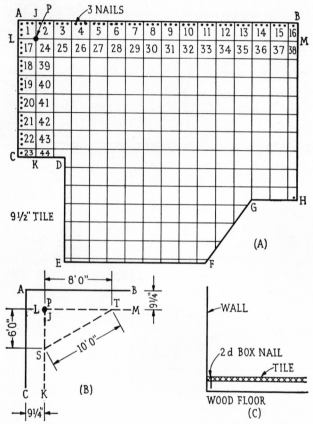

FIGURE 7. Layout for plastic tile applied over old wood floor.

of tile would be placed at corner *A*. Other such sketches, assuming that the first full piece of tile will be placed at *B, H, E,* and *C,* should also be made as a means of obtaining the best appearance, especially in terms of partial pieces of tile along the walls. Here, we can assume that it is best to place a full piece of tile at corner *A*. The squares represent pieces of tile.

The following layout work should be done on the kitchen floor:

Measure 9½ inches from wall *AB* and draw (or snap a chalk line) line *LM*. Then draw line *JK* so that it is 9½ inches from wall *AC*. Lines *LM* and *JK* must form an angle of 90 degrees at *P*. To test the angle, use the method shown in the *B* part of the illustration. Starting at point *P*, where the lines *LM* and *JK* cross, measure 6 feet to *S* and 8 feet to *T*. If lines *LM* and *JK* meet at 90 degrees, the line *ST* will be exactly 10 feet long. If any error exists, move lines *LM* and *JK* slightly until line *ST* is exactly 10 feet long.

TILE APPLICATION. Unpack the tile and allow several hours of time during which they will accommodate themselves to room-temperature and humidity conditions. Tile should not be laid when room temperatures are less than 70°F.

Start with tile 1, as indicated in the *A* part of Figure 7. Lay it so that its corner is exactly over point *P*. Use three 2d box nails along both the *AJ* and *AL* edges. Place the nails close to the wall, as shown in the *C* part of the illustration. Do not drive the nailheads into the tile as that would distort it.

Lay tile 2 along line *LM* and tightly against tile 1. Use three nails as indicated in the *A* part of the illustration. Next, lay tile 3 through 15 and use three nails in each. Tile 16 will have to be cut to fit and then securely nailed.

Next, lay tile 17 through 22 along line *JK* and nail them as indicated. Tile 23 will have to be cut to fit.

Only tile next to walls should be nailed.

Next, lay tile 24 through 37. Before laying and nailing tile 38, place a little block of wood at the edge of tile 37 and tap it gently to tighten the tile in that row. Make sure all joints coincide with joints in the first row laid.

Lay all other rows alternately, trimming the tile next to walls and making sure that all joint lines coincide.

If any of the tile buckle after a few days, place a heavy weight on them and the buckle will disappear. Place quarter round along the walls to hide the nails. Use metal toe strips at the door where the tile stops.

Wax and clean as recommended by the manufacturer of the tile used.

SOFT RECREATION-ROOM FLOOR

The following project is typical of all cases where insulation, hardboard, and asphalt tile are to be applied over existing concrete floors. The project is presented in terms of a typical problem and its solution.

PROBLEM 2. RECREATION-ROOM FLOOR. For the purpose of this problem, we can assume that part of the basement space indicated in Plate II and set forth in Problem 3 in Chapter 4, is to be remodeled to provide a recreation area. The problem is to install an asphalt-tile floor which will be soft and warm. The tile are 12 inches square.

SOLUTION. It can be assumed that the concrete floor is never wet but that it is damp and cold.

PLANNING. The design shown in Figure 8 will assure ample insulation effectively to reduce dampness and chill. It will create a soft foundation and provide a firm base for the tile. Both the insulation and hardboard should be laid, using hot asphalt emulsion as an adhesive. The tile should be cemented to the hardboard using the kind of adhesive recommended by the manufacturer of the tile.

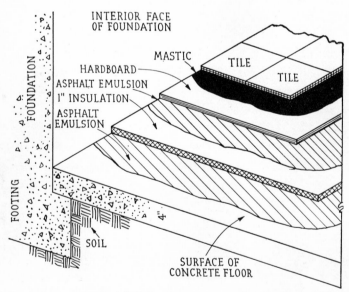

FIGURE 8. Soft recreation-room floor.

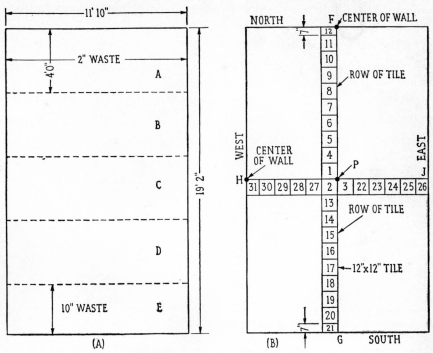

FIGURE 9. Layout of insulation and tile.

LAYOUT. Rigid insulation may be purchased in sheets which are 4 by 8, 4 by 10, or 4 by 12 feet in width and length and $^{25}\!/_{32}$ inch thick. In this case, a size should be used which can be applied easily and with as little waste as possible. As shown in the *A* part of Figure 9 and in Plate II, the recreation room is 11' 10" wide and 19' 2" long. We can use 4- by 12-foot sheets, as indicated at *A, B, C, D,* and *E,* in such a manner that there is a waste of only 2 inches at the ends of the sheets and 10 inches of waste along the side of sheet *E.*

The hardboard can be planned in the same manner.

In order to plan the position of the first piece of tile, we must make a scaled sketch of the recreation room, such as indicated in the *B* part of Figure 9, and then find the center point *P* by means of lines *HJ* and *FG.* As a trial, we can place the first piece of tile so that its southeast corner is at *P.* The first two rows of tile can then be drawn as shown in the sketch. From this layout it can be seen that only 1 inch will have to be cut from tiles 26 and 31 and that only 5 inches, which is less than half the tile width, will have to be cut from tiles 12 and 21.

Other such layouts may be drawn, but the one shown in the *B* part of the illustration is satisfactory because none of the tile near the walls have to be cut more than half their widths.

By means of chalk, or a chalk line, draw or snap lines *FG* and *HJ* on the concrete floor. Then check the layout by placing uncemented tile on the floor in the same positions as shown in the sketch.

APPLICATION OF TILE. Use a notched trowel (available where the mastic recommended by the manufacturer is sold) to apply a light coat of mastic to the floor area to be covered by the first two rows of tile.

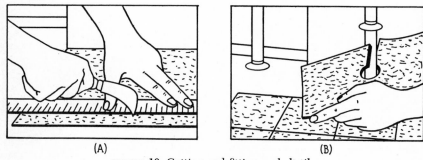

(A)   (B)

FIGURE 10. Cutting and fitting asphalt tile.

Allow the mastic to dry before placing tile on it. To test for drying, press thumb against mastic. If the mastic does not stick, it is ready for tile.

Before placing tile, unpack and stack them so that they are all right side up. The top surface of the tile is smoothest. Tile should always be laid with the marbelized grain of one piece alternating in direction at right angles with the next piece.

Lay two crossrows of tile, as shown in the *B* part of Figure 9, first. Use lines *FG* and *HJ* as guides. Carefully set each piece in position. Do not slide them into place as that may force the mastic up between the pieces. After two rows have been laid, cover one of the remaining quarters of the floor with mastic. When the mastic is dry, place tile in this section, working from center of room to border. Cover one-fourth of the floor at a time until entire floor is laid. Never use a cleaning fluid on asphalt tile. A dull-edged knife or No. 00 steel wool can be used to remove any excess mastic.

When trimming pieces of tile to fit against a wall or around a post where a tight fit is desired, warm the tile enough to make it pliable but not so hot that it cannot be handled with bare hands. The *A* and *B* parts of Figure 10 show how to cut and fit tile.

PARQUET OR BLOCKS OVER CONCRETE

The following project is typical of any and all cases where parquet or block are to be applied over existing sound and dry concrete floors. The project is presented in terms of a typical problem and its solution.

PROBLEM 3. RECREATION-ROOM FLOOR. For the purpose of this problem, we may assume that part of the basement space indicated in Plate II, as explained in the previous problem, is to be converted to a recreation area. The problem is to apply blocks directly to the concrete floor.

SOLUTION. We can assume that the existing concrete floor is sound and that it is always dry.

PLANNING. Because the room is of good size, we can plan to use 12- by 12-inch blocks of the type shown in Figure 2, and the squared pattern illustrated by Figure 5 of Chapter 4.

LAYOUT. As previously explained in connection with layout procedures, the first step consists of making a scaled sketch which can be used to plot the center point of the room and the positions of the first two rows of blocks. Figure 11 shows such a sketch. Lines *AB* and *CD* were drawn from the mid-points of walls *EH* and *FG* and *EF* and *HG* to find the center point *P* of the room. Blocks 1, 2, 3, and 4 were grouped around the center point, and the first and second rows of blocks were indicated. This constitutes a satisfactory layout because blocks 9 and 14 will require little cutting and blocks 26 and 34 will be more than half their original size after cutting.

By the use of chalk or a chalk line, the *AB* and *CD* lines should be drawn or snapped on the floor. Then the layout should be tested by placing uncemented blocks in the positions of the first two rows shown in the sketch.

APPLICATION OF BLOCKS. Using a notched trowel, spread thin coats of the adhesive recommended by the manufacturer on the floor areas to be covered by the first two rows of block. If lines *AB* and *CD* cannot be seen through the adhesive, they should be redrawn or snapped on it. Lay blocks 1, 2, 3, and 4 first. Press them into position, making sure that the tongues engage the grooves enough to make the joints between blocks tight and flush. Next, lay blocks 18 through 25, using line *AP* as a guide. Tap the edge of each block just enough to force its tongue into the groove of the previous block. Block 26 must be cut so as to provide a ½-inch

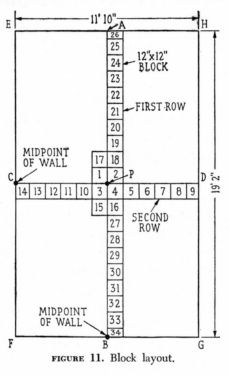

FIGURE 11. Block layout.

expansion space between its edge and the wall. Blocks 16 through 34 should next be laid using line *PB* as a guide. Biock 34 must also be cut so as to provide a ½-inch expansion space. Blocks 10 through 14 and 5 through 9 should be laid along line *CD* to complete the first two rows. Blocks 9 and 14 should also be cut to provide ½-inch expansion spaces. Cover one-fourth of the remaining floor at a time until the whole floor is complete, remembering to provide ½-inch expansion spaces between all blocks next to the walls. The expansion spaces can be covered by a base or other molding.

SANDING. After the blocks have been laid for several days, they must be sanded by means of a heavy electric sanding machine. The finest grit sandpaper obtainable should be used for the last sanding because the smoother the surface, the more beautiful the final finish will be.

PLANK FLOOR OVER WOOD SUBFLOOR

The following project is typical of any and all cases where plank flooring is to be laid on existing subflooring such as in attic spaces. The project is presented in terms of a typical problem and its solution.

PROBLEM 4. ATTIC FLOOR. It can be assumed that an attic space in an old house is being remodeled in order to provide one or more new bedrooms. The problem is to lay plank flooring on the existing subfloor.

SOLUTION. We can assume that the type of flooring shown in Figure 3 is to be used and that both nails and screws must be employed for fastening the plank to the subfloor.

PLANNING. The first step consists of checking the existing subfloor to make sure that all the boards are tightly nailed. If additional nailing is required, use screw-type nails at least 2½ inches long. Their heads should be driven slightly below the surface of the boards. If any of the boards are dished, the edges should be scraped, planed, or sanded flush with other parts of the boards.

If possible, plank flooring should be laid at 90 degrees to the floor joists and in the direction of the longest dimensions of a room but never parallel to the subflooring. If two or more rooms are involved, the planks should, if possible, be laid in the same direction in all of them and extend from one to the other to form a continuous surface. A pattern such as indicated in Figure 3 should be used and end joints should be staggered as shown in the A part of Figure 12. A good grade of heavy waterproof building paper should be laid over the subflooring from wall to wall with joints overlapped at least 6 inches. At the time of laying the planks, the interior temperature must be at least 70°F. This is highly important as a means of preventing shrinkage cracks.

LAYOUT. When laying tongued-and-grooved plank flooring, the first board should be placed at the junction of the side wall and the floor and should be parallel to the side wall with the grooved edge next to the wall. An expansion space of at least ½ inch must be provided between the first board and the wall. However, such a space should not be wider than can be covered by a baseboard or quarter round. As shown in the B part of Figure 12, the baseboard or quarter round should be so installed

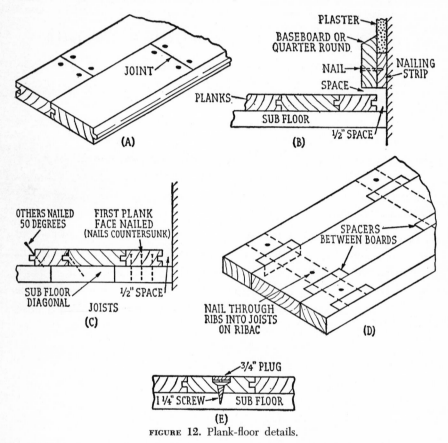

FIGURE 12. Plank-floor details.

that lower edges are slightly above the finished floor level. Fastening should be done as indicated. Never nail baseboards or quarter rounds to the planks.

APPLICATION OF PLANKS. The first board, next to the wall, should be face-nailed as shown in the C part of the illustration. Then the tongue edge should be blind-nailed with the nails driven at an angle of about 50 degrees. When blind-nailing, the head of each nail should be countersunk, using a nail set. Nails should be 8d, of the screw type, and spaced 8 inches apart.

In order to allow for any possible movement or expansion of the planks, a small space (approximately $\frac{1}{32}$ inch) should be left between each board. For this purpose spacer strips, as shown in the D part of the illustration, should be inserted every 8 inches so that the nailing does not draw the planks up too tightly. Do not remove spacers until 6 runs of plank have been laid, then continue in this manner across the room, moving forward the rear row of spacers. Plank flooring is grooved on both ends, and splines are furnished which are to be inserted at the time of installation.

As shown in the A and E parts of the illustration, countersunk screws should be used at each end of every board. Screws can also be used at intervals along the length of boards if they seem necessary as a means of assuring tight fastening. An ordinary brace and bit may be used for drilling the holes for the screws and the plugs. To save time, a counterbore performing all operations at one time is recommended. The most popular size of plug is $\frac{3}{4}$ inch. A $1\frac{1}{4}$-inch flathead screw is recommended. Oak or walnut plugs may be glued into the holes. Basically, the more nails and screws used, the more satisfactory the results.

SANDING. The finest grit sandpaper obtainable should be used for the last cut. The smoother the floor, the better the finish and final appearance.

TILE OR PLANKS OVER PLYWOOD

The following project is typical of any and all cases where tile or planks are to be applied to plywood.

PROBLEM 5. It can be assumed that an attic space in any house is being remodeled in order to make one or more new bedrooms. It can also be assumed that no subflooring exists in the attic space. The problem is to apply plywood that can be used as a base for tile or planks.

SOLUTION. It can also be assumed that $\frac{3}{4}$-inch plywood is to be fastened directly to the floor joists and that a blanket type of insulation is to be placed between the joists as a means of reducing sound transmission between the new bedrooms and the rooms below them.

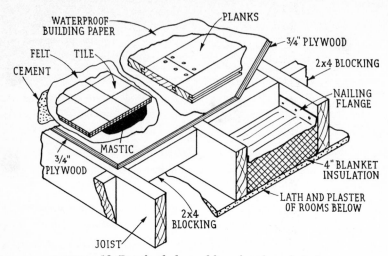

FIGURE 13. Details of plywood base for tile and planks.

FIGURE 14. Application of insulation between attic-floor joists.

APPLICATION OF INSULATION. Blanket-type insulation having a thickness of about 4 inches may be installed between the joists as shown in Figures 13 and 14. Both illustrations show the insulation packed just above the lath and plaster of the rooms below. In Figure 14, the mechanic is applying short pieces of the insulation which will serve as a draft stop between the knee-wall plate and the top of the insulation between the joists.

APPLICATION OF PLYWOOD. As indicated in Figure 13, the plywood can be nailed directly to the top edges of the joists. However, it should be noted that wherever plywood joints occur, 2 by 4 blocking must be installed. Use 2½-inch screw-type nails, spaced 8 inches apart, to nail the plywood to all joists and blocking. Countersink the nailheads just below the surface of the plywood. (Also see plywood section in Chapter 1.)

APPLICATION OF TILE. Same as explained in the solution to Problem 1.

APPLICATION OF PLANKS. Same as explained in the solution to Problem 4.

TILE ON PLYWOOD OVER WORN-OUT
WOOD FLOORS

The following project is typical of any and all cases where plywood and tile are to be applied over an old single floor.

PROBLEM 6. ANY FLOOR. For the purpose of this problem, we may assume that an old single floor (finish floor without a subfloor) is badly worn and unsightly and that we want to use plywood, over it, as a base for a new tile surface. The problem is to apply the plywood. NOTE: A project of this kind should not be contemplated unless all of the rooms, on a first or second floor of a house, are to be given the same treatment.

SOLUTION. It can also be assumed that ⅝-inch plywood is sufficiently strong for the purpose of this project.

APPLICATION OF PLYWOOD. First, the existing floor should be renailed. This is a precaution against squeaking and other difficulties. Use 2½-inch screw-type nails and drive two of them in every board at all joist locations. Countersink the heads. If the boards are dished, after the renailing, they should be planed or sanded until all edges are flush.

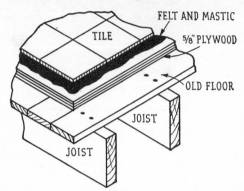

FIGURE 15. Details of plywood and tile over old single flooring.

As indicated in Figure 15, the plywood can be applied directly to the old flooring. Use 2-inch screw-type nails spaced 8 inches apart at all joist locations and along all edges of the plywood. Countersink the nail-heads.

APPLICATION OF TILE. Same as explained in the solution to Problem 1.

HARDWOOD FLOORING ON CONCRETE

The following project is typical of any and all cases where hardwood flooring is to be applied over an existing concrete slab.

PROBLEM 7. BASEMENT-RECREATION-ROOM FLOOR. For the purpose of this problem, we can assume that a basement space is being remodeled to serve as a recreation area. The problem is to apply new hardwood flooring over the existing concrete slab.

SOLUTION. We can also assume that the concrete floor is occasionally damp but never actually wet or cold.

PLANNING. It is best to plan the hardwood flooring so that the boards run in the direction of the longest dimension of the room.

There is definite opportunity for wise economy in using short lengths of either oak or maple flooring. Pieces of short lengths provide the same strength, durability, and smoothness as a floor laid with standard long lengths. For recreation-room requirements, the short lengths are ideal, even if they do require a little more laying time.

There is also definite opportunity for economy in using what is classed as Second Grade flooring. Tests have shown that second-grade flooring is equal in every performance and endurance qualities to first-grade flooring. At times, second-grade lumber is preferred over the first grade because of its pleasingly varied colorations and interesting grain patterns which tend to give a floor more pronounced character. Appearance is by no means sacrificed. Manufacturers give careful attention to selecting only attractive boards.

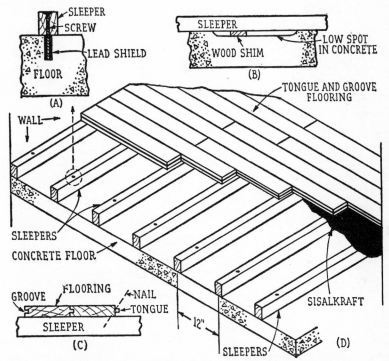

FIGURE 16. Details of hardwood floor over an old concrete floor.

LAYOUT. Wood sleepers which have dimensions of at least 2 by 2 inches, must be fastened to the concrete at 12-inch intervals, somewhat as shown in the *D* part of Figure 16. The new floor boards must be placed so that they are at 90-degree angles to the sleepers.

APPLICATION OF SLEEPERS. As explained in Chapter 2 and as shown in the *A* part of the illustration, the sleepers can be fastened, as necessary to make them secure, by means of lead shields and screws; or a gun-type fastener can be used to "shoot" nails through the sleepers and into the concrete. Sometimes concrete nails work to advantage. The top surfaces of all sleepers must be at exactly the same level. Where necessary, and as indicated in the *B* part of the illustration, shims may be used to force sleepers up to level.

Before the sleepers have been placed, some type of mastic or asphalt should be applied to the concrete floor. This coating will act as insulation and keep dampness away from the new surface of the floor.

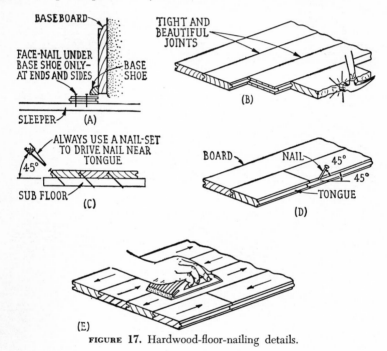

FIGURE 17. Hardwood-floor-nailing details.

APPLICATION OF FLOORING. In order to provide additional insulation, so far as dampness is concerned, Sisalkraft should be spread on the tops of the sleepers and well lapped.

Place and nail the first floor board as explained in the solution to Problem 4 and as shown in the *A* part of Figure 17. Use two 2- or 2½-inch screw-type nails at each sleeper.

After the first board has been nailed, use a scrap piece of flooring, as shown in *B* part of illustration, to force grooves over tongues of successive boards for tight joints. The *C* and *D* parts of the illustration indicate how nails are to be driven. Use one nail at each sleeper location.

SANDING. Most hardwood flooring comes from the mill smoothly surfaced, but in laying any floor, slight inequalities, scratches, and scars are bound to occur. Scraping or sanding removes these. A really smooth sanding is the most important part of a good floor-finishing job. Scrape and sand with the grain lengthwise (see *E* part of Figure 17), using either a cushioned hand-sanding block or a power sander, of the belt or oscillating type—never one of the disk type; No. 2 or 2½ sandpaper is suggested for leveling off high spots and joints, and No. 1 for the second cut. The final step—most important of all—is the finish-sanding with No. 0 or 00 paper (or both, if necessary). Do not be content with anything less than perfect sanding.

HOW TO KEEP HARDWOOD FLOORS BEAUTIFUL

The secret of keeping hardwood floors beautiful is proper care. After they have been newly finished and waxed, it is a simple matter to keep them bright and spotless by daily dusting with an untreated mop and by cleaning and waxing them periodically. Once a floor has been neglected to the point where the finish is worn in spots or dirt has become embedded, nothing short of refinishing will restore its original beauty.

The first rule for proper floor maintenance is: Never use soap and water to clean hardwood floors.

This is highly important because soap and water will injure both the finish and the wood of hardwood floors. Water will sometimes even cause the floor to buckle.

Water spilled on a wood floor should be wiped up and the floor dried immediately. If allowed to remain, it will produce an unsightly white spot which is almost impossible to remove without complete sanding and refinishing.

Several wax cleaning compounds are available which contain no water. They literally dry-clean floor surfaces through the action of solvents which remove the top layer of old wax in which dirt and grime have become embedded, then replace the old wax with a coating of new wax that polishes readily to a lustrous sheen.

SAFETY FEATURES IN CONNECTION WITH THE LAYING OF NEW HARDWOOD FLOORS

Do not:

Lay flooring immediately after its delivery. Store it for a few days in the house where it is to be laid.

Bring flooring into a damp house.

Lay flooring in a damp or cold house. The temperature in the house should be at least 70°F.

Stack bundles of flooring too close together. Do allow ample air circulation between bundles.

Close windows. This is important. Opening windows at tops aids in ventilation.

ASPHALT TILE OVER CONCRETE

The following project is typical of any and all cases where asphalt tile is to be applied over an existing concrete floor, such as in a basement.

PROBLEM 8. BASEMENT-RECREATION-ROOM FLOOR. For the purpose of this problem, we can assume that a basement space is being remodeled to serve as a recreation area. The problem is to apply asphalt tile over the existing concrete.

SOLUTION. PLANNING. Existing concrete floors must be clean and free from all coverings, adhesives, and other surface finishes. All oil, grease, and wax must be removed. Expansion joints, cracks, score marks, and depressions must be filled in to produce a smooth, even surface. The concrete must be thoroughly dry and free from moisture before the asphalt tile is laid. If the floor is unusually porous or dusty, it should be given a coat of hot asphalt before the tile adhesive is spread.

LAYOUT. Few rooms are perfect rectangles. As the field (area within the border) of an asphalt-tile floor must be laid within a perfect rectangle, it is necessary to establish center or guidelines which are at right angles to each other from which tile can be laid. When laying out a room, we should measure only from the principal walls, such as *AB* and *BC* shown in the *A* part of Figure 18. Offsets and other breaks, as shown at

DEF, should be disregarded. In all cases, we must start laying the tile at the center of a floor and work toward the walls, where the width of the border can be adjusted as desired.

To square the area to be covered, first find the center of one end of the floor. Locate the same point at the other-end wall. Snap a chalk line

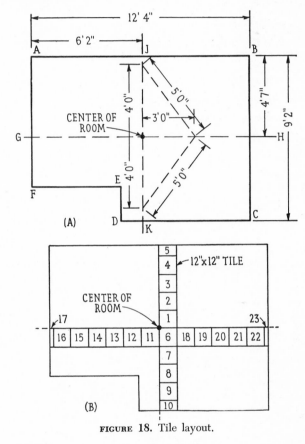

FIGURE 18. Tile layout.

between these points to mark the center line of the floor. Then measure to find the middle point of the room, as shown in the illustration, on this line. At this middle point, mark off a line across the room at right angles to the first line. This can be done by means of the 3-4-5 triangle method as shown in the illustration.

Measure 4′ 0″ toward each side wall from the center point. Then measure 3′ 0″ from the center point along the longer line. Measure exactly 5′ 0″ from the 3′ 0″ mark on the center line to the 4′ 0″ mark on the crossline. Snap a chalk line across the room between this point and one that is similarly located on the other side of the center line. This line will be at right angles to the first line.

APPLICATION OF TILE. Test the layout by placing tile as shown in the *B* part of the illustration. Another test may be made by placing the first tile so that it straddles the center point. The layout shown is best.

It is wise to use the adhesive recommended by the manufacturer of the tile. The adhesive should be applied to the concrete using a notched trowel having notches $\frac{1}{16}$ inch deep and spaced on $\frac{3}{16}$-inch centers.

Asphalt tile should be laid starting at the center of the floor, working toward the wall, as shown by tiles 1 to 4, 6 to 9, and 11 to 16. Any desired width of border may be obtained by trimming the tile next to the walls. Any asphalt cove base can be cemented to the walls.

CHAPTER SEVEN

Basements

Basements have gone through many years of interesting development.

Some 60 or more years ago, they were practically unknown. There was no need for them, owing to the fact that heating systems consisted of base burners and other stoves which were set up wherever heat was desired. However, small cellars were used for the storage of food. They were located under houses but could only be reached by means of outside entrances.

The advent of hand-fired gravity furnaces, along with hot-water heating systems, brought about the first great improvement in cellars. Such equipment functioned only when located below the floor level of the rooms to be heated. Thus it became necessary to deepen the cellars and otherwise enlarge them, to make room for the equipment and accompanying coalbins. Even in those days families needed more room; so it was only natural that some household activities, such as laundry work, were shifted from kitchens to what soon became known as basements. At best, however, the early basements were dusty and dirty, owing to the use of coal and the removal of ashes.

The arrival of modern heating plants, with automatic fueling, brought about another great improvement. Dust and dirt no longer had to be contended with and basements took on the appearance of the one shown in Figure 1. Such basements could have been remodeled and made into usable living spaces if the old washtubs could have been removed and if clothes could have been dried in ways other than by hanging them on lines.

FIGURE 1. Typical old basement.

FIGURE 2. Same basement after remodeling.

With the coming of automatic clothes washers and dryers, even small basements were suitable for remodeling. Figure 2 shows what was done with the basement illustrated in Figure 1. Such remodeled and attractive space can be used for any number of purposes all in keeping with modern living.

Thousands of homeowners realize the possibilities of their basements and are probably anxious to turn them into attractive and worthwhile living spaces. The purpose of this chapter is to explain important remodeling considerations, to show how many related projects can be accomplished and to illustrate the planning and actual construction work involved in typical remodeling work.

PURPOSE OF REMODELING

Before the actual planning for any basement remodeling begins, we should give a great deal of thought to the following fundamentals:

What is the purpose of the remodeling?
What are the requirements?
Financial considerations.
Will the remodeling be worthwhile?

Ordinarily, remodeling motivation stems from a desire to create additional space or spaces which can be used for one or more of the following typical purposes:

A recreation room	A workbench area
A party room	A darkroom
A new laundry	General storage facilities
Modern storage facilities for food	A workshop

A new bedroom (if 50 per cent of basement is above grade)

Whatever the purpose of remodeling is, it should be firmly established so that the basement can be studied accordingly. No planning can logically be done until or unless the purpose has definitely been set up as a goal. Without a definite purpose, planning would be haphazard and at the risk of disappointing final results.

The requirements of remodeling are closely allied to the purpose. For example, if a recreation area is the purpose, will it satisfy the requirements so far as children or other planned uses are concerned? This aspect also requires careful thought. All requirements of such a space should be written so that they can be studied.

Financial considerations are always important and should be studied. However, this aspect of the remodeling cannot be determined accurately until final plans have been made. In the meantime, we should set up a maximum allowable expenditure to use as a guide.

The question as to whether or not remodeling will be worthwhile should be given careful preliminary consideration. Some of the items to consider are listed in the following:

1. Will the remodeling make a house more desirable from the standpoint of living conditions?

2. Is the general structural condition of a house sound enough to merit the planned remodeling? Unless all other parts of a house are in good condition, the remodeling of any one area might not be a good investment.

3. Will the remodeling add to the value of the house from the standpoint of its possible sale?

4. How much will remodeling increase the real estate taxes?

5. Is the neighborhood such that property values are apt to increase or decrease?

6. Are the prospects for the neighborhood such that continued residence in it is assured?

7. Will the remodeling help to rent a house?

8. Can the cost of remodeling be handled without undue financial strain.

REMODELING PRECAUTION

Inexperienced mechanics and homeowners are apt to do a great deal of preliminary planning without taking into consideration several aspects of the probable cost. This is a common mistake that always leads to unexpected expense or probable disappointment. As a means of helping readers to avoid such a mistake, the following typical remodeling plan is explained.

The *A* part of Figure 3 shows an ordinary basement plan of a type common to many houses. The plan lacks convenience and is poorly

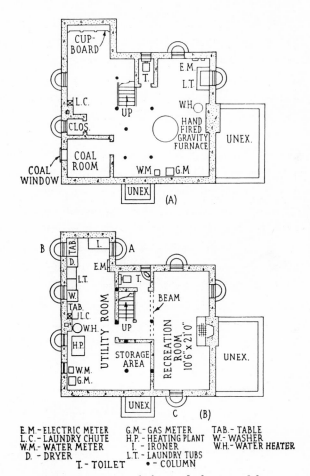

E.M.–ELECTRIC METER   G.M.–GAS METER   TAB.–TABLE
L.C.–LAUNDRY CHUTE   H.P.–HEATING PLANT   W.–WASHER
W.M.–WATER METER   I.–IRONER   W.H.–WATER HEATER
D.–DRYER   L.T.–LAUNDRY TUBS
T.–TOILET   •–COLUMN

FIGURE 3. Basement before and after remodeling.

designed. For example, the laundry chute is located far away from the laundry tubs, and the hand-fired gravity furnace is too far from the coal-bin, yet, the design is typical of many basements.

The *B* part of the illustration shows the proposed remodeling plan. At first glance, and without careful thought, this plan seems well designed.

The heating plant, laundry tubs, and other utility equipment are all located in one section of the basement, and the stairway leads directly into the recreation area. However, there are several aspects of the plan which would cost a great deal to accomplish.

Fireplace. The fireplace constitutes a most desirable feature. But, not many existing chimneys, such as shown in the *A* part of the illustration, contain the extra flue necessary for a fireplace. Thus, a great deal of expense would be involved in rebuilding the chimney so as to provide the needed flue. Even if the extra flue is available, the cost of building a fireplace at the base of the chimney is apt to be excessive.

New Heating Plant. A new forced-air heating plant would certainly give added comfort and, unlike the old gravity furnace, could be placed as shown, so as to be out of the way. However, two items of extra expense should be understood. First, the new heating plant would cost several hundred dollars. Second, an entirely new duct system would probably be necessary. That would cost considerably more money. Additional expense would also be involved in patching the floors where the old warm- and cold-air inlets and outlets were located.

New Windows. The windows shown at *A, B,* and *C* would be expensive, especially because of the cost of cutting the solid concrete foundations.

Piping. Moving the gas and water meters would mean expensive pipe relocations.

Water Heater. Moving the water heater would also mean expensive pipe relocations.

Water Closet. Moving the position of this fixture only a few feet would mean relocating both sewer and vent lines.

Washer. New hot- and cold-water pipes, vent and sewer pipes would have to be installed for the new washer. The same is true for the new location of the laundry tubs. In fact, relocating or adding new pipes in connection with any of the plumbing work is very expensive.

Lavatory. The new lavatory would require hot- and cold-water pipes, a vent, and connections to the sewer.

Some of the new ducts, in connection with the new heating plant, would have to be located below the level of the ceiling joists and would be difficult to hide in the recreation area. The same is true for the relocated gas and water pipes.

All of the foregoing items constitute extra expense which could easily amount to a much greater total than a homeowner could or would care to assume in connection with a remodeling project. There are probably few cases where such expense could be justified when only a recreation area results. Most remodeling, so far as basements are concerned, should be planned so that only new walls, ceiling, and floor surfaces, and new partitions are required.

PRELIMINARY CONSIDERATIONS

After the purpose of a basement remodeling project has been definitely established, the next step consists of studying the actual conditions to determine what must be done to make the remodeling possible. Here, we shall discuss some of the most commonly encountered items. In subsequent pages, we shall see how the required work is accomplished.

Ceiling Height. Fortunately, most basements were built to allow at least a distance of 7' 0" between floors and ceilings. This distance constituted the lowest ceiling height recommended. Anything lower gives occupants of rooms a cramped feeling and lessens the enjoyment of the new areas. Higher ceilings do not offer much of a problem, except that more wall-surface materials are required. If ceiling heights are more than 9' 0", they can be lowered, as explained in Chapter 4.

When ceiling heights are less than 7' 0", some excavation can be done. Several methods are explained in subsequent pages.

Columns. Basement columns or posts are for the purpose of supporting walls and floors above them. In most cases, they are located exactly where required. They should not be moved or changed in any way. As shown in Figure 3, remodeling should be planned around them or so that they will be within new partitions.

Bearing Partitions. Sometimes existing basement partitions support floor joists. In such cases, they should not be removed or altered in any way until temporary supports are created. In subsequent pages, such a condition is explained.

Floors. If an old basement does not contain a concrete floor, the re-modeling work must include such an allied project.

See Chapter 6 in regard to floor treatment.

Windows. As previously mentioned, the installation of windows in existing concrete foundations is apt to create considerable expense. Power tools are required. In concrete-block walls, the procedure is much easier because blocks can be removed by the process of breaking the thin joints between them.

Basement Water. A *wet* basement is defined as one where water actually flows in through the foundations. A *damp* basement is defined as one where the foundations become damp after hard rains.

WET CONDITIONS. Sometimes basements are built on what appears to be dry ground, but at a later date it is discovered that a static head of water, as shown at *Y* in Figure 4, is present for long periods of time each year. This condition is frequently encountered in basements built on low ground near rivers or other bodies of water. In such cases, the water actually builds up a pressure against foundations and seeps through them. Although masonry foundations are strong and durable, they are some-what porous and will absorb moisture under pressure. This is especially true as regards concrete block. If the joints between block are carelessly made, the water *runs* through the cracks.

DAMP CONDITIONS. Concrete-block foundations are sometimes subjected to dampness immediately after hard rains. Any one or more of three causes could be at fault. First, downspouts from roofs may dispose of water near the foundations so that the water can soak into the soil, as indicated by the arrows at X in Figure 4, and contact the foundations. Second, the backfill against the foundations may contain old cans, bits of wood, plaster, brick, and other odds and ends of rubbish. If the surrounding soil is hard clay or not easily permeable, the rubbish creates a reservoir of water against foundations and the water will gradually seep through them. Third, the soil may be inherently wet enough to keep water against the foundations.

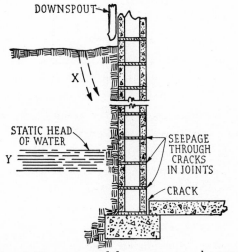

FIGURE 4. How water and dampness enter a basement.

Ways and means of avoiding wet and damp basement conditions are explained in subsequent pages.

Stairs. Basement stairs are frequently rough in appearance. However, they constitute part of remodeling work and should be improved as explained in subsequent pages.

Wall Surfaces. If foundations are always dry, or if they can be moistureproofed, there are especially made paints which can be used, all as explained in subsequent pages.

See Chapter 5 for new wall surfaces.

Pipes. It is rare, indeed, that ducts or pipes can be moved. Thus, they must be covered as indicated in Figure 2.

Sweating Pipes. During warm weather, one or more of the cold-water pipes in a basement may sweat and drip water. This can be avoided by applying special pipe insulation to them. Such insulation is available at all lumberyards.

Furnace Location. Unless an entirely new heating system is contemplated, remodeling projects should be planned to avoid any changes in furnace locations, pipes, or ducts.

Basement Temperatures. In general, basement temperatures, without artificial heating or cooling, tend to be cooler in summer and warmer in winter than other parts of a house. For example, on a hot summer day the temperature in a first-floor room may be about 86°F, whereas the basement temperature is apt to be about 68 or 72°F. On the other hand, the winter temperature of an unheated first-floor room may be about freezing, whereas the basement temperature may be as high as 40 or 45°F.

From the foregoing it can be seen that basement recreation areas are apt to be quite comfortable during the hottest summer weather. It can also be seen that keeping a recreation area warm during the winter can be accomplished without too much trouble. However, thick masonry walls are apt to radiate a cold sensation during the winter months. How to remedy such a situation is explained in subsequent pages.

Sagging Floors. In some of the older houses the floor joists over the basement areas may have deflected to the extent that the floors they support sag near their mid-points. Such conditions, as explained later in this chapter, should be corrected before basement remodeling is started.

Games. If recreation areas are to include standard pool or billiard tables, the dimensions shown in Figure 5 must be considered. The cues are 57 inches long. Therefore, the tables must be at least 5′ 0″ from the walls, chairs, or other obstructions.

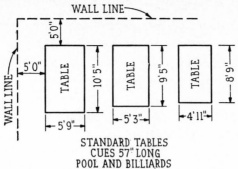

FIGURE 5. Clearance for pool and billiard tables.

Ceilings. Where ordinary wood joists are used in the ceiling above a basement space, any of the surface materials explained in Chapter 4 can be used.

Hot-water Tank. An automatic hot-water tank, containing its own heating mechanism, can be moved to any convenient location at only the cost of additional lengths of pipe. However, a hot-water tank hooked up to a furnace should not be moved away from the furnace.

Electrical Outlets. Lights, switches, and convenience outlets can be moved or added with ease by the use of BX or Romex wire. Local building codes should be studied to ascertain electrical requirements.

RELATED PROJECTS

The following projects are typical examples of commonly encountered preparatory or related work which must be done in connection with most basement remodeling.

Ceiling Height. In many old houses, especially those dating back to the cellar era, basement ceiling heights are apt to be less than 7 feet. Figure 6 shows several suggested ways of lowering floors so that additional ceiling height can be created.

PART *W* OF FIGURE 6. Here, we can assume that the ceiling height, *A*, is only 6′ 6″. We shall also assume that the existing floor and footing are

4 and 8 inches thick, respectively. Four more inches of ceiling height may be obtained by placing a new concrete floor, as shown at *F,* so that its surface is flush with the top of the footing. Or, a total of 12 additional inches can be obtained by placing a new floor, as shown at *H,* so that its surface is even with the bottom of the footing. In this case, the corner of the footing could be furred and trimmed with wood to create an attractive base around the space. When new concrete floors are laid on damp soil, a waterproof portland cement should be used as part of the concrete mix.

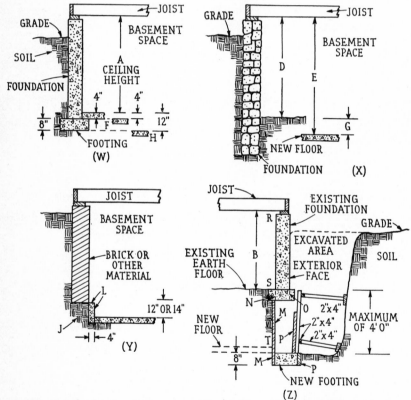

FIGURE 6. Details showing how more ceiling height can be provided in basements.

PART *X* OF FIGURE 6. Some old houses, located in the central regions of the country, have rubblestone foundations, with or without footings, which generally extend to depths far below the earth floor levels. Let us suppose that the existing ceiling height, *D,* is only 6′ 0″. The depth of the foundation can be checked by means of a small excavation in the basement. Depending upon the depth of the foundation, soil can be excavated to a depth G, so as to provide a suitable ceiling height, E.

PART Y OF FIGURE 6. Some old houses, especially in the Eastern regions of the country, have brick foundations without footings. If the soil under the foundation shown at J is a firm clay, the floor can be lowered 12 or 14 inches. A 4-inch retaining wall, as shown at L, should also be placed. The exposed surfaces of the retaining wall can be furred and trimmed with wood to create an attractive base around the space.

PART Z OF FIGURE 6. In some cases, ceiling heights, such as shown at B, are no more than 4 or 5 feet. This poses a much more complicated situation, but there is a way of providing suitable ceiling heights. The necessary work can be done so that a depth of only a few feet of the existing foundation is affected at any one time.

First, excavate down to the level where the new footing is to be placed. Also, excavate under the existing footing to the same depth. Cut off part of the old footing, as shown at O, by means of a cold chisel. Erect form boards, as shown at M and P, and brace them as indicated. The space between M and P is then ready for concrete.

The concrete should consist of 1 part portland cement, 2 parts clean sand, and 4 parts of clean gravel or crushed rock. Use enough water to make the mix free-flowing. Pour the concrete through the opening at O and spade it carefully as a means of making sure that it fills the space, especially under the old footing. Allow the new concrete to cure and harden at least a week before removing the exterior forms.

After the exterior forms have been removed, backfill the soil against the foundation. Be sure to compact the soil as the backfilling is in progress. Such packing will help to avoid dampness on the basement face of the foundation.

When the backfilling has been completed, the interior excavation work can be carried on and the N part of the old footing cut off by means of a cold chisel.

Place the new concrete floor, using a mix composed of 1 part portland cement, 3 parts of sand, and 5 parts of gravel or crushed rock. Use enough water to make the mix plastic but not running-wet.

The basement side or surface of the new foundation, especially the portion between S and T, is likely to be somewhat rough so far as appearance is concerned. However, the whole surface between R and T can be furred and a surface material applied as explained in Chapter 5.

Bearing Partitions. The X part of Figure 7 shows a section view of a basement in which a brick bearing partition is used to divide the space and to support the floor joists. In two-story houses, such bearing partitions also support walls above the first-floor level.

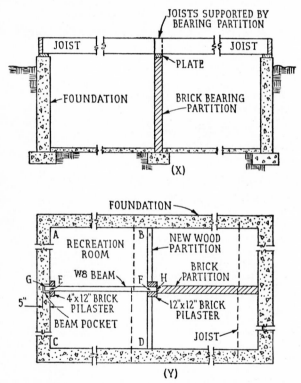

FIGURE 7. Use of W8 beam in place of bearing partition.

The Y part of the illustration indicates a plan view of the same basement. The area $ABCD$ is to be turned into a recreation area. To create one large room, the brick partition must be removed between E and F. However, some means must be provided for supporting the joists between E and F when the partition is removed.

The *X* part of Figure 8 indicates how the brick partition supports the joists and the *Y* part shows that a steel W8 beam can replace the brick partition.

The first step of such a project consists of measuring the distance *GH* as shown in the *Y* part of Figure 7, to determine the required length of the beam. When such beams are not more than 12 feet long, an 8-inch

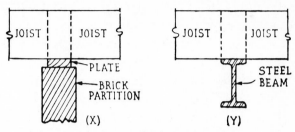

FIGURE 8. Details of joist support.

size is sufficiently strong. When longer lengths are required, local dealers will suggest the sizes to use.

Before the brick partition can be torn out between *E* and *F*, the joists must be provided with temporary supports. As indicated in Figure 9, such support can be provided by means of 4- by 4-inch timbers. The *A* and *B* horizontal timbers, on both sides of the bearing partition, should be as long as the width of the ceiling. The vertical timbers should be spaced about 4 feet apart.

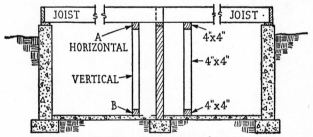

FIGURE 9. Temporary support for joists.

When the partition between *E* and *F*, as shown in the *Y* part of Figure 7, has been removed, a beam pocket, as shown at *G*, must be cut into the foundation. This pocket must have a depth equal to the depth of the beam. At the *H* end of the remaining part of the brick partition, a 12-

by 12-inch brick pilaster must be laid up as support for the *F* end of the beam. If the beam pocket can be at least 5 inches wide, so as to provide a 5-inch bearing for the beam, a brick pilaster at the *E* end of the beam is not necessary. If the pocket is less than 5 inches wide, a 4- by 12-inch pilaster is required.

Before the beam is placed into position, the bottom of the beam pocket and the tops of the pilasters should be covered with a bedding of cement and sand mortar. This will assure a firm bed for the beam. Make sure that the top flange of the beam is snugly fitted to the bottom edges of the joists.

The space left in the floor by the removal of the brick partition can be patched and a new over-all floor covering applied as explained in Chapter 6. The surfaces of the new partition and foundation can be finished as suggested in Chapter 5. The ceiling can be sheathed as set forth in Chapter 4.

Floors. If existing concrete floors are free from cracks and dusting, and are always dry, either paint or stain can be applied in any one of a variety of decorator-styled colors.

Often seemingly dry concrete floors are too damp for good painting results. One method of testing is to lay a rubber mat on the floor and leave it undisturbed for at least two days. If, at the end of that time, moisture shows under the mat, the floor is probably too damp for paint and should be furred as explained in Chapter 6.

PAINT. Concrete floors in a recreation area are often subjected to heavy traffic, especially in connection with pool or billiards, and demand more than ordinary oil paint. Coatings for this type of surface must be extraordinarily adhesive and tough and have the qualities of good aging, rapid drying, and high resistance to soap or other cleaning agents. Paints such as Medusa rubber-base coatings are recommended.

A concrete floor should be thoroughly cleaned of all traces of soap or grease by means of a lye solution. After cleaning, the floor should be etched with a 10 per cent solution of muriatic acid. Pour the solution on the floor, let stand for 10 minutes, rinse, and allow to dry. Hands should be washed in cold water after using the muriatic acid solution.

After the floor is etched, test for porosity by placing a few drops of water on the surface. If the water is readily absorbed, the surface is ready for painting.

Most such paints are applied as they come from the containers, usually in two coats. Three coats are suggested for areas which will be subjected to heavy traffic. When the first coat is dry to touch, apply the second coat. If a third coat is applied, it should be brushed out more than either of the first two coats. Wax will protect the paint and give it more luster.

STAIN. In some instances, stain is a longer-lasting color than paint. Several commercial forms are available, any of which can be applied to concrete that has not been previously painted, oiled, or sealed against penetration.

The floor should be etched as previously explained. The dye should be scrubbed into the surface and forced into the pores. Apply a second coat if the first coat dries without a uniform color. Wax will give the floor added luster, protect the dye, and assure easier cleaning.

Windows. In order to install a window in an existing concrete-block wall, several courses of block must be removed to provide space for the window and so that jamb block, a sill, and a lintel can be laid up around the window opening.

The first step consists of studying the joists over the window location. For example, refer to Section *C-C* in Plate II. This view shows that joist ends are supported by the foundation over the window opening. In a case like this, at least three of the joists on both sides of the window location should be temporarily supported, somewhat as shown in Figure 9, while the window is being installed. If the joists are parallel to the foundations, temporary support for them is not necessary.

The *B* part of Figure 10 shows an elevation view of a typical concrete-block foundation that is similar to the one illustrated in Section *W*-1 of Plate V. It can be assumed that an opening, *ABCD*, in the foundation must be provided for the window. The *A* and *C* parts of the illustration show both wood- and steel-sash windows in a concrete-block wall. We can further assume that steel sash is required.

The next step is to remove the necessary block from the foundation. Joints between block can generally be broken by means of a cold chisel

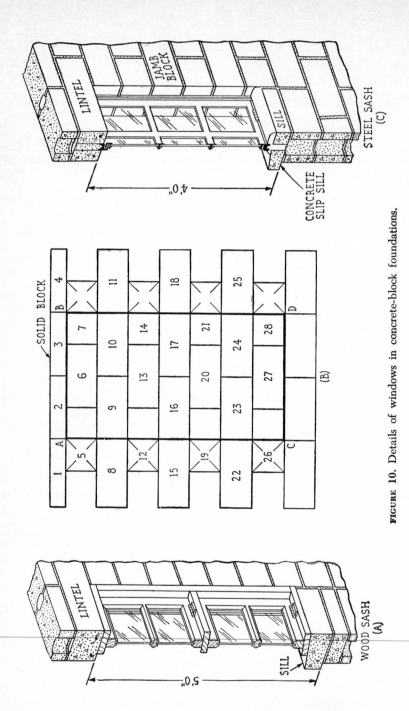

FIGURE 10. Details of windows in concrete-block foundations.

202

or a steel claw bar. Remove blocks 1, 2, 3, and 4 first. Then remove blocks 5 through 28.

In place of ordinary block, we will need steel-sash jamb block on both sides of the window opening. We will also need a sill and lintel, such as shown at *C* in the illustration.

The mortar for laying block can be composed of 1 part of portland cement and 3 parts of sand. In place of blocks 26 and 28, we will lay the sill and two half jamb blocks. Blocks 22 and 25 should be whole

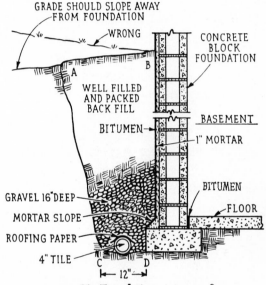

GRADE SHOULD SLOPE AWAY FROM FOUNDATION

WRONG

CONCRETE BLOCK FOUNDATION

WELL FILLED AND PACKED BACK FILL

BITUMEN

BASEMENT

1" MORTAR

BITUMEN

GRAVEL 16"DEEP

FLOOR

MORTAR SLOPE

ROOFING PAPER

4" TILE

12"

FIGURE 11. Foundation waterproofing.

jamb block. In place of blocks 19 and 21, we will lay two half jamb blocks, etc. In place of blocks 5, 6, and 7, we will install the lintel. Finally, the solid block, 1, 2, 3, and 4, can be laid above the lintel. This completes the window opening.

Basement Water. As previously explained, basements may be subject to either wet or damp conditions.

WET CONDITIONS. When wet conditions such as caused by severe static pressure exist, a drastic remedy must be applied.

First, excavate a trench all around the foundation somewhat as indicated by the section view in Figure 11. The bottom of the trench should be at the same level as the bottom of the footing. Brush and wash all traces of soil from the foundation.

Second, prepare a mortar composed of 1 part portland cement and 3 parts clean sand. A total thickness of 1 inch of mortar should be applied to the foundation in 3 separate coats. Allow 3 days of hardening time between coats. Spray the first and second coats with water before the second and third coats are applied. Use the same mortar mix to build up a slope, as shown in the illustration, between the foundation and the top of the footing.

Third, mop a thick coat of hot bitumen on the surface of the mortar.

Fourth, lay lines of plain-end drain tile, spaced about ½ inch apart, around the foundation as indicated in the illustration. All lines of tile should have a gradual slope to one location where a connection to a sewer or other means of disposal can be made. Spread heavy roofing paper along the tops of the tile.

Fifth, fill in at least 16 inches of gravel or crushed rock over the tile.

The earth backfill should be free of rubbish and well compacted. The slope of the grade should be as shown in the illustration.

If there is a crack between the floor and the foundation, it should be filled with hot bitumen.

DAMP CONDITIONS. When damp conditions occur, the remedy is less drastic.

After a hard rain, mark the areas where dampness appears on a foundation.

If the foundation has been painted previously with an oil paint, remove with a solution of 1½ pounds of caustic soda in 1 gallon of hot water. If painted previously with whitewash, calcimine, or cold-water paints, remove by scrubbing surfaces with 1 part muriatic acid and 5 parts water. Clean off loose dirt and dust by means of a stiff wire brush.

On the areas marked, scrub in with a scrubbing brush a coat of a good portland-cement paint. Extend paint several feet beyond the marked areas. Work paint into all voids and depressions with a circular motion of the scrub brush.

Wait until the next hard rain to ascertain whether the foundation has been made sufficiently watertight to stop dampness. Then, give the entire surface a first coat of the same paint. Cure by applying a fine spray of water two or three times during the following 18 to 24 hours. Apply a second coat of the paint for thorough protection.

New Foundation Surface. In cases where the basement sides of masonry foundations have poor appearance, in addition to being slightly wet or undesirably damp, new cement plaster surfaces can be applied which will be attractive and waterproof. The following suggestions are typical.

The old surface should be roughened using a stone mason's hammer, drills, or similar tools, exposing a new surface, and leaving ¼- to ⅜-inch-deep holes every 2 or 3 inches, so as to provide a better bond for the cement plaster.

Apply a solution to the wall of 1 part muriatic acid to 10 parts of water, using a fiber or acid brush. Allow the acid solution to exhaust itself, which requires about 10 minutes. Hose off the acid thoroughly with water.

Remove any remaining loose pieces by going over the walls with a wire brush.

If the foundation is made of brick or concrete block, instead of following the foregoing directions, rake out all mortar joints to a depth of ½ to ¾ inch.

Then remove all loose mortar, dirt, grease, paints, and efflorescence. Whitewash, calcimine, cold-water paints, and efflorescence are easily removed by means of a solution composed of 1 part muriatic acid and 5 parts of water. Oil paint can be removed by applying freely a solution composed of 1½ pounds of caustic soda and 1 gallon of water. Rinse with clear water and be sure that all loose particles are removed, preferably by means of a wire brush.

Spray the entire foundation surface with water. Then use a fiber brush to apply a thin waterproofing grout coat composed of portland cement and water mixed to a creamy consistency. Brush the grout thoroughly into all holes and irregularities in the foundation surface.

The next step consists of applying cement plaster to the surface of the foundation. The plaster should be composed of 1 part portland cement and 2½ parts of clean sand. Mix with water to a stiff workable consistency.

Apply the first coat of cement plaster ⅜ inch thick and be sure to trowel the plaster well into the surface to secure a proper bond. Scratch the first coat with a "scratcher." An old broom or a wire brush can be used. Do not use nails or trowels. The scratches should be about $\frac{1}{16}$ inch deep.

As soon as the first coat has set, spray the surface with water and apply the second coat $\frac{3}{8}$ inch thick. Trowel the plaster with sufficient pressure to obtain a tight, close-grained finish.

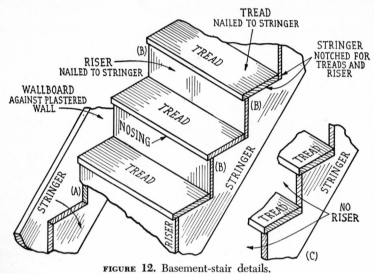

FIGURE 12. Basement-stair details.

Care should be exercised not to trowel any more than is absolutely necessary to obtain the proper finish. Excess troweling results in poor plaster.

If there is continual seepage through a foundation, one or more holes should be bored and small pipes inserted to concentrate the flow of water while the plaster is being applied. After the plaster has set, plug the holes with plaster.

Stairs. Many basement stairs, especially in older houses, are rough and unsightly. Such stairs can be given a face lifting at only a fraction of the money new stairs would cost.

Figure 12 shows several details of typical basement stairs. The more common type is shown at *B,* where two or more stringers are notched so treads and risers can be nailed to them. When stairs are against a wall, or between two walls, wallboards may exist as shown at *A*. More economical stairs, as shown at *C*, do not have risers between the treads. Generally, such stairs are nailed together and the wood is not smooth.

Because of ordinary wear, nosings and treads may be rounded and dished to the extent that new paint would not greatly improve their appearance. They should be sanded until the nosings are near their original condition and the treads should be leveled. Sanding will remove old paint. Sanding may be done without removing the old treads by using a small electric hand sander. Some scraping will be necessary with a regular hand scraper.

Better results can be obtained if the treads are removed and taken to a shop where they can be sanded smooth and true with heavy cabinetmaker's equipment.

After the sanding is done, apply a good coat of shellac to the treads before nailing them in place to prevent any tendency to warp. Use finishing nails and a nail set to drive them below the surface.

Risers, stringer, and wallboards can be prepared for new paint by filling all cracks and dents with Spackle or water-base putty. Casein-type cement of the kind used to fill plasterboard joints can also be used. Apply with a wide putty knife. Allow to dry for at least 24 hours. For a good job, apply a primer coat of paint before the undercoater and final coat.

An enamel color may be used. The undercoater can consist of half flat and half enamel paint, but the final coat should be all enamel. When the enamel is dry, nail the treads in place and give them a coat of hard but flexible varnish. For best results, sandpaper lightly on the varnish, wipe away dust, and apply a second varnish coat. A natural finish is achieved with shellac and varnish.

When treads are in so poor a condition that they cannot be repaired, the stairs can be carpeted or new treads added. Lumber dealers can furnish the material, cut it to size, and add the nosing required. Where no risers exist, as shown at *C,* they may be added along with new treads on the old stringers.

Wall Surfaces. If the surfaces of concrete or concrete block are fairly smooth and are otherwise in good condition so far as appearance is concerned, they can be painted any one or combination of several colors using a good grade of cement paint. Such paint creates attractive appearance and also provides a high degree of dampproofing.

If surfaces have been previously painted, paints other than cement paint must be removed. Oil paint, oily stains, soot, grease, shellac, and glue size can be removed by applying caustic soda mixed to the proportion of 1½ pounds with 1 gallon of hot water. Apply freely, wash with water after film softens, and follow with rinsing. Whitewash, calcimine, cold-water paints, and efflorescence (white powdery deposits) may be removed with 1 part muriatic acid mixed with 5 parts of water. Scrub with brush and rinse.

All surfaces should be wire-brushed. Small cracks should be cleaned and filled with a paste made by mixing dry paint and water. Large cracks should be filled with cement mortar.

Before painting, spray the surface with a fine mist of water. Apply first coat of paint with a bristle or calcimine-type brush. Use a horizontal motion, keeping the brush full of paint. Do not brush the paint after application.

Cure the first coat by means of a fine spray of water applied several times during 12 hours. This is important and should not be neglected.

The second coat may be applied on the second day. Cure this coat as previously explained.

See Chapter 6 in connection with new surface materials.

Cutting Structural Details for Pipes and Ducts. In the framing for floors and walls, the joists and studs each support a definite amount of weight and contribute to the stiffness of the framing. Thus we must consider each joist or stud individually and understand that if one of them fails, an undue stress is forced on the others and may cause defects in floors and walls.

PIPES. Sometimes joists have to be notched, somewhat as shown in the *A* part of Figure 13, in order to run pipes to required locations. If a 2 by 10 joist has a notch 5 inches deep in it, the whole joist is no stronger than at the notch. In other words, the strength of the joist is reduced to the strength of a 2 by 5 joist. In order to avoid loss of strength and stiffness, some means of strengthening the joist must be employed. As shown in

the *B* part of Figure 13, we can nail 2 by 4 pieces on both sides of the
joist to reinforce it. The 2 by 4 pieces should be at least 6 feet long or
even the full length of the joist. Use 3½-inch nails and space them not
more than 6 inches apart along the length of the reinforcing members.

If, as indicated in the *C* part of Figure 13, holes have to be drilled in
studs, they should be reinforced by means of stiff metal straps on both
sides of the holes. The straps should be at least 12 inches long and have
five or six nail holes.

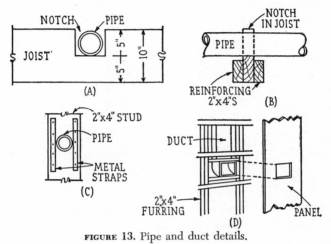

FIGURE 13. Pipe and duct details.

DUCTS. The ducts used in connection with either gravity or forced-air
heating systems are generally run along the under edges of joists or between studs so that notching is not required. However, when notching is
required, the same reinforcing as explained in connection with joists
should be provided. The *D* part of Figure 13 shows how 2 by 4 furring
can be used when a basement forced-air duct is required.

Existing Floor Drains. If existing floor drains are to be covered over
with furring and new surface materials, such as suggested in Chapter 6,
they must be effectively plugged by means of cement mortar. This is to
avoid the entry of sewer gas after the water in the drain seals has
evaporated.

Basement Temperature. If there is a possibility of cold drafts being
radiated from foundations, especially when parts of them are above

grade as indicated in Figure 14, effective insulation can be provided as indicated.

The first step of such a project consists of applying 2 by 2 or 1 by 2 furring strips spaced 16 inches apart. They can be fastened to the foundation and made level as explained in Chapters 2 and 5.

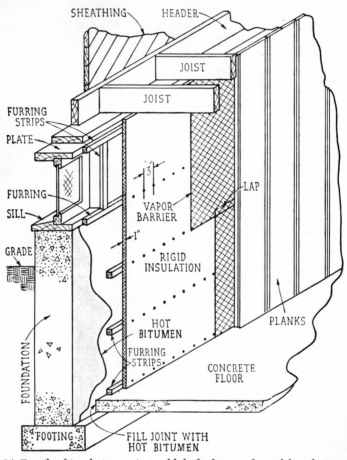

FIGURE 14. Details of insulation against cold drafts from surface of foundation surfaces.

After the furring strips have been applied, the surface of the foundation should be mopped with hot bitumen. This constitutes effective dampproofing.

Next apply 1-inch thick panels of rigid insulation to the furring strips. Place the nails about 3 inches apart. Then tack well-lapped waterproof buildei paper over the insulation. This constitutes the required moisture barrier.

The interior surface material, such as planks, can be applied as explained in Chapter 5.

Sagging Floors. The *A* part of Figure 15 shows an exaggerated example of deflection (sagging) in a floor joist. Such deflection affects all joists alike and can cause several troubles including vibration, squeaking, cracks in surface materials, and out-of-plumb conditions so far as furniture and other household equipment is concerned.

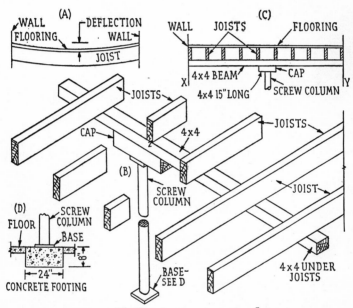

FIGURE 15. How to correct sagging floors.

The *B* and *C* parts of the illustration indicate how a 4 by 4 timber, a 4 by 4 cap, and a screw-type column can be used to correct deflection and provide permanent support for the weakened joists. If the 4 by 4 timber must be more than 10′ 10″ long, two screw columns should be used. When only one screw column is necessary, it should be placed at the mid-point of the timber.

Because of the weight screw columns support, they require a strong concrete footing of the size suggested in the *D* part of the illustration.

The timber can temporarily be held up against the joists by means of 2 by 4's used somewhat as shown in Figure 9. Then the cap and column can be placed with just enough adjustment of the column to make the whole assembly tight. Screw the column up a little, not more often than once every two or three days, until the floor is level. Such gradual adjustment avoids any chance of cracks in joists or flooring. When the column has been finally adjusted, the cap and joists can be toenailed to the timber.

If a screw-type column must be placed within a recreation area, cartwheel shelving, as shown around the column in Figure 2, can be used to partially hide the column and to provide decorative storage.

TYPICAL REMODELING PROJECTS

For the purpose of the following projects, we shall assume that the house indicated in Plates I through VI actually exists and that the basement is to be remodeled. The projects are presented in the form of problems and their solutions.

PROBLEM 1. We can further assume that the purpose of remodeling is to provide the following items:

1. A large area to be used as a general recreation room
2. A workbench area where the man of the house can engage in a woodworking hobby
3. A general storage area
4. An area for deep-freeze equipment and food storage

The problem is to plan the best use of the basement space.

SOLUTION. From the standpoint of practical expense, we must consider that the boiler and stairs cannot be moved from their original locations.

Our first inclination would be to place the recreation area in the west portion of the basement, as indicated in Figure 16. Partitions on both sides of the chimney would enclose an area 11′ 10″ wide and 19′ 2″ long. This plan provides a recreation area of fair size and a well-placed workbench area. However, there are several serious objections:

1. The plan does not provide logical space for general storage.
2. Entrance to the recreation area is through an unfinished part of the basement.

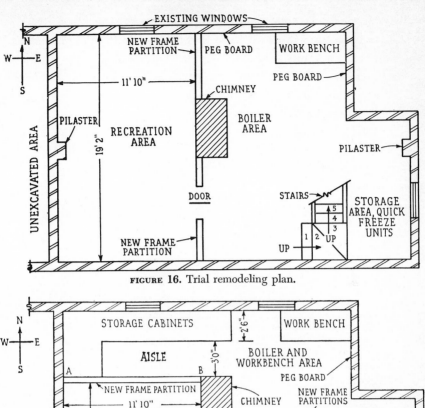

FIGURE 16. Trial remodeling plan.

FIGURE 17. Second trial remodeling plan.

3. The recreation area seems detached because of the distance from the stairs.

4. The width of the recreation area is too narrow as compared to the length. Furniture arrangement and conversation would be difficult.

The plan shown in Figure 17 avoids all of the objections to the plan shown in Figure 16:

1. There is ample and desirable general storage space.

2. The stairs are within the recreation room so that the unfinished part of the basement is not visible.

3. The recreation room does not seem detached.

4. The shape is such that furniture can be arranged to advantage and easy conversation is possible. See Figure 18.

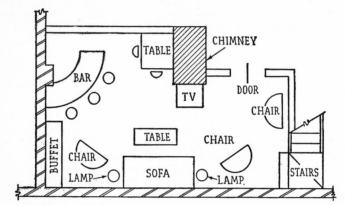

FIGURE 18. Possible furniture arrangement for plan shown in Figure 17.

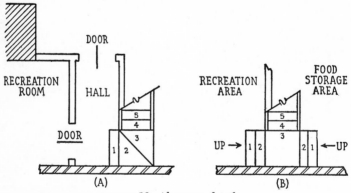

FIGURE 19. Alternate details.

However, there are two objections to the plan:

1. The new windows add considerably to the cost.

2. Traffic to other parts of the basement must go through one end of the recreation room. This objection could be avoided but only by means of the additional expense items shown in Figure 19.

PART *A* OF FIGURE 19. A hall between the stairs and the recreation area would provide access to the unfinished part of the basement and avoid such traffic through the recreation area. However, considerable additional expense would be involved, all of which seems out of proportion to the advantage gained.

PART *B* OF FIGURE 19. The steps could be rebuilt so as to provide access to both the recreation area and the food-storage area. However, the additional expense involved seems out of proportion to the advantage gained.

We can assume that the plan shown in Figure 17 is acceptable.

PROBLEM 2. The problem consists of erecting 2 by 4 framing for the partition shown between *A* and *B* in Figure 17.

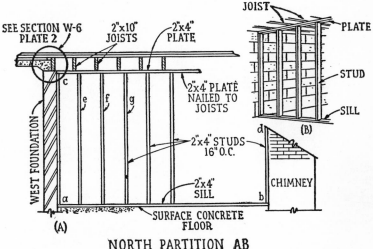

NORTH PARTITION AB
FIGURE 20. Partition framing.

SOLUTION. The first step in the framing is to place the 2 by 4 sill shown between *a* and *b* in the *A* part of Figure 20. Measure the exact distance and cut a piece of 2 by 4 to the length required. Place it on the floor so that it is at 90 degrees to the foundation and flush with the corner of the chimney. Fasten it to the concrete floor by means of powder-actuated nails spaced no more than 16 inches apart.

Next, erect the stud marked *ac*. Its length is 1½ inches less than the distance from the top of the sill to the under edges of the joists. Place it against the foundation and make sure it is plumb. Powder-actuated nails can be used for fastening it to the foundation. Erect stud *bd*, next to the chimney, in the same manner. Place the plate in position and nail it to the under edges of the joists.

Next, cut the studs, such as shown at *e*, *f*, and *g*, to be placed between the sill and plate. Space them 16 inches on centers, starting at the chimney corner. The resulting frame will appear like the framing shown in the *B* part of the illustration.

PROBLEM 3. The problem consists of erecting 2 by 4 framing for the partition shown between *C* and *D* in Figure 17.

SOLUTION. The first step consists of marking the position of corner *D* on the concrete floor. Also mark the position and width of the door opening. It is helpful to have the door frame at hand so that its width can be measured.

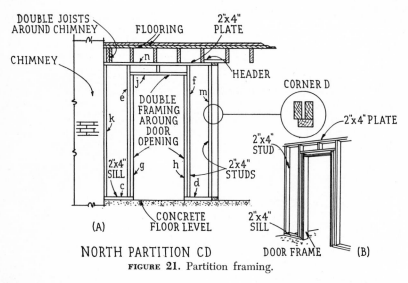

FIGURE 21. Partition framing.

Because of corner *D*, the sill for partition *DE* must be placed along with the sill for partition *CD*.

Place the sills as previously explained except that pieces *c* and *d*, shown in Figure 21, are short so as to allow for the door opening.

Erect the stud marked *k* as previously explained.

Because of the corner *D*, it is advisable to erect the plate *n* before any other studs are erected.

Stud *m* should be placed keeping in mind that it must be part of a three-member corner assembly. Studs *e* and *f* should be erected, in the positions indicated, so that studs *g* and *h* can be set in at the ends of sill pieces *c* and *d*. Piece *j* should be placed as indicated in the *B* part of the

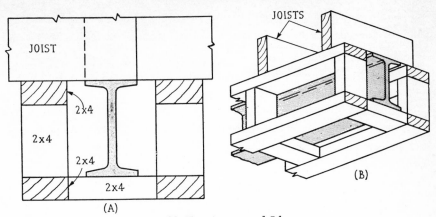

FIGURE 22. Framing around I-beam.

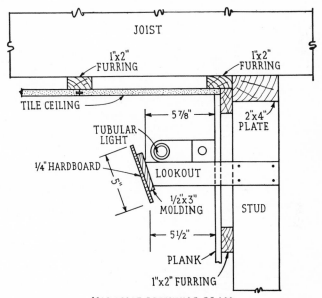

VALANCE LIGHTING PLAN

FIGURE 23. Details of valance.

illustration. The framing around the door opening should leave ample room for the door frame to be placed and plumbed by means of shims.

The plate for partition *DE*, shown in Figure 17, should be fastened to headers as indicated in Figure 21.

PROBLEM 4. Plate V specifies that 8-inch I-beams must extend from the chimney to the foundations on the west and east sides of the basement. The two beams are indicated in Figure 17. The problem is to erect framing around the beam in the recreation area so that ceiling-surface material can be applied.

SOLUTION. The *A* and *B* parts of Figure 22 show suggested erection details.

PROBLEM 5. It can be assumed that valance lighting is required along the partition marked *AB* in Figure 17. The problem is to design and erect the valance.

SOLUTION. The details in Figure 23 show design and erection suggestions.

CHAPTER EIGHT

Kitchens

Aside from basements and bathrooms, there is nothing that so definitely dates houses, and nothing that so positively determines their convenience, attractiveness, and general desirability as the design and equipment of their kitchens.

Many exceptionally old houses, especially in rural areas, have kitchens which resemble the one shown in the upper part of Figure 1. Such kitchens date back to the cookstove era and to times before the first useful kitchen equipment was manufactured. Kitchens of such age are dismal places where the work required of housewives actually amounts to hard labor.

With the advent of the first electric refrigerators, improved sinks and cupboards became available and kitchens were somewhat improved. However, the equipment had to be scattered about kitchens wherever floor and wall space existed; this is shown in the upper part of Figure 2. Such kitchens are brighter and more cheery, but they lack convenience and efficiency.

With the coming of improved gas and electric ranges, along with better sinks and cupboards, kitchens like the one shown in the upper part of Figure 3 became possible. More attractive floor and wall surface materials brought about better over-all appearance. Yet, such kitchens are far from efficient. They require a great deal of walking and reaching, retain the feeling of a work area, and are not inviting so far as family activities are concerned.

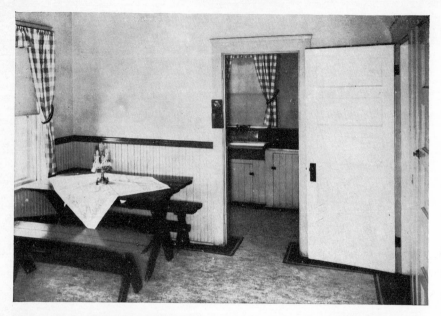

FIGURE 1

FIGURE 2

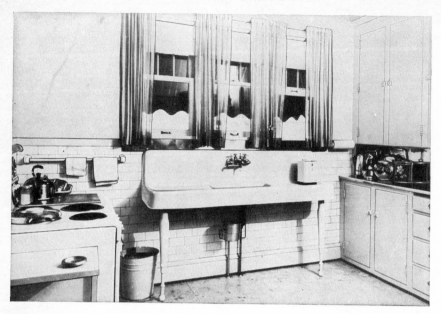

FIGURE 3

The remodeled kitchens shown in the lower parts of Figures 1, 2, and 3 prove that any old kitchen can be remodeled and thus transformed into a cheery, beautiful, and efficient area.

For housewives, kitchens are activity centers where they spend a large part of every day. To them, remodeling means a great deal. For example, research has proved that a modern kitchen can reduce walking, movement, and reaching by at least 70, 74, and 60 per cent, respectively. Thus, remodeled kitchens are efficient activity areas where all tasks can be accomplished with much greater ease and in far less time.

For families, remodeled kitchens often become pleasant gathering places both during and between meals. In fact, statistics prove that where such kitchens exist, 85 per cent of the families are eating most of their meals amid such attractive surroundings.

Kitchen remodeling is a fascinating project. This chapter proposes to outline the items relating to such a project which require careful consideration, to call attention to modern equipment, and to show how to go about transforming old-fashioned kitchens into cheery and efficient areas.

BASIC KITCHEN TYPES

After a great deal of research and experimentation, the manufacturers of modern kitchen cabinets were able to design four basic kitchen types which suit the needs of any and all kitchen areas. In other words, no matter what shape or size a kitchen area may be, at least one of the types can be used in connection with it and in such a manner as to ensure convenience, efficiency, and attractiveness.

U Type. See part *A* of Figure 4. In the U-type kitchen, the major appliances and storage work cabinets are arranged on three sides of the area. Figure 5 shows a typical U-type kitchen in a small area.

L Type. See part *B* of Figure 4. In the L-type kitchen, the equipment is located on two adjacent walls. Corner wall and base cabinets are often

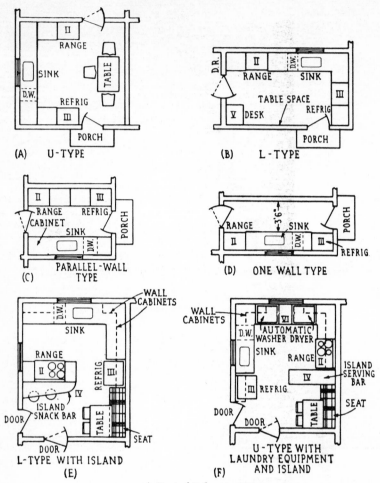

FIGURE 4. Basic kitchen patterns.

used in these kitchens so that corner space, which otherwise might be wasted, becomes usable. Figure 6 shows a typical L-type kitchen in one corner of a large area.

Parallel-wall Type. See part *C* of Figure 4. In the parallel-wall-type kitchen, the arrangement is particularly well adapted to a long, narrow area. This type of kitchen is seldom necessary and is therefore not illustrated by means of a picture.

FIGURE 5. A typical L-type kitchen in a small area. (*Courtesy General Electric Company*)

FIGURE 6. A typical L-type kitchen in one corner of a large area. (*Courtesy General Electric Company*)

FIGURE 7. A typical one-wall kitchen.

One-wall Type. See part *D* of Figure 4. In the one-wall-type kitchen, all equipment is lined up along one wall. This type of installation, somewhat as shown in Figure 7, is often used in small, minimum-cost houses where kitchen areas are only a few feet wide and when doors are necessary in both of the short walls.

Variations. There can be any number of variations from the four basic types, depending upon the sizes and shapes of kitchen areas.

The *E* part of Figure 4 shows the use of an island (sometimes known as a peninsula) in connection with an L-type kitchen in a large area.

The *F* part of Figure 4 shows where automatic laundry appliances and a serving bar (sometimes known as a snack bar) can be placed in a U-type kitchen, where space permits.

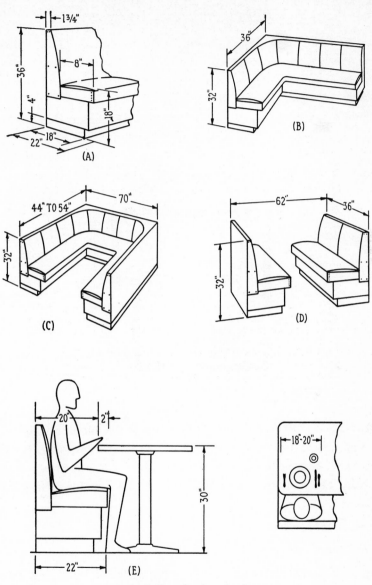

FIGURE 8. Details of nook plans.

DINING NOOKS

Built-in dining nooks usually follow three basic plans. The space available generally determines the appropriate type. In many cases, however, the layout is such that there is a choice. It then becomes a matter of selecting the type best suited to the needs.

Standard dimensions are shown in the *A* part of Figure 8. The recommended and standard 36-inch over-all height can be varied to meet particular conditions, such as a low window or other obstructions. However, it is best not to modify this dimension more than 5 or 6 inches.

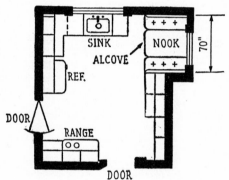

FIGURE 9. A U-type nook in a variation of a U-type kitchen.

L Type. See part *B* of Figure 8. This type is flexible in that it can be used equally well in large or small corners, such as shown at *E* and *F* in Figure 4. With one side acting as a room divider, an interesting variation is possible. The table used with this nook can be movable or fastened to the floor.

U Type. See part *C* of Figure 8. This type of nook is best suited for large alcoves such as shown in Figure 9. The table should be movable.

Parallel Type. See part *D* of Figure 8. The type of nook can be used in a small alcove or in one corner of a kitchen. It requires a space 5′ 2″ wide and adequately seats four adults. The table should be movable.

As is shown in the *E* part of Figure 8, approximately 18 to 20 inches of table space is needed for a full-service setting. Table tops less than 24 inches wide are too narrow.

All of the foregoing nook equipment may be purchased ready to install.

ADVANTAGES OF REMODELING

The advantages obtainable, even by fairly economical remodeling, are extraordinary. The difference between old and modern kitchens is so great that such projects are the most interesting home-planning activity we can possibly engage in.

Study the top part of Figure 3. Notice in it the items listed in the following summary, keeping in mind that such items are typical of most old kitchens.

1. The sink is old-fashioned and offers little by way of modern conveniences. There is no place for storing cleaning supplies and the exposed plumbing is ugly. The two legs constitute a stumbling hazard. There is no counter space around the sink where soiled dishes, incoming vegetables, or bottles of milk can be placed prior to and immediately after washing.

2. The old-fashioned cupboards require too much reaching and were not designed for convenience or efficiency. Note that many appliances and other kitchen equipment must be stored on the cupboard counter where they constitute an eyesore and are difficult to reach.

3. The table is not shown in the picture. However, it is inconveniently placed in a corner across the kitchen. In preparing a meal, hundreds of steps must be taken from corner to corner because the limited storage space is all on one side of the room.

4. There is no work surface adjoining the range. To transfer cooked foods from cooking utensils to serving dishes, the food must be carried from the range to the table where serving dishes must be placed. Then the utensils must be returned to the range or taken to the sink to be rinsed. This flow of work requires hundreds more steps and unnecessary motions. Such inefficiency makes a housewife's work tedious and tiring.

5. The old tile walls, reaching from the floor level to the window sills, echo every sound and cause the kitchen to be noisy. Also, the tile design and installation are uninteresting.

6. The garbage-can corner is untidy, appears dirty, and certainly is not in keeping with modern standards of cleanliness considering that food is being prepared and served.

7. The window sills are too close to the sink and the height of the windows is out of good proportion.

8. The room lacks cheerfulness and gives the impression of a workshop rather than a pleasant area.

9. The old-fashioned floor covering appears to be worn and lacks any trace of beauty.

10. The ceiling is too high and makes the room look out of proportion.

11. There are no convenient electric outlets to use in connection with modern appliances.

12. There is no toe space under the cupboards.

Other items could be mentioned, but this brief summary shows the inconvenience of preparing, serving, and cleaning up after a meal in this old kitchen.

Now study the bottom part of Figure 3. The advantages of remodeling are immediately apparent. Hundreds of steps are saved as soon as the new cabinet sink (with or without an automatic dishwasher or a food disposer) is made the center of activity. Since its position does not have to be changed, plumbing costs are kept at a minimum. New cabinets, properly located, make the kitchen much more efficient in both storage space and work surface. The sink is flanked by handy wall and base cabinets on either side along with undercabinet storage space.

The refrigerator and range remain in the same position, but now ample counter space is conveniently placed beside each one. The floor covering has been replaced and the windows remodeled.

Note, too, that work has been simplified in this remodeled kitchen. Groceries can now be placed on the cabinet next to the sink. There is no retracing of steps to rinse food, store staples, or put perishables into the refrigerator. Ample work space as well as storage space has been provided.

By reducing steps, the remodeled kitchen cuts down on expenditure of much time and energy. It is much easier to maintain high standards of homemaking in such a kitchen, and the area is a pleasant place to be in.

Figures 1 and 2 can be studied for like contrasts.

WORK CENTERS

In order to accomplish convenience and efficiency, the various appliances and cabinets must be arranged accordingly. In other words, all kitchen items should be grouped so that work can be done to the best of advantage and in a manner somewhat similar to production lines in an industrial plant. For this purpose, the sink and its accompanying cabinets should be grouped into what is called a *work center*. The following centers are typical:

I. Sink center provides space for:

Dishwasher	Dishes	Linen

II. Cooking center provides space for:

Pots and pans	Coffee and tea	Toaster
Griddle	Canned goods	Coffeemaker
Cooking cutlery	Dry packaged foods	

III. Food-preparation center provides space for:

Mixing bowls	Mixers	Staples
Baking pans	Spices	Perishables
Cutlery	Canned Goods	Vegetables

IV. Serving center provides space for:

Dishes	Trays	Glasses
Bowls	Silverware	Island snack bar

V. Planning center provides space for:

Cookbooks	Telephone
Writing materials	Chair or stool

VI. Laundry center provides space for:

Soaps	Bleach
Starch	Irons

Work centers are indicated in the *A* to *F* parts of Figure 4 by means of the same Roman numerals shown in the foregoing lists.

CHOICE OF EQUIPMENT

Cabinet manufacturers offer standardized cabinet sizes in 3-inch multiples. Therefore, cabinets are available to fit almost any wall or floor space. The size and style of kitchens and financial budgets are the chief factors in determining what equipment shall be installed. (NOTE: Planning procedures are explained in subsequent pages.)

Sinks. Modern sinks are shown in Figures 1, 2, 3, 5, 6, and 7. A food-waste disposer is virtually a necessity in modern kitchens. Dishwashers are most convenient but not a necessity. The type of sink is an important factor and should be given special attention in terms of family size and habits.

Ranges. When families already own ranges which are in usable condition, they can be installed in remodeled kitchens. Future replacements and additions should be planned for when new kitchens are being installed.

Refrigerators. Same explanation applies as for ranges.

Base Cabinets. Modern base cabinets are shown in Figures 1, 2, 3, 5, 6, and 7. Ample storage and counterspace are necessities in up-to-date kitchens. Steps and time are saved if small appliances and utensils are located at spots where each is used most frequently. Also, when ample counter space is provided, work can proceed quickly and efficiently.

Merry-go-rounds. The best way to utilize corner spaces, such as shown in Figure 3, is by means of merry-go-rounds. When given a light push, the shelves spin around, bringing shelf contents to the front. In Figure 10, merry-go-rounds are shown in both base and wall positions.

Cutting-board Cabinets. The *A* part of Figure 11 shows a convenient cutting-board cabinet. When the drawer is pulled out, the drawer head drops down and an edge-grained maple board moves up. It can be used for cutting and chopping, and as a base for a grinder.

FIGURE 10. Typical merry-go-rounds in base and wall positions.

Mixer Cabinets. The *B* part of Figure 11 shows a solution to the question of where to store a mixer. The bottom area of such cabinets can be used for the mixer bowls.

Wall Cabinets. Modern wall cabinets are shown in Figures 1, 2, 3, 5, 6, and 7. Such cabinets are primarily for storage space and should be planned for easy access to articles that are used daily. They can be obtained in widths ranging from 15 to 54 inches and in heights of 15, 18, and 30 inches. Double or single doors are available.

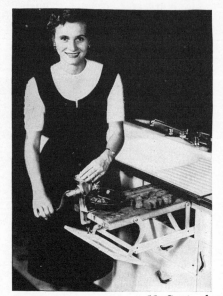

FIGURE 11. Cutting board and mixer cabinets.

FIGURE 12. Electric range and base cabinets form an island in this kitchen. (*Courtesy General Electric Company*)

Islands. Islands are indicated in the *E* and *F* parts of Figure 4. In Figure 12, an electric range and base cabinets constitute an island. Note the use of a hood and hidden fan to catch and exhaust cooking odors.

Suggested Cabinets and Accessories. The following suggestions relate to the work centers previously explained:

I. Sink Center. Suggested items:

Sink cabinet	Pan-storage cabinets	Vegetable bins
Drawer and pan cabinets	Tray-storage cabinets	Cabinets over sink
	Dishwasher	

II. Cooking Center. Suggested items:

Drawer cabinets	Cutlery cabinets	Range-base cabinets
Pan cabinets	Above-range cabinets	

III. Food-preparation Center. Suggested items:

Mixer cabinets	Base cabinets
Cutting-board cabinets	Spice racks
Wall-storage cabinets	Deep-freeze unit
Above-refrigerator cabinets	

IV. Serving Center. Suggested items:

Island snack bar	Base-drawer cabinets
Base-tray cabinets	Tray cabinets

V. Planning Center. Suggested items:

Desk	Wall-storage cabinets

VI. Laundry Center. Suggested items:

Automatic washer	Ironer
Automatic dryer	Wall cabinets

CABINET DIMENSIONS

Typical cabinets and cabinet sizes are shown in Figure 13. Manufacturers of such equipment publish the dimensions for their full line of cabinets. It is wise to secure such data before starting to plan a remodeled kitchen.

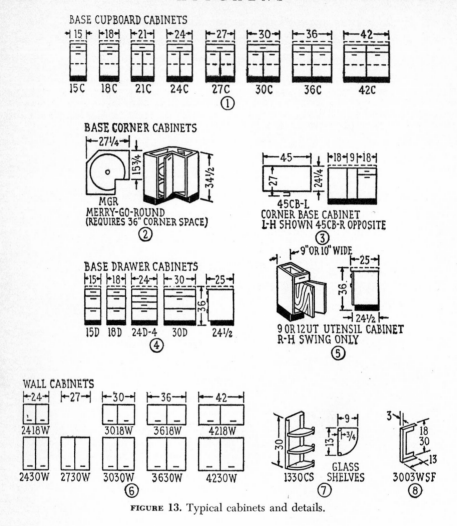

FIGURE 13. Typical cabinets and details.

OTHER KITCHEN FACTORS

There are several other kitchen factors which must be kept in mind as we start to consider a remodeling project.

Lighting. Good lighting by both day and night is a most important consideration. If windows give adequate daytime lighting at the main preparation center, the situation is ideal. Sink and work counters are not necessarily placed directly under a window. However, they should be arranged so that the housewife does not work in a shadow.

There are many types of modern lighting fixtures to give well-distributed artificial illumination. Good overhead lighting is needed for general illumination. In addition, separate fixtures in each work area add to the comfort and efficiency of kitchens.

Electrical Convenience Outlets. When planning the lighting for kitchens, the available electrical outlets should be considered. With the ever-increasing use of electrical appliances, adequate wiring facilities are necessary in the modern kitchen.

It is best to plan the necessary electrical connections before the new installation is started. In some existing houses, an additional circuit may be required. This can be installed much more reasonably before other work is done. If future plans include major electrical appliances, such as a freezer, washing machine, or dishwasher, the electrical requirements of these should be considered and provided for in order to save future costs.

Future Plans. Since a modern kitchen is built to last a lifetime, future needs should be visualized. For example, a 27-inch base cabinet can be placed against a sink in order that an automatic dishwasher may be installed in its place at some future time. In the same manner, enough spaces near ranges and refrigerators can be planned so that larger models may be installed some time later without tearing out base or wall cabinets.

CABINET-TOP MATERIALS

Manufacturers of kitchen cabinets generally offer a selection of cabinet-top materials including such materials as Formica, linoleum, and maple wood. Any of these materials can be specified.

WALLS AND FLOORS

Since remodeled kitchens often become additional living rooms, as much thought should be given to the decorating of them as is given to decorating and planning other rooms in houses.

Walls. See Chapter 5 for suggested soilproof types of wall-surface materials.

Many plastic wall coverings, in the form of wallpaper, are also available in a great variety of patterns and colors. Such materials resist all types of staining and can be washed repeatedly.

Floors. See Chapter 6 for suggested floor coverings.

Coverings such as linoleum, asphalt tile, and plastic tile are colorful and easy to keep clean. They also offer a certain amount of resilience which helps to make them comfortable surfaces on which to stand.

SOFFITS

In Figure 6, the light band between the tops of wall cabinets and the ceiling is the soffit. In other words, the tops of the wall cabinets do not reach the ceiling and we must provide soffits to fill the intervening space.

Ordinarily, the tops of wall cabinets are about 7′ 0″ above the floor. Thus, in a kitchen area having an 8′ 0″ ceiling height, we would need soffits about 1′ 0″ deep. Ceiling heights vary and soffit depths differ accordingly. However, if a ceiling is more than 8′ 6″ above the floor, it should be lowered, as explained in Chapter 4. Otherwise, the new cabinets will make the room appear out of good proportion. Such a condition can be visualized by imagining that the soffit had been omitted in Figure 6.

The *A* part of Figure 14 shows a section view of a soffit built in an existing kitchen area. The framing is composed of 2 by 4′s and the sheathing is ¼-inch plywood.

The first step in the construction of such a soffit is to determine the distance that point *a* must be above the floor. This will vary according to the brand of steel or wood cabinets to be installed. Next, determine the required length of the soffit—how many cabinets (as indicated in Figure 6) it must cover. The widths of soffits also vary according to the brand of cabinets to be installed but are never much less or much more than 13 inches.

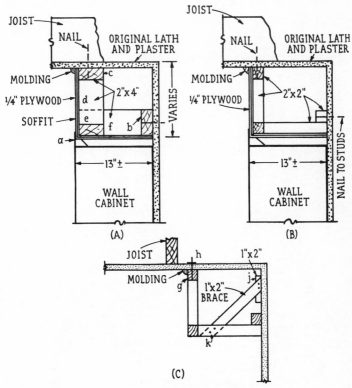

FIGURE 14. Details of soffit.

Nail the 2 by 4 marked *b* over the wall plaster, making sure that the 3½-inch nails are driven at locations where they will enter the studs. Nail the 2 by 4 marked *c* over the ceiling plaster, making sure that the nails are driven at locations where they will enter the joists.

Cut short pieces of 2 by 4 to fit at *d* between *c* and *e* pieces. These short pieces should be spaced 16 inches on centers. The pieces at *f* should be spaced 16 inches on centers, notched to fit over piece *e*, and nailed to piece *b*.

The plywood sheathing can be applied as explained in Chapter 5. Use a piece of molding where the plywood meets the ceiling.

The *B* part of the illustration indicates how 2 by 2's can be used for the framing.

Both the *A* and *B* parts of the illustration show the soffits at right angles to the ceiling joists. But, if soffits must be constructed on two adjacent sides of a kitchen area, the joists will be in a different position on one side.

The *C* part of the illustration indicates a case where the joists are parallel to the soffit and not spaced so that the piece marked *g* can be nailed to one of them. In a case like this several short pieces, such as the one marked *j*, should be nailed to the studding so that braces can be nailed to them. The other ends of the braces should be nailed to the lower framing member of the soffit, as shown at *k*. A few toggle or molly bolts (see Chapter 2), can be placed as shown at *h* to secure the piece *g* in proper position.

FIGURE 15. Hanging cabinets over an island.

HANGING CABINETS

Figure 15 shows an island composed of a range and a planning center. The cabinets above the island must be hung from the ceiling because they are away from the wall.

Figure 16 indicates one method by which off-wall cabinets (Figure 15) may be securely hung. The elevation view shows the wall line and

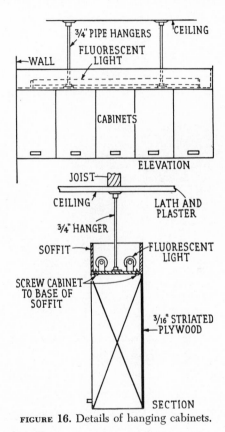

FIGURE 16. Details of hanging cabinets.

the two pipe hangers necessary. The section view indicates the construction of the soffit and the casing for the cabinets. Note that the tops of the pipe hangers must be so located that the fastening screws will penetrate a ceiling joist.

As shown in Figure 16, the soffit can be used to house indirect-lighting equipment, or it can be extended to the ceiling as indicated in Figure 15.

FILLER STRIPS

To make possible the installation of standard-sized wall and base cabinets in any kitchen area, regardless of its dimensions, filler strips of varying widths and heights are available. Such fillers create a finished appearance and do away with dust-catching gaps between cabinets. They are also valuable as a means of overcoming the difficulties caused by out-of-plumb structural details. Typical sizes and types are shown in Figure 17. A typical application is illustrated in Figure 24.

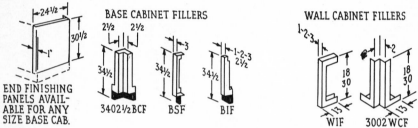

FIGURE 17. Base- and wall-cabinet filler strips.

KITCHEN-AREA REMODELING

The kitchen areas in most old houses are closely associated with pantries, laundry rooms, or back porches.

The pantries date back to an era prior to the introduction of useful storage cabinets. They are inconvenient to use, cause hundreds of extra steps, and are difficult to keep clean. In connection with modern kitchens, such spaces can be used otherwise and to much better advantage.

The laundry rooms also date back to an early era when hot water came from reservoirs in kitchen cook stoves and when "washing" was a major chore. Such rooms can now be used for other purposes and to much better advantage.

Back porches date back to a time when architects thought a great deal of "gingerbread" decoration added to the beauty of houses. In our modern way of life, we have no need for such porches.

In order to discuss the remodeling of old kitchens as a means of preparing them for modern equipment and to make them convenient and

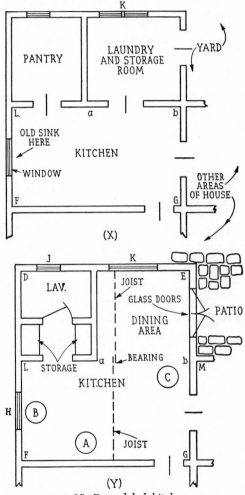

FIGURE 18. Remodeled kitchen area.

efficient, let us assume the floor plan shown in the X part of Figure 18. Let us further assume that the dimensions of the kitchen are approximately 8′ 0″ wide and 14′ 0″ long, that the pantry is about 6′ 0″ by 7′ 0″, and that the laundry room is close to 8′ 0″ by 7′ 0″.

The kitchen dimensions are ample, so far as the needs of modern equipment are concerned (see Figures 22 and 23). A modern sink can be placed in the same location as the old sink in order to save plumbing expense. Plumbing is an important item, so far as remodeling expense is concerned, and we should always try to use existing water pipes, vents, and sewer connections.

A first-floor lavatory, including a water closet and washbowl, is a handy addition to any old house. Part of the pantry space could be used for such a purpose. Plumbing connections are not far away. Thus, the new piping would not cost too much.

Because of the two doors which lead to other areas of the house, the corner of the kitchen where they are located cannot be used for a dining area. However, the old laundry room will not be needed as such and could therefore be converted into a pleasant dining area. The partition between a and b could be removed and the door enlarged so that the area could be closely associated with a new patio in the yard.

The Y part of the illustration indicates how the floor plan will appear after the remodeling previously discussed is completed.

The old pantry area has been transformed into a convenient lavatory and two spaces for large storage cabinets. The partition between a and b has been removed. Glass doors have been installed so that they afford a view of and open out into the new patio. A new single window has been installed at K. Windows H and J were not changed.

Work centers can be installed in the locations marked A, B, and C. The center at C can be a combination of range and snack bar, somewhat similar to the island center shown in the E part of Figure 4.

Structural Considerations. If the joists in the kitchen ceiling extend continuously from wall EG to wall DF, the removal of partition ab can be accomplished without complications. However, if shorter joists, such as the ones indicated by the dashed lines, have their bearing on partition ab, then a beam must be substituted for the partition.

The A part of Figure 19 shows how the partition ab supports the ends of such joists as indicated in the Y part of Figure 18. When the partition is removed, a beam such as shown in the B or C parts of Figure 19 must be used. Either of these beams will support the joists and will not extend below the ceiling surface. The ends of a beam, such as shown at B, must be supported by two 4 by 4 columns placed in each wall at a and b. The ends of a beam, such as shown at C, must be supported by one 4 by 4 column placed in each wall at a and b.

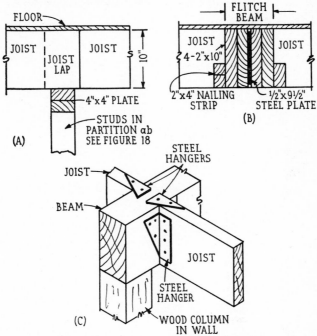

FIGURE 19. Details of joist support when bearing partitions are removed.

Before the partition can be removed and while the beam is being installed, the joists must be temporarily supported as explained in Chapter 7.

In order to install a new and wider door in the partition between E and M, as shown in the Y part of Figure 18, the old studs must be removed and a new rough frame for the door constructed, as indicated in Figure 20. If the joists run from wall DF to wall EG, their ends, over the door opening, must be temporarily supported while the new framing is being installed.

If balloon framing (studs continuous for two stories) is encountered, the header shown in Figure 20 must be extended to R and S.

In order to replace the two double-hung windows, shown at K in the

X part of Figure 18, with one large window, the old window frames can simply be removed and a new frame, having the same over-all dimensions, substituted for them.

The partition and door opening for the new lavatory should be constructed as shown in Figure 20, except that two 2 by 4's can be used instead of the 4 by 8 beam.

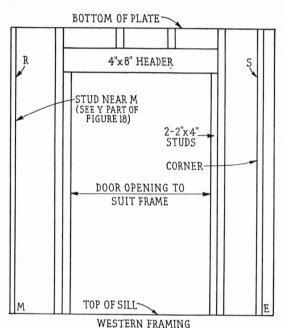

WESTERN FRAMING

FIGURE 20. Details of opening for new door in frame wall.

PRELIMINARY PLANNING

In the foregoing explanations, we discussed the remodeling of a kitchen area. However, the remodeling work did not change the size or shape of the kitchen proper. In such cases, all of the explanations in the balance of this chapter are next in regular order.

In cases where the sizes or shapes of old kitchens are to be changed, the planning order should be as shown in the following four steps, all of which are explained in this chapter under like headings:

1. Preliminary planning
2. Kitchen-area remodeling
3. How to plan a new kitchen
4. Financial considerations

Plan to Save Steps. Most of the kitchen time of the average housewife is spent either working at or walking between four major appliances: sink, range, refrigerator, and dishwasher. Therefore, they should be placed as close to each other as possible. However, adequate counter surface and storage room near these pieces of equipment should not be sacrificed. For economy in installation, the dishwasher should be placed next to the sink.

Where very large, old kitchens are to be remodeled, it is important to consider condensing the areas. The use of an island or peninsula, as indicated in the *E* part of Figure 4 or as suggested in connection with the *Y* part of Figure 18, tends to partition such areas effectively. Another arrangement is shown in Figure 15.

Plan for Convenience. Every housewife has her own way of doing things. Every family has peculiar likes and dislikes. Thus, kitchens should be planned to suit the convenience of all concerned.

Plan for Efficiency. Provide such equipment as will help to best advantage in all the work done in kitchens. Any housewife can write a list of the kitchen work she does and then make plans for her new kitchen accordingly.

Check Points. The following points will be of help in preliminary planning work:

1. Provide plenty of electric outlets for toasters, mixers, clocks, coffeemakers, etc.

2. Keep main work centers small but not confining.

3. Plan refrigerator locations so that their doors do not obstruct activities.

4. Do not stint on counter surfaces.

5. As nearly as possible, kitchen arrangements should be planned so that traffic stays out of main work centers.

6. Keep all accessories close to the point of their use.

7. Provide space for long-handled items.

8. Make sure that all necessary utensils and other small equipment can be stored when not in use.

9. Keep any known future requirements in mind and make provisions for them.

HOW TO PLAN A NEW KITCHEN

The following explanations relate to the planning or arrangement of appliances and cabinets within a kitchen area.

Such planning must be done in one of two ways, depending on whether the shape and size of the kitchen is *known* or *unknown*. For example, the shape and size of the kitchen indicated in Figure 18 is *known,* owing to the fact that the remodeling plans did not include changing the original dimensions. The shape of a kitchen would be *unknown* if remodeling plans included reducing the size of a very large old kitchen.

When the shape and size are *known,* we can plan the arrangement of appliances and cabinets without further consideration. When the shape and size are *unknown,* we must carry on such planning for *two* reasons: to determine the required shape and size and to determine arrangement.

Known Shape and Size. When we know the shape and size of a kitchen area, we can use the *template* or *drawing* method of planning the arrangement.

TEMPLATE METHOD. Once we have decided what appliances and cabinets we want in a new kitchen, this process consists of drawing a plan view of the kitchen to the ½″ = 1′ 0″ scale and also drawing plan views of all equipment and cabinets to the same scale on stiff paper or cardboard. We can then cut out such equipment and cabinet representations and move them around on the plan view of the kitchen. In this manner, we can try out any number of different arrangements until we find one that is satisfactory. Refrigerators and ranges should be separated from cabinets by 1-inch-wide spaces, dishwashers by ½-inch. Base- and wall-cabinet arrangements can be planned in this manner.

DRAWING METHOD. This process consists of drawing a plan view of the kitchen to the $\frac{1}{2}'' = 1'\ 0''$ scale and then drawing the plan views of the appliances and cabinets on the same drawing. Pieces of tissue paper can be placed over the first drawing and other trials made.

Unknown Shape and Size. When we do not know the shape and size a remodeled kitchen will have, the *drawing* method is best suited to the purpose.

Use the $\frac{1}{2}'' = 1'\ 0''$ scale to draw a partial plan view of the old kitchen. Select two walls, such as *FL* and *FG* in the *X* part of Figure 18, which are not likely to be changed. Then, by the use of tissue paper, make several trial arrangements of the desired appliances and cabinets. By this procedure, the minimum size of the kitchen and its shape can be determined. This is a most important part of the planning and must be done accurately. Otherwise, any one or more of several costly and disappointing mistakes could happen. This work is not at all difficult and anyone can accomplish it with ease.

PROBLEM 1. It can be assumed that we want the following appliances in a new kitchen: (NOTE: The cabinet numbers shown here are illustrated in Figure 13.)

Appliances:

    Refrigerator, 28 inches wide
    Range, 40 inches wide
    Sink, 24 inches long
    Dishwasher, 24 inches wide

Base Cabinets:

One 24C, 24 inches wide	One 45CB-R, 46 inches wide
One 27C, 27 inches wide	One 18D, 18 inches wide
One 45CB-L, 46 inches wide	One desk, 38 inches long

Wall Cabinets:

    One 3618W, 36 inches wide (to be used above refrigerator)
    One 2430W, 24 inches wide (to match 24C base cabinet)
    One 4218W, 42 inches wide (to be used above range)
    One 2730W, 21 inches wide

One 4230W, 42 inches wide

Three 3030W, each 30 inches wide

One 1330CS, 9 inches wide

It can also be assumed that the size and shape of the kitchen area is *known* and as shown in Figure 21. The problem is to plan the arrangement of the appliances and cabinets to suit our needs and convenience.

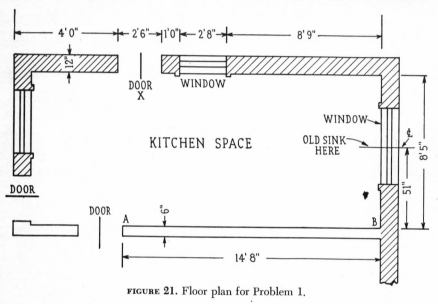

FIGURE 21. Floor plan for Problem 1.

SOLUTION. Our first inclination would probably be to place the refrigerator near to door X where it would be handy so far as incoming milk and other perishable groceries are concerned. However, there is a window next to the door on one side, and the space on the other side of it is obviously not suited for appliances or cabinets.

In order to take advantage of the existing plumbing, the new sink should be placed in the same position that the old one occupied. The new sink, however, should be placed to provide space for the dishwasher.

The corner cabinets should be placed in the corners next to the dishwasher and the sink.

The range and its two side cabinets require a total of more than 8 lineal feet and should therefore be placed along wall *AB*.

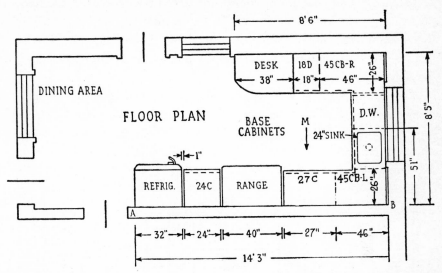

FIGURE 22. Final arrangement of appliances and base cabinets in answer to Problem 1.

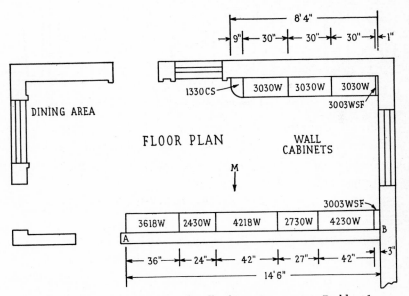

FIGURE 23. Final arrangement of wall cabinets in answer to Problem 1.

We can assume that after two or three trial drawings we decided upon the arrangement shown in Figure 22, which allows space for a nook or a table and chairs in one corner near the doors. The arrangement is good because all work centers are conveniently placed and because efficiency is possible.

The arrangement of wall cabinets can be planned by means of more trial drawings. The short cabinets, 4218W and 3618W, are to be placed over the range and the refrigerator. Other wall units can be placed where they will be convenient and according to their widths and the widths of base units directly under them.

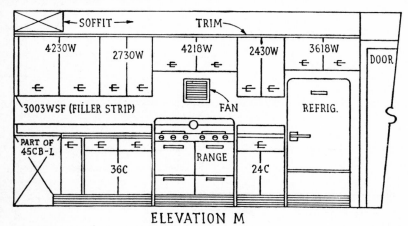

ELEVATION M

FIGURE 24. Elevation *A* in answer to Problem 1.

Figure 23 shows the final arrangement.

Figure 24 shows an elevation view of all the equipment as it is to be placed along wall *AB*. This view can be visualized if we imagine that we are standing at *M* in Figures 22 and 23.

Note that a filler strip is required to finish off one side of cabinet 4230W.

Note, too, that a soffit is indicated above all wall cabinets.

HOW TO INSTALL CABINETS

The following explanations and illustrations have to do with typical cabinet installation procedures. There are some variations so far as various brands are concerned, but for the most part, all procedures are similar.

Figure 25 shows placement dimensions for base and wall cabinets. These dimensions will be helpful in laying out cabinet positions. Note that the tops of wall cabinets should not be more than 82 inches above the floor.

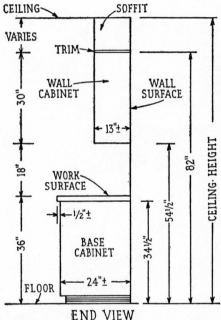

END VIEW

FIGURE 25. Cabinet-placement dimensions.

Fastening Cabinets to Walls. There are two methods of fastening cabinets to walls. Either method may be used for all ordinary installation work.

HANGER METHOD. Manufacturers supply steel hanger rods which can be fastened to studs by means of wood screws. The cabinets are then hung on the hangers. When masonry walls are encountered, the hangers must be attached to them by means of such masonry fasteners as explained in Chapter 2.

DIRECTLY TO STUDS. A somewhat less complicated method consists of screwing the cabinet backs directly to the studs. The screws should be long enough to go through the plaster and penetrate well into the studs.

Checking Walls. As old-fashioned cupboards are being removed from walls, the plaster should be checked to locate possible low spots. Wherever such irregularities exist, shims must be used so that the cabinets will be level and plumb. Figure 26 shows how a long straightedge can be used for the checking operation.

FIGURE 26. Checking wall irregularities in old kitchen.

Layout. After all old cupboards, the sink, and baseboards have been removed, the exact locations of the new cabinets and appliances should be outlined on the plaster as shown in Figure 27. The top line must be 82 inches above the floor (see Figure 25) and should be drawn with the help of a carpenter's level. Hold the level against the wall and draw the line along its top edge. The 82-inch dimension should be measured from the highest point on the floor. Note that the exact location of each appliance and cabinet is indicated by a rectangle and by its name or number. The locations should be carefully checked as a means of making absolutely sure that they are correct.

Installing Wall Cabinets. Wall cabinets should be installed first, beginning with corner units such as indicated in Figure 28. Place the hanger bars on top of the 82-inch line and screw them to the studs. If hangers are not being employed, drill holes through the cabinet backs and use 1½-inch No. 12 wood screws. Check the cabinet levelness and plumbness after only one screw has been put in. As each cabinet is installed next to a preceding one, put in the top screws (as indicated in the cabinets) only

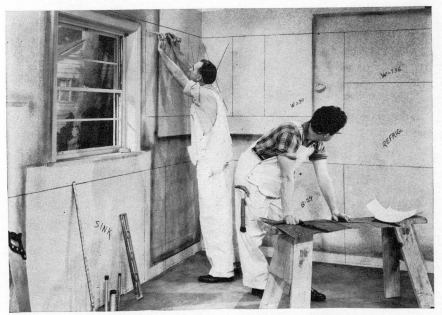

FIGURE 27. Marking locations of cabinets on walls.

and bolt the adjacent cabinet sides together. Follow this procedure until the location for the first filler strip, if one is needed, is reached. Fillers generally have four holes that line up with holes in the cabinets. The filler is attached to an adjacent cabinet as shown in Figure 29. After all wall cabinets have been hung, leveled, plumbed, and bolted together, insert bottom screws in the backs of them.

Installing Base Cabinets. As in the case of wall cabinets, corner base cabinets should be installed first in U- and L-shaped kitchens. Follow the same procedure as outlined for wall cabinets. Hold the cabinets in posi-

FIGURE 28. Corner cabinets should be installed first.

FIGURE 29. Installation of filler strip.

FIGURE 30. Installation of sink cabinet.

FIGURE 31. Complete installation.

tion so that their top edges are even with the chalk lines on the wall (note the 34½- and 36-inch dimensions in Figure 25). Drill holes in the cabinets where necessary to contact studding. Make sure that the cabinets are level and plumb. Use shims as may be required. Anchor all cabinets to studs using at least two 2-inch No. 10 wood screws, and bolt them together through their adjoining sides.

Installing Sink Cabinet. See Figure 30. To install the sink cabinets, remove the knockouts from the bottom so that the holes coincide with the locations of existing pipes, or make new holes as may be required. Set the cabinet level and plumb. Use shims where necessary.

Figure 31 shows the completed kitchen.

FINANCIAL CONSIDERATIONS

There are three ways in which remodeling may be carried on and paid for. Any one of them can be employed, depending upon homeowners' budgets and preferences.

Outright Payment. If a homeowner desires to pay the remodeling cost all at one time, the following procedures are recommended:

1. Do the planning as previously explained. Then make up drawings, such as indicated in Figures 22 and 23, which show all appliances and cabinets by name and number.

2. Take the drawings to two or more kitchen-cabinet dealers and ask them to make up an estimate of total cost including just the materials or materials and labor, as may be desired.

Unit-by-Unit Purchase. Some homeowners may prefer to buy and pay for one or more appliances or cabinets at a time and in that manner gradually accomplish the remodeling. In such cases, the following steps are recommended:

1. Do the planning as previously explained. Then make up drawings such as shown in Figures 22 and 23.

2. Ask a kitchen-cabinet dealer for an estimate of cost for each of the appliances and cabinets. Such an estimate will be helpful when planning a unit-by-unit installation.

The following unit-by-unit plan is based on Figures 22 and 23.

1. Buy and install the new sink, dishwasher, and sink cabinet first. These appliances constitute a basis for all other and later installations and they will be greatly enjoyed.

2. Next, install the 27C and 45CB-L units to complete one corner. The range and refrigerator can then be moved to their permanent locations and the base units for the *AB* wall will be mostly complete. Also, work surfaces will have been provided.

3. The 45CB-R and 18D units can be the next step. These units will provide more storage and counter surface.

4. The 24C unit can be added next because it provides a chopping and cutting surface.

5. The wall cabinets are less expensive than the base units and can be purchased in groups. For example, the three 3030W units can be installed next.

In like manner, the balance of the units can be purchased and installed as budgets permit. In the meantime, more and more convenience and efficiency are provided.

Extended Payment. If homeowners desire to install all of the appliances at one time and pay the total cost over an extended period, the following procedures are suggested:

1. Make up drawings as previously suggested.

2. Obtain estimates from kitchen-cabinet dealers.

The following financing plans are available in most regions of the country:

1. Remodeling loan from a bank.

2. Open-end mortgage. Remodeling cost added to an existing mortgage. Number of payments increased.

3. Open-end mortgage. This plan increases the size of monthly payments.

4. Refinanced mortgage. Many homeowners have paid off so much of

their original mortgage that the mortgagor will be interested in re-financing to include remodeling costs.

TYPICAL PROJECTS

The following projects can be made in home workshops. All required materials are easily available:

Serving Bar. Figure 32 shows the details for the serving bar indicated in the *F* part of Figure 4. Only 2 by 4's, ¼-inch-hardwood plywood and formica, or equivalent plastic laminate, are required.

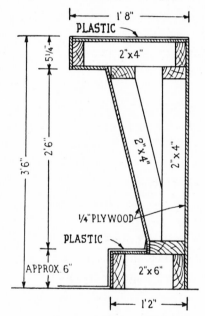

FIGURE 32. Details of serving bar.

Seat. The *A* part of Figure 33 shows the details for a corner seat which can be used along with a table in a dining area such as shown in Figure 22. The same details can be used to make a seat such as indicated in the

B part of Figure 33. Only 2 by 4's, ¼-inch hardwood plywood, 2-inch foamed rubber or plastic, and seat-cover material are required.

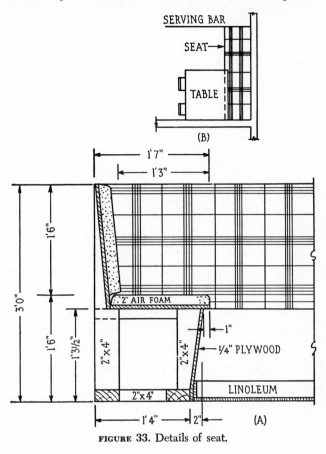

FIGURE 33. Details of seat.

CHAPTER NINE

Attics

It is surprising how the wasted space in attics can be transformed into efficient and attractive living areas to serve the needs of growing families and to make old houses suitable for our modern way of life.

Millions of old houses around the country were built during an era when popular design features included high roofs. Such houses are usually of sound construction and constitute economic advantages in terms of current building costs. The high roofs are generally irregular in shape, but large attic spaces are available for remodeling purposes.

In order to visualize remodeling possibilities and to see how various roof and attic shapes can be used to advantage, we shall briefly study a few examples.

The upper part of Figure 1 shows part of the attic space in connection with an L-shaped house. The entrance to the space is located on the left-hand side but is not visible in the picture.

The sloped roof is partially supported and held in position by means of vertical 2 by 4 studs and by horizontal 1 by 5 collar beams. The space is amply long and wide. Three windows assure enough light and ventilation. The distance between the collar beams and the floor constitutes a satisfactory ceiling height. Therefore, the space is ideal for remodeling purposes.

The lower part of the illustration shows the same attic space after it was transformed into a small apartment. Every foot of available space was used. An efficient but compact kitchen was built into one wall. Space for a bed-type couch was provided in a picture alcove. A com-

FIGURE 1

FIGURE 2

FIGURE 3

bination desk and dressing table was built into another wall. The sloping part of the ceiling was made attractive by means of a dark-colored fascia board and light-colored tile. The remodeled area is completely modern and a worthwhile addition to the house. Such an apartment may be used by a young couple or by elderly members of a family.

The upper part of Figure 2 shows an attic space under an exceptionally high valley-type roof. The lower part of the same illustration shows the results obtained by the erection of a lower ceiling and knee walls. Such an area is ideal for recreation and hobby purposes.

The upper part of Figure 3 shows an attic space under a gable and valley roof. The lower part of the same illustration proves that such a space can be transformed into a pleasant bedroom.

Remodeling an attic is an interesting and rewarding project that can be accomplished at reasonable cost. This chapter proposes to outline the items relating to attics which require careful consideration and to explain typical examples of the planning and structural work required.

REASONS FOR REMODELING

The items listed in the following summary constitute practical reasons for attic remodeling:

1. Separate bedrooms for growing children
2. Recreation area for small children
3. Secluded and quiet apartment for elderly members of a family
4. A second bathroom
5. A music or hobby room
6. A study or office for the man of a family
7. Rentable space
8. Additional and clean storage space
9. A sewing room

REMODELING CONSIDERATIONS

Inexperienced mechanics and homeowners are apt to do a great deal of preliminary planning and thinking without taking into consideration several aspects of cost or allied work. This is a common mistake that always leads to unexpected expense, delays, and probable disappointment. As a means of helping readers to avoid such a mistake, the following summary of preliminary considerations is set forth:

Dormers. In many instances, attic spaces do not have enough windows to provide ample light and proper ventilation, especially when partitions are employed to create more than one room. For example, let us assume that the *V* part of Figure 4 shows the plan view of a typical attic space. Two small windows are indicated, one at either end of the space. The *W* part of the illustration indicates a possible remodeling plan that includes two rooms with a hall between them. Both rooms would be adequately lighted, but unless all of the doors were kept open, proper ventilation could not be possible. Good ventilation is of great importance in attic rooms, owing to the fact that appreciable summer heat gets through even well-insulated roofs.

In order to provide the necessary light and ventilation in such cases, additional windows must be provided. This is accomplished by means of *dormers.*

TYPES OF DORMERS. The *X* part of Figure 4 illustrates what is called a *continuous dormer.* Two or more windows can be installed, depending upon the length of a house. This type of dormer can also be constructed so that the top of its roof, as shown at *m,* intersects the main ridge of the house, as indicated at *n.* Also, the vertical wall, as shown at *t,* can be extended to the vertical plane of the main house wall indicated at *r.* In like manner, the gables of the dormer, as shown at *x,* can be extended to the same vertical plane as the main gable shown at *y.* Such a dormer tends to detract from the exterior appearance of a house and should therefore be constructed only on the rear elevation.

The *Y* part of Figure 4 illustrates what are called *individual dormers.* Depending upon the length of a house, as from *a* to *b,* two or more such dormers can be constructed to provide as many windows. This type of dormer can be constructed on either the front or the rear elevation of a house.

As indicated by *GHJ* in the *Z* part of the illustration, the shape of an attic space is triangular when a gable roof is involved. Near the walls, as at *G* and *H*, the roof is so close to the floor that part of the space, such as between *G* and *L*, is not usable. As shown at *EF*, knee walls are therefore necessary. Thus, the usable space is bounded by the letters *L K C D E F*. If an extended, continuous dormer is constructed, the usable space will be

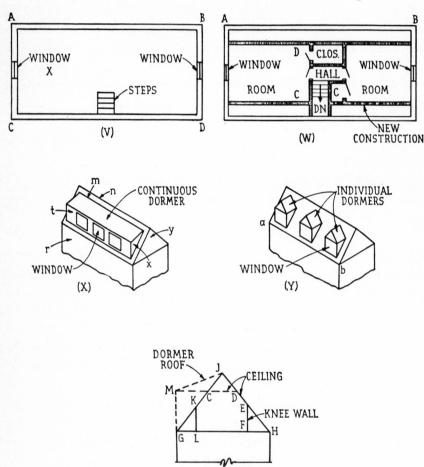

FIGURE 4. Types of dormers.

increased to that bounded by the letters *G M C D E F*. Such a dormer could be constructed on the *AB* side of the plan shown on the *W* part of the illustration to provide more space, light, and air for both rooms.

Individual dormers do not provide an appreciable increase in usable space.

Dormers of both types are expensive, unless a homeowner plans to eliminate labor cost by doing the work himself.

Area of Attic Space. Unless an attic space, such as bounded by the letters *L K C D E F* in the *Z* part of Figure 4, has an area equal to that of an average-sized room, remodeling is not recommended.

The probable area of remodeled attic space can be estimated by assuming that knee walls should not be less than 4 feet high. Hold a tape measure at vertical points along a rafter until a length of it 4 feet long just touches the floor. This will locate the knee-wall positions. The distance between such walls multiplied by the length of the attic will give the probable area. This area can be compared with the area of an average-sized room.

The width of a remodeled attic area, such as between *L* and *F*, should be at least 10 feet. If the width is less, the area cannot be used to good advantage so far as furniture is concerned.

After estimating the positions of knee walls, it is wise to make a fairly accurate drawing. Use the $\frac{1}{8}'' = 1' \ 0''$ scale. Then, as explained in Chapter 8, cut out templates representing required furniture. Place the templates on the drawing to determine if the available space is ample.

Ceiling Height. Most gable roofs require collar beams such as shown in the upper part of Figure 1 and by *CD* in the *Z* part of Figure 4. Such structural members should not be moved.

Unless the distance between the bottom edges of the collar beams and the floor is at least 7' 6", the space is not suitable for remodeling.

In cases where the bottom edges of the collar beams are more than 9' 0" above the floor, a new ceiling exactly 8' 0" above the floor is recommended. Figure 5 shows an assumed case where the bottom edges of the collar beams are 10' 0" above the attic floor. As indicated, new ceiling joists can be erected so that the ceiling will be 8' 0" above the floor. This ceiling height creates much better room proportions and allows the use of standard-length wall planks and panels.

If the distance from *A* to *B* is not over 15' 0", 2 by 4's can be used as joists. They should be spaced the same distance apart as the rafters. Nail them at both ends to the rafters. As each joist is erected, measure the distance above the floor and use a level so that all joists will be in the same horizontal plane. Nail two continuous 1 by 4's along the top edges of the joists to stiffen them.

If the distance from *A* to *B* is more than 15' 0", 2 by 6's should be used as joists.

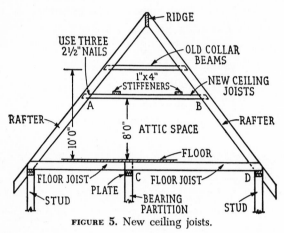

FIGURE 5. New ceiling joists.

SIZE OF FLOOR JOISTS. In most houses, attic floor joists are supported at one end by means of a bearing partition somewhat as indicated in Figure 5. The distance from *C* to *D* is called the *span* of the joists.

It is not uncommon to encounter instances where 2 by 4's are used as attic floor joists. However, when such spaces are to be used as living areas,

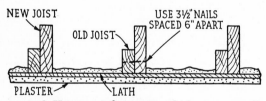

FIGURE 6. How to reinforce joists which are too small.

2 by 4 joists are too small and are not permitted by city building codes. Thus, they must be reinforced as indicated in Figure 6.

When spans do not exceed 12 feet, 2 by 6's may be used as reinforcement. For spans ranging from 12 to 16 feet, 2 by 8's are recommended. For longer spans, 2 by 10's should be used.

To install the new joists, scrape away enough of the plaster keys so that the joists contact the lathing. This scraping must be done with care so as to avoid cracking the ceiling plaster. Nail the new joists to the old ones using 3½-inch nails spaced no more than 12 inches apart. Make sure that the ends of the new joists are properly seated on the bearing surfaces, such as shown at *C* and *D* in Figure 5.

If joists of any size are spaced more than 16 inches on centers, additional joists must be placed between the old ones so that the floor boards do not have a span of more than 15 inches between joists.

Condition of Roofing. Existing roofing materials, such as shingles, should be inspected to make sure that no roof leaks are possible. Once an attic space is remodeled and decorated, even small roof leaks could raise havoc.

A leak in a shingle roof can be located by examination of the attic side during the time rain is falling. The point where water drips may not be at the leak, for water will often run for long distances along rafters before falling. The path of the water should be traced back to the leak.

A leak from a shingle that is split, or otherwise defective, can be closed with a piece of single-ply tar paper. Raise the end of the defective shingle slightly, using a putty knife, and slip the paper under it. Paste the paper in place by means of roofing cement.

A badly curled shingle should be flattened by splitting, a piece of tar paper placed beneath the split, and the parts of the shingle nailed through its exposed ends, using rustproof shingle nails.

Reroofing. When shingles are in obviously bad condition, reroofing is a logical procedure. This will avoid any possibilities of trouble in the future and give a house a smart, sleek appearance. New asphalt shingles can be applied directly over the old shingles.

Where old wood shingles are involved, the reroofing procedure is as follows.

1. Redrive all protruding nails.

2. Add new nails where necessary to fasten all of the old shingles securely. This is an important part of the work and must be done thoroughly.

3. Slit all curled shingles and nail down the parts.

4. Replace missing shingles with new ones.

5. As indicated in Figure 7, cut back the old shingles at the eaves far enough to permit the application of a 1- by 4-inch wood edging. This board is not shown in the illustration but is under the metal drip edge. Nail the edging firmly to the existing roof boards so that its outside edge projects beyond the edge of the roof boards the same distance that the old wood shingles did.

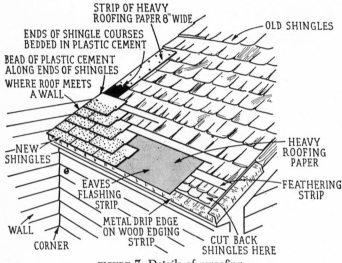

FIGURE 7. Details of reroofing.

6. Apply pieces of beveled siding, as feathering strips. This procedure assures a smooth and practically level surface on which to apply the new shingles.

7. Nail the metal drip edge in the positions shown in the illustration.

8. Nail the eaves flashing strip over the old shingles as indicated. This strip should be at least 12 inches wide.

9. Apply heavy roofing paper along valleys. For this purpose the paper should be at least 24 inches wide.

10. In cases where a roof intersects a wall, apply a strip of heavy roofing paper, as indicated in the illustration.

11. Apply the new shingles as recommended by the manufacturer. Use rustproof nails which are at least 1¾ inches long.

If an old, badly weathered asphalt-shingle roof is being re-covered, nail down or cut away all loose shingles; remove or redrive all loose and protruding nails, and remove all badly worn edging strips and replace them with new ones.

When asphalt shingles are to be laid on top of old roll roofing, these three steps are recommended:

1. Slit all buckles and nail the segments down smoothly.

2. Remove all loose and protruding nails.

3. If some of the old roofing has been torn away to expose the deck, inspect exposed deck areas carefully for loose or pitchy knots and excessively resinous areas. Cover any defects with sheet-metal patches made from galvanized iron, painted tin, zinc, or copper, approximately 26 gage.

Regardless of the kind of old roofing being prepared for asphalt shingles, the last step is to sweep the roof thoroughly clean of debris. A smooth, sound deck surface is a basic requirement for fully satisfactory asphalt-shingle application.

Climbing Suggestions. No climbing should be done without the type of ladders recommended by the American Ladder Institute and the National Safety Council. Lightweight extension ladders may be used for practically all purposes on one- and two-story houses. They are available in wood and lightweight metal.

When using an extension ladder against a house, the foot of it should be placed away from the house a distance equal to one-fourth the length of the ladder, as shown at Z in Figure 8. For example, if a house is 16 feet high, the foot of the ladder, *d*, should be placed a distance *ad*, or 4 feet, from the wall of the house. The ladder height should be adjusted to at least 20 feet, or 4 feet longer than the height it is to reach.

If possible, the top of a ladder, such as shown at C in the Z part of the illustration, should reach about 3 feet above the corner of the roof. Never try to get on a ladder that reaches only to or below a cornice.

As shown at W, a so-called chicken ladder should be made and used to reach various parts of a roof. A ridge piece, such as shown in the X part of the illustration, should hook over the ridge of the roof. The X part of the illustration also shows how the rails of the chicken ladder should be nailed or screwed to the 2 by 6 ridge piece. An extension ladder and a chicken ladder may be moved from place to place where roof work is required.

Make sure that the rails (feet) of a ladder are level. The *Y* part of the illustration shows how a block of wood can be used to assure safety.

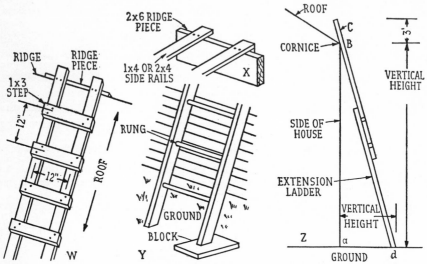

FIGURE 8. Proper use of climbing equipment.

Stairs. The importance of stairs should not be overlooked at the time remodeling is being considered. This one item will have a great deal to do with the enjoyment and use of remodeled attic space.

It is not uncommon to encounter attic stairs which are steep and difficult to walk up or down. Such stairs may have narrow treads and high risers both of which pose a definite hazard.

Figure 9 shows recommended dimensions for attic stairs. To be safe, the treads on such stairs should be at least 10 inches wide. The risers should be about 7½ inches high. Headroom should be no less than 6½ feet so that people of average height will not bump their heads at *A*. If treads are less than 10 inches wide or if risers are much more than 8 inches high, stairs are difficult to use and somewhat dangerous.

Unless attic stairways are at least 2½ feet wide, the movement of furniture up or down them is likely to be either difficult or impossible.

In most cases, attic stairs cannot be rebuilt without seriously disturbing surrounding partitions, joists, studs, or other structural details. Therefore, rebuilding is not recommended.

Readers are urged to study their attic stairs in the light of the foregoing explanations and to decide for themselves if the stairs are suitable and safe.

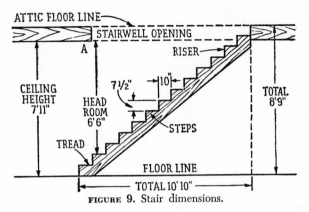

FIGURE 9. Stair dimensions.

Disappearing Stairs. In extreme cases where attic steps do not exist, disappearing (folding) stairs may be installed in openings cut into and between attic-floor joists. When not in use, such stairs can be folded into the opening where they are out of the way and out of sight.

Such stairs may be purchased in ready-built assemblies, ready for installation. They can be installed so that they unfold into halls or at other convenient locations.

Heating. The heating of remodeled attic space constitutes another problem that must be given careful attention before final remodeling plans are made. In order to illustrate the problem, we shall assume a one-story house.

The *X* part of Figure 10 indicates how either gravity ducts, starting at *B*, or forced-air ducts, starting at *A,* would have to be installed in partitions to reach the grilles or registers in the attic space. In this case, the first-floor and attic partitions are in the same vertical plane. In order to provide space for the ducts in the sills and plate, portions of partitions and floors would have to be torn out. Such a process is difficult and the patched partitions and floors forever after exhibit the scars.

The *Y* part of the illustration indicates an even more difficult situation that is encountered when attic partitions are not in the same vertical plane as first-floor partitions. A section of attic floor would have to be removed all in addition to the other work previously mentioned.

In either of the foregoing situations, duct installation is difficult and expensive. A better, easier, and less expensive procedure would be to install gas heaters, of the wall type, in the rooms of a remodeled attic. Gas lines could be installed without too much difficulty and the necessary vents could be extended through the roof. In regions where electricity

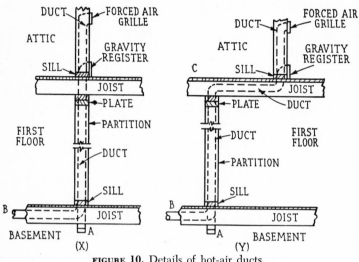

FIGURE 10. Details of hot-air ducts.

is not expensive, electric heaters could be used to advantage. Or, window-type air conditioners of the type that supply both heated and cooled air could be used.

Insulation. In Chapter 3, there is a full explanation of insulation as applied to remodeled attic spaces.

Chimneys. There are several aspects of chimneys which should be given careful consideration before final remodeling plans are completed.

LOCATION. The location of a chimney may have an important influence on attic remodeling. For example, suppose that a chimney is located at the point indicated by X in the V part of Figure 4. Such a location would make part of the plan shown in the W part of Figure 4 impossible. Therefore, it is wise to measure the size and location of a chimney and to keep such dimensions in mind.

FLASHING. The flashing around a chimney could be rusted or in otherwise bad condition to the extent that some leaking takes place during heavy rainstorms. Such leaking might not be serious enough to have caused concern prior to the time remodeling was contemplated. How-

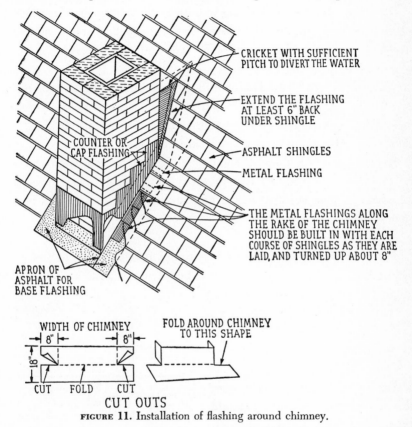

FIGURE 11. Installation of flashing around chimney.

ever, even small leaks would ruin the ceiling and wall-surface materials in a remodeled area. Therefore, all flashing should be examined, and if necessary reflashed.

Figure 11 illustrates typical flashing around a chimney. To reflash a chimney, the procedure is as follows:

1. Cut two pieces of metal flashing about 18 inches wide and long enough to bend back to fit the sides of the chimney. The length will

depend on the width of the chimney. These are known as the front-apron and rear-base flashing.

2. Imbed these pieces in roofing cement and nail into place.

3. Step-flash the sides with metal flashing or with metal shingles cut and bent so that they will extend under each course of shingles at the lower end and also into the mortar joints in the chimney.

SWEATING. If a masonry chimney is used as a vent for gas-fired heating equipment, it is quite likely to sweat unless metal flue linings have been installed. Such sweating would ruin wall and ceiling-surface materials in a remodeled area.

MORTAR JOINTS. The National Board of Fire Underwriters recommends that the mortar joints in old brick and concrete-block chimneys should be examined to make sure that they are completely filled with mortar and that the mortar is not cracked or loose.

If joint mortar is loose, it should be scraped out and replaced with new mortar composed of 1 part portland cement and 3 parts clean sand. Moisten the joint surfaces before applying the new mortar and be sure that each joint is completely filled.

Joist Direction. If attic-floor joists are not at right angles to new partitions, 2 by 4 headers must be nailed between the joists as indicated in Figure 12. The headers should be toenailed to the joists using two 3-inch nails on each side and at each end of the headers.

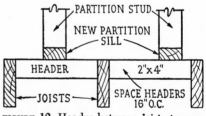

FIGURE 12. Header between joists to support new partition.

Subflooring. All of the floor area involved in remodeling should be covered with a subfloor composed of boards which have a thickness of at least ⅝ inch. Such flooring should be nailed to the joists as suggested in Chapter 2. The nailing is important as a means of preventing floor squeaks.

Dormer Flashing. On some dormers an apron at the bottom and a valley on the roof, as well as side flashing are required (see Figure 13).

The metal apron flashing shown at *A* on the dormer is placed after the shingle course, shown at 1, has been placed. This is followed by placing shingle course 2 and the flashing or shingle tin *B* against the wall. Shingle tins measure about 5 by 7 inches over-all and must be bent at right angles so as to fit tightly against the dormer wall and the roof. Shingle course 3 is then laid and shingle tin *C* placed on top of it. In this manner, each shingle tin is covered by a shingle course. This will cause water to run down on top of the shingle course below.

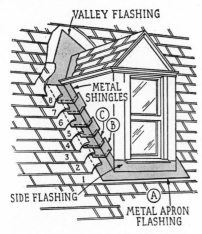

FIGURE 13. Flashing around dormer window.

After shingle course 8 has been placed, the valley flashing for the roof is fastened into position and the shingling is continued in the same manner as for any roof valley. On the dormer side wall the wood covering will overlap the wall flashing. To ensure drying, the wood covering of the dormer should be cut short enough so that about 1 inch of the metal flashing will be exposed where the dormer meets the roof.

Plumbing. When attic remodeling is being contemplated, an additional bathroom is often one of the desired features. However, the following facts should be understood and kept in mind.

In an average house, the kitchen and bathroom are so situated that all of the plumbing fixtures in both rooms can be served by one soil stack. In other words, there is a mutual partition between the two rooms in which one soil stack is located.

Unless it is possible to plan the position of an additional bathroom so that the plumbing fixtures in it can be conveniently connected to an existing soil stack, a *great deal* of extra labor and material expense will be involved.

In many cities and towns all plumbing installations are subject to strict plumbing codes. Such codes should be studied before any plans for new bathrooms are made.

HOW TO PLAN AND DO ATTIC REMODELING

The following problems and their solutions are typical examples of the visualization, planning, and construction work involved in attic remodeling. We shall make a few assumptions and then discuss the necessary procedures.

PROBLEM 1. It can be assumed that we are going to remodel the attic space of a rectangularly shaped house and that the requirements include two bedrooms, closet space, and individual dormers.

SOLUTION. The various parts of the solution are explained under the following headings all of which are set forth in the order of proper procedure.

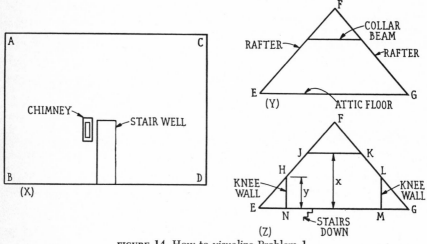

FIGURE 14. How to visualize Problem 1.

HOW TO VISUALIZE THE AVAILABLE SPACE. The first step consists of drawing a single-line sketch such as shown in the X part of Figure 14. This sketch should be drawn to scale and indicate the outline of the house ($ABCD$) and the stair and chimney locations.

The second step consists of drawing a single-line section view such as shown in the Y part of the illustration. This sketch should indicate the shape of the attic space (EFG) and the location of the collar beams.

The third step consists of drawing in the knee walls as shown in the Z

part of the illustration. The shape of the available space can now be visualized. It is bounded by the letters *NHJKLM*. The ceiling and knee-wall heights should be indicated at *x* and *y*. At this stage of the planning, we can scale our single-line sketches to determine all of the dimensions in connection with the length and general shape of the available space.

HOW TO VISUALIZE CONSTRUCTION. In order accurately to visualize the structural details involved, it is good practice to draw a section view such as shown in Figure 15. This view should show the floor, the rafters,

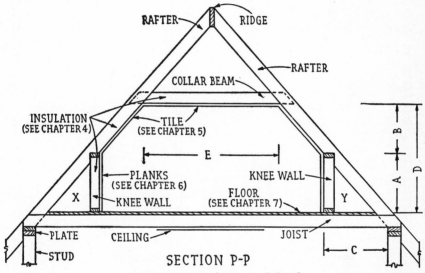

FIGURE 15. Principal structural details.

the knee walls, and the collar beams. The drawing provides a better picture of the space and helps in other planning. Actual dimensions should be shown at *A, B, C, D,* and *E*.

PRELIMINARY PLAN VIEW. Using the data obtained from Figures 14 and 15, we can now draw a preliminary floor plan of the space. In Figure 16, the *ABCD* space is the same as shown in the *X* part of Figure 14. The main walls of the house should be indicated as shown at *r, t, x,* and *y*. The stairwell and chimney should also be indicated. Dormers should be spaced so that they constitute good proportion so far as the elevation view of the house is concerned. We shall try them as shown. The floors of the dormer spaces should be flush with the main floor and their walls should be indicated in the same manner as other walls. The depth m depends upon the type of dormer construction to be used. See subsequent illustrations.

Now that the preliminary floor plan is complete, we can study it and discuss the revised plan to be made from it.

Obviously, the bedrooms should be located at E and F. In order to provide privacy for such rooms, some sort of a hall should be planned in

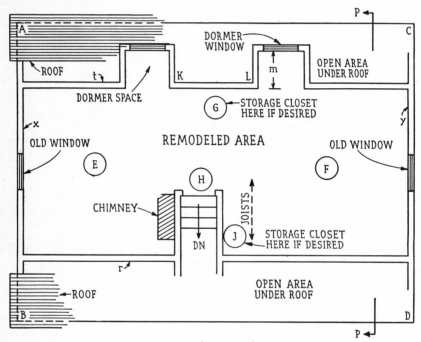

FIGURE 16. Preliminary plan view.

connection with the space at the head of the stairs near H. The hall should be at least 4′ 0″ wide. A closet can be planned near G, in the dark space between the two bedrooms. It should be at least 3′ 0″ wide. After scaling the width of the plan view, we can assume that there is enough space for the hall and the closet. However, if the closet is located along wall KL, its left-hand end wall will not line up with the left-hand wall of the stairwell. Therefore, the dormer locations must be changed.

REVISED PLAN VIEW. Figure 17 shows the revised plan view. The dormer locations have been changed, without destroying good propor-

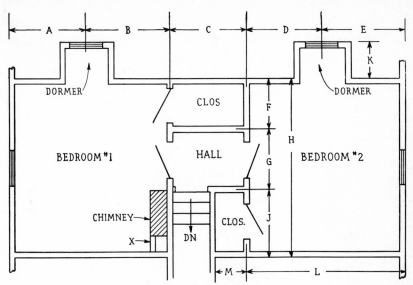

FIGURE 17. Revised plan view.

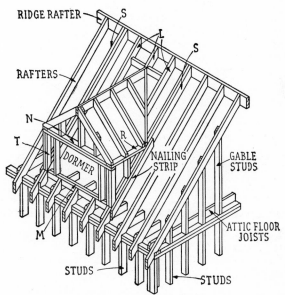

FIGURE 18. Typical dormer construction for small windows.

tion, and the hall and closets are indicated. This constitutes a satisfactory plan. Notice that the short partition shown at *X* eliminates the small corner alongside of the chimney. In an actual remodeling project, accurate dimensions should be shown at *A, B, C, D,* etc.

Typical Dormer Construction. Figure 18 shows the structural details for a dormer in which a small window is to be installed. The height of the

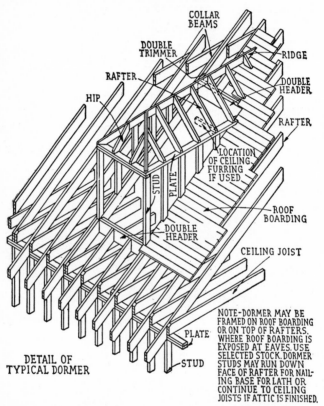

COLLAR BEAMS

DOUBLE TRIMMER

RIDGE

RAFTER

DOUBLE HEADER

HIP

RAFTER

LOCATION OF CEILING FURRING IF USED

STUD

PLATE

ROOF BOARDING

DOUBLE HEADER

CEILING JOIST

PLATE

NOTE—DORMER MAY BE FRAMED ON ROOF BOARDING OR ON TOP OF RAFTERS. WHERE ROOF BOARDING IS EXPOSED AT EAVES. USE SELECTED STOCK. DORMER STUDS MAY RUN DOWN FACE OF RAFTER FOR NAILING BASE FOR LATH OR CONTINUE TO CEILING JOISTS IF ATTIC IS FINISHED.

STUD

DETAIL OF TYPICAL DORMER

FIGURE 19. Typical dormer construction for large windows.

studs at *T* depends upon the exact height required for the window frame. The length of the plate *R* depends upon the horizontal and level distance between the stud corner post and the double rafter *S.*

To construct such a dormer in an existing roof, the roofing and roof boards must be removed around the area of the opening. Then the original rafters, marked *L,* must be taken out. The rafters marked *S* are

doubled. The header at *M* can then be nailed into place. Next, the front
studs and corner posts, such as at *T*, can be erected. The plate *N* can be
installed next. The balance of the work is obvious. All pieces are cut to
fit as the assembly is erected. Roof boards can be replaced on the main
roof and applied to the roof of the dormer. The sides of the dormer can
be sheathed the same as regular exterior walls.

On the inside of the dormer, ceiling joists can be installed. Studs can
then be placed under the double rafters to complete the framing.

Figure 19 shows the structural details for a dormer in which a window
of ordinary height can be installed. The general construction procedure
is the same as previously explained.

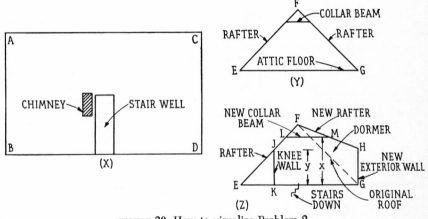

FIGURE 20. How to visualize Problem 2.

PROBLEM 2. It can be assumed that we are going to remodel the
attic space of a house which has considerably less width than the house
specified in Problem 1. The remodeling requirements include: two
bedrooms, two closets, and a bathroom.

SOLUTION. We shall assume that an extended, continuous dormer is
to be constructed in order to provide more usable space.

HOW TO VISUALIZE THE AVAILABLE SPACE. We shall also assume that
the *X*, *Y*, and *Z* parts of Figure 20 were drawn somewhat as explained
for similar single-line drawings in the solution to Problem 1. In the *Z*
part, the dashed line *FG* indicates the original roof and the letters *FMHG*
outline the dormer. The shape of the available space is bounded by the
letters *KJLMHG*.

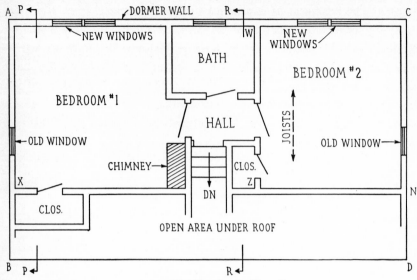

FIGURE 21. Plan for Problem 2.

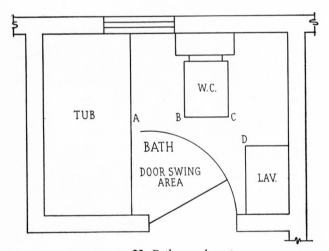

FIGURE 22. Bathroom layout.

FLOOR PLAN. Figure 21 shows what we can think of as the revised floor plan. As explained in the solution to Problem 1, such a plan should be the result of a preliminary plan and careful study. Note that the dormer contains five new windows, that two closets have been provided, that a hall separates the two bedrooms, and that space for a bathroom

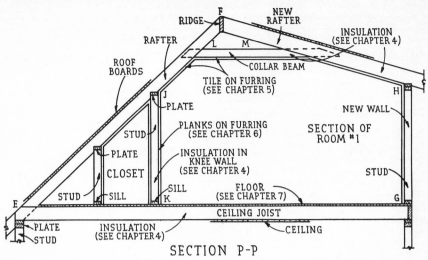

SECTION P-P

FIGURE 23. Structural details in connection with section *P-P* of Figure 21.

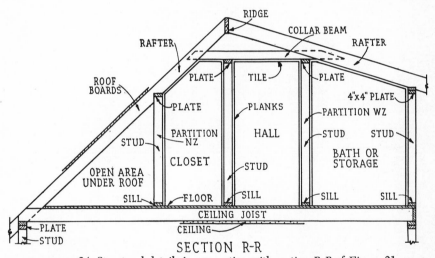

SECTION R-R

FIGURE 24. Structural details in connection with section *R-R* of Figure 21.

is possible. In an actual plan of this kind, all major dimensions should be shown.

BATHROOM SPACE. In order to make sure that the bathroom space is large enough to accommodate a bathtub of at least 5 feet, a standard water closet, and a lavatory of convenient size, a drawing such as shown in Figure 22 should be prepared. Use the ¾″ = 1′ 0″ scale.

Several such drawings may have to be prepared before a suitable arrangement is found. It should be kept in mind that distances between fixtures, such as indicated at *AB* and *CD*, must be sufficient to allow easy access around them. The door-swing area must also be kept in mind.

If the planned space proves to be too small, the floor plan will have to be studied and changed accordingly.

STRUCTURAL DETAILS. If we imagine that the attic space can be cut through along the *P-P* and *R-R* cutting lines shown in Figure 21, and

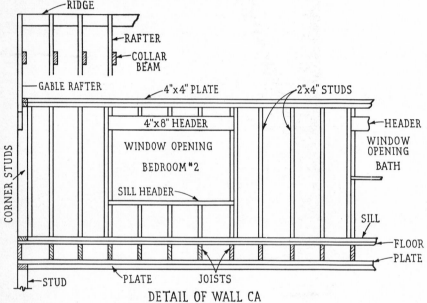

DETAIL OF WALL CA

FIGURE 25. Details of wall *CA* shown in Figure 21.

that we can look at the cut surfaces, we can then "see" the section views illustrated in Figures 23 and 24. Such views should be drawn because they help us to visualize the required structural details and because they serve to check the partitions indicated in the plan views. The views also serve as a construction guide.

Figure 25 shows the structural details for part of the wall indicated by *CA* in Figure 21. Drawings of this kind should be prepared because they are helpful when planning the studs, the plate, the sill, and the framing around window openings. (NOTE: The size and types of headers used should conform to local building codes.)

Figure 26 shows the structural details for the partition indicated by *WZ* in Figure 21. Such drawings are helpful in planning the studs, the sill, and the framing around door openings. Note that three-member corner assemblies are necessary at *A, B, C,* and *D,* where other partitions and walls are intersected.

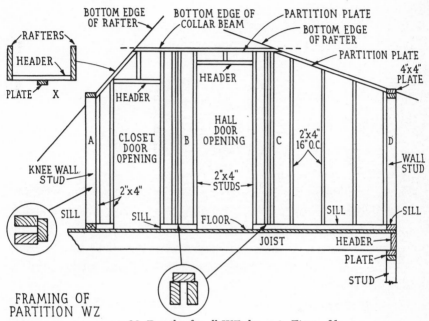

FIGURE 26. Details of wall WZ shown in Figure 21.

The door-opening heights are controlled by the rafters and collar beams. Therefore, stock doors to suit the conditions should be selected and the framing around the openings planned accordingly.

The reader is referred to *Plan Reading for Home Builders,* by the author, and *Practical House Carpentry,* by J. Douglas Wilson, both companion volumes to this one and published by the McGraw-Hill Book Company, Inc.

CHAPTER TEN

Bathrooms

Bathrooms, like basements and kitchens, have gone through many years of interesting development.

Our grandfathers can remember an era when "plumbing facilities" consisted of backyard installations and when bathing was confined to laundry tubs beside kitchen cookstoves. Few, if any, houses had any provisions for what we now call bathrooms. Plumbing fixtures were unheard of and washbasins were kept in bedrooms and kitchens for the purpose of washing hands and faces.

As cities grew in population, municipal water supplies and sewage disposal were seen to be essential for the prevention of various epidemics. With the advent of the first water mains and sewers, quaint ancestors of our present-day plumbing fixtures made their appearances. Bathtubs were constructed mostly of wood, but had sheet-metal linings. They were unsanitary, inconvenient, and ugly. Other fixtures, including high-tank water closets, were just as crude. However, some progress had been made, and bathrooms became regular parts of many houses.

As time went on, manufacturers took more interest in fixture design, especially from the sanitary standpoint. They produced all-metal and enameled equipment such as shown in the upper part of Figure 1. However, bathrooms were drab and unpleasant areas. Pipes were visible, lighting was crude, and decoration had not been given much thought.

Before long, further improvements in fixture designs came about and more attention was given to the decoration of walls and floors in bath-

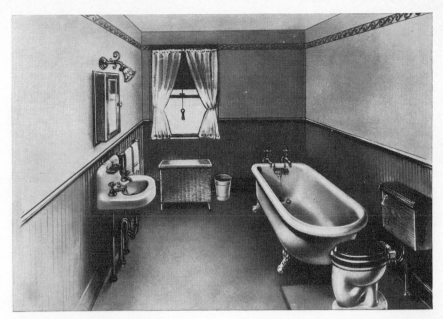

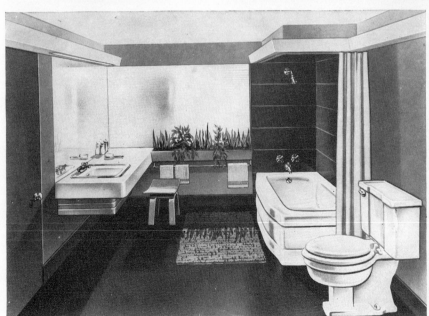

FIGURE 1

FIGURE 2

rooms. The upper part of Figure 2 illustrates some of the changes. Yet, bathrooms were still inconvenient, unpleasant, and difficult to keep clean.

Over the years tremendous strides have been made in the design of bathroom fixtures and other equipment. In keeping with such progress, bathrooms have also been improved to the point where they are beautiful, functional, adequate, and easy to maintain in sanitary conditions. The lower parts of Figure 1 and 2 indicate some of the improvements we can accomplish by remodeling.

Many old houses are still without bathrooms, and a great number have old-fashioned bathrooms which are inconvenient, inadequate, un-pleasant, and unsanitary. This chapter proposes to outline the items relating to modern bathrooms which require careful consideration, to call attention to modern equipment and to show how new or remodeled bathrooms can be planned.

HOW TO VISUALIZE PLAN VIEWS OF BATHROOMS

In order to understand many of the illustrations in this chapter and in order to create such drawings we must learn how to visualize existing, new, or remodeled bathrooms by means of their *plan views*. In other words, we must be able to interpret plan views the same as pictures. An example of this requirement is indicated in Figure 3.

The X part of the illustration shows a plan view of an older-type duplex bathroom formerly recommended for large families. Note that all fixtures and equipment are named. The following information is indicated:

1. The over-all size of the bathroom is 14′ 6″ by 10′ 9″.

2. The general space is divided into two areas. One area is 8′ 0″ wide and the other is 6′ 0″ wide.

3. In the 8′ 0″ area there is a bathtub, a water closet and a lavatory. In the 6′ 0″ area there is a water closet and a lavatory.

4. The two areas are separated by a sliding-door partition.

5. Entrance to the general space is by means of one sliding door and one hinged door.

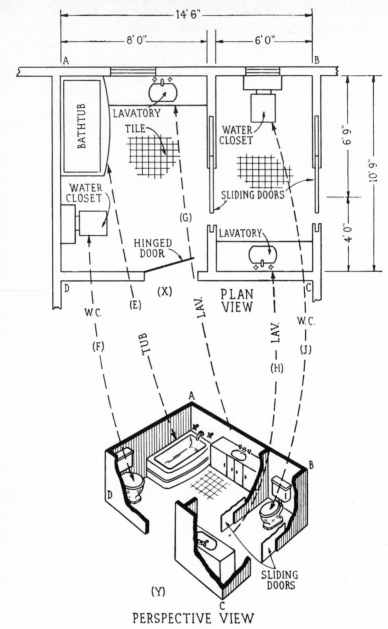

FIGURE 3. How to visualize plan views of bathrooms.

6. There is one window in each area.

7. A tile floor is specified.

8. The two areas afford such privacy that two people may use the general area at the same time.

The *Y* part of the illustration shows a cutaway perspective view (picture) of the general space. Note the *A, B, C,* and *D* corners in the plan and perspective views. The dashed lines *E, F, G, H,* and *J* connect plan and perspective views of the bathtub, water closets, and lavatories.

The two views in Figure 3 should be studied until the perspective view, or picture, can be visualized when looking only at the plan view. Once we have learned such visualization, the planning of new or remodeled bathrooms can be carried on to much better advantage.

BATHROOM SAFETY

Several important safety precautions should be carefully considered and kept in mind when new or remodeled bathrooms are being planned.

Nonslip Flooring. Ceramic tile floors are beautiful and easy to keep clean. Yet, unless special precautions are exercised, they tend to be slippery, especially when wet. Many housewives like to place cloth or other types of small rugs on such floors. Unless the under surfaces of the rugs are treated with rubber or some other nonslip preparation, they are apt to slide on tile and therefore constitute a hazard. The same fact applies to bath mats.

Various forms of asphalt tile and rubber tile or linoleum may be used without as much slipping hazard.

Bathtub Bottoms. Old bathtubs, and even some of the cheaper varieties now available, have curved bottoms which are decidedly dangerous. The one shown in the upper part of Figure 1 is a good example. Such curved surfaces are especially slippery when covered with soap and water. A step too near the side of such a bathtub could result in a serious fall and broken bones.

Flat-bottomed bathtubs, such as the one shown in the lower part of

Figure 1, are recommended by the National Safety Council and by all casualty insurance companies.

Grab Bars. Securely fixed grab bars should be provided on walls for both bathtubs and shower stalls. Metal grab pipes from floors to ceilings should also be installed in front of bathtubs to provide maximum safety for elderly people. Such accessories may add a little to the cost of new or remodeled bathrooms, but the safety they assure is worth whatever they cost.

Thermostatic Valves. Thermostatically controlled valves on shower hot-water outlets may prevent serious scalding.

Towel Bars, Etc. Towel bars, soap dishes, and all fixture handles should be made of metal, since serious cuts may result from broken china.

Light Switches. Locate all light switches near entrance doors and where they cannot be operated from bathtubs or lavatories.

If individual lights are operated by pull cords, the cords should be insulated. Electric switches, cover plates, etc., should be made of insulating materials. Electric heaters should be of the built-in or recessed types.

Medicine Cabinets. Special locked and lighted compartments should be provided for drugs—high enough to be out of children's reach. Ordinary medicine compartments are not safe enough for most drugs. Special wall slots should be provided for the disposal of used safety-razor blades.

Radiators. Steam- and hot-water-heating radiators should be enclosed to prevent any possibility of burns. Casings of various kinds are available for such purposes.

REMODELING CONSIDERATIONS

Inexperienced mechanics and homeowners are apt to do a great deal of preliminary planning and thinking without taking into consideration several aspects of cost or allied work. This is a common mistake that always leads to unexpected expense, delays, and probable disappointment. As a means of helping readers to avoid such a mistake, the following summary of preliminary considerations is set forth.

Piping Economy. Figure 4 illustrates a typical plumbing system such as found in most houses where old bathrooms include water closets,

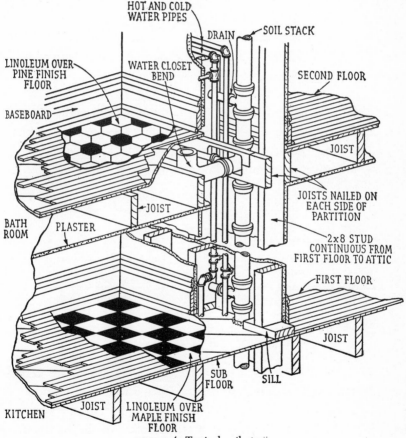

FIGURE 4. Typical soil stack.

bathtubs, and lavatories. All such fixtures are connected to soil stacks which are generally 4-inch cast-iron pipes.

Ordinarily, soil stacks are located in partitions between kitchens and bathrooms or, as shown in Figure 4, in partitions which constitute one wall of kitchens and bathrooms. Note, too, that hot- and cold-water pipes are installed close to soil stacks.

Soil stacks are expensive to install, even at times when houses are under construction and access to the space between studs is easily possible. They are much more expensive if existing partitions have to be opened up so that they can be installed.

In order to economize on piping costs, the locations of new bathrooms should be planned so that existing soil stacks can be used and so that the lengths of water-closet bends do not exceed the length permitted by local building codes. When remodeled bathrooms are being considered, the location of water closets, bathtubs, and lavatories should be planned so that existing drains and closet bends can be employed.

Bathtub Locations. When a modern bathtub is filled with water, the total weight involved constitutes a load that must be carefully considered so far as joists are concerned. Unless due precautions are observed, plaster cracking and other undesirable results are probable.

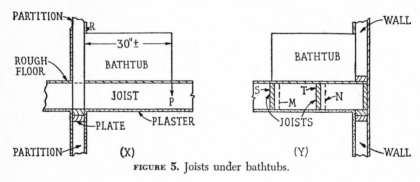

FIGURE 5. Joists under bathtubs.

The *X* part of Figure 5 shows a situation where joists are at right angles to the length of a bathtub that is located next to a partition. In such cases, most of the load from the bathtub is applied to the joists near the points where they are supported by the plate in the partition. As indicated by the arrow at *P,* some of the bathtub load is applied to the joists at a point approximately 30 inches from the plate. Ordinarily, a situation of this kind may cause the joists to bend only enough to cause small cracks at *R*.

The *Y* part of the illustration shows a situation where joists are parallel to the length of a bathtub that is located next to a wall. In such cases, most of the load from the bathtub is applied to joists S and T. If those joists have a span (distance between points of support) of 12 feet or more, they are apt to bend enough to pull the tub away from the wall and seriously to crack the ceiling plaster attached to their bottom edges. In order to prevent such undesirable reactions, additional joists can be installed, as indicated at M and N. The joists M and N should be nailed to joists S and T using 3½-inch nails spaced about 12 inches apart.

Bathtub Hangers. In cases where new partitions are being installed or where the lath and plaster are to be removed from existing partitions, metal bathtub hangers can be employed to support much of the weight of a bathtub. Such hangers are hung from, or attached to, studs and bathtubs are supported by them.

Codes. Most cities and towns have regulations relating to the installation of all types of plumbing fixtures and to the piping in connection with them. Such codes should be studied before new or remodeled bathrooms are planned.

Windows. Any bathroom should have at least one window. Where duplex bathrooms are involved, each area should have a window.

Condensation. Bathrooms are subject to warm and humid air, and as a result condensation is likely to occur on the walls and ceilings. With this fact in mind, either enamel or waterproof surface materials should be used.

Roughing-in Drawings. All plumbing manufacturers will supply roughing-in drawings which show where water-supply pipes, waste pipes, and vents must be placed in order to connect with various fixtures when they are set in place. These are very important, especially when we remember that most fixtures are set after all other work is finished.

Cabinets. When new or remodeled bathrooms are being planned, provisions should be made for ample cabinets or other storage spaces, where towels and all other bathroom supplies may be stored.

Heating. See the discussion relating to heating in Chapter 9.

Figure 6 shows several good and poor locations for bathroom hot-air registers.

PART A. The floor register is under a window where the rising warm air mixes with the cold downdraft from the window and outer wall, producing uniform temperature from floor to ceiling.

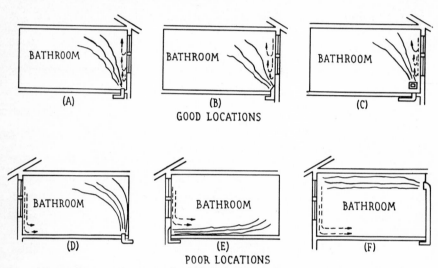

FIGURE 6. Vertical section through a bathroom showing register locations.

PART B. The baseboard register is under a window so that hot air is blown upward where it mixes with the cold downdraft from the window and wall to produce uniform floor-to-ceiling temperature.

PART C. The wall register is low on a partition near an outer wall. It blows warm air across the outer wall and the window where it mixes with the normal downdrafts to produce uniform floor-to-ceiling temperatures.

PART D. The floor register is near an inside wall. Heat rises to the ceiling, with the cold drafts from the window and outer wall dropping down and crossing the floor. This causes undesirable heating, especially in bathrooms.

PART E. The baseboard register blows air across the floor and creates an unpleasant draft at the floor level.

PART F. The wall register is high in an inside wall. The heat is delivered at the ceiling level and allows cold drafts from the window and outer wall to sweep across the floor.

Sliding Doors. When bathroom space is limited or where a swinging door conflicts with fixtures, sliding doors can be used to advantage. However, and as indicated in Figure 3, there must be enough partition space for such doors to slide into.

Size of Bathrooms. Bathrooms need not be large. Small bathrooms are easier to keep clean and are considerably less costly. The smaller they are, the less floor-, wall-, and ceiling-surface materials required. However, there should be ample room for each of the fixtures and enough room between them for easy access.

Shutoff Valves. It is a good idea to install shutoff valves in the pipelines, near each fixture, so that faucet repairs can be made without shutting off the entire water supply.

ADVANTAGE OF REMODELING

The advantages obtainable, even by fairly economical remodeling, are fascinating. The difference between old and modern bathrooms is so great that such projects are exceptionally worthwhile.

Study the top parts of Figures 1 and 2. Notice in them the items listed in the following summary, keeping in mind that such items are typical of most old bathrooms:

1. Old-fashioned bathtubs are ugly and dangerous.

2. Visible pipes are unsightly.

3. The wood dado (wall covering) is unattractive, unsanitary, and difficult to keep clean.

4. It is difficult to clean the floors under and in back of old-fashioned bathtubs.

5. Inadequate and ugly lavatories.

6. Unsanitary wood baseboards.

7. Insufficient lighting.

8. Inadequate shower facilities.

9. Unsanitary cracks around lavatories.

10. Unsightly and difficult-to-reach medicine cabinets.

11. Old-style water closets.

12. Poor wall and ceiling decorations.

13. Lack of cabinets and storage spaces.

14. Lack of grab bars.

15. Lack of counter space.

16. Unsanitary bathtub drains.

17. Old-fashioned floor coverings.

18. Old-fashioned windows.

19. Unsanitary toilet seats.

20. Wasted space.

Now study the lower parts of Figures 1 and 2. The great advantages of remodeling are immediately apparent. All of the foregoing disadvantages and undesirable items have been removed or corrected. The remodeled bathrooms are more convenient and they are beautiful. For example, note the following improvements shown in the lower part of Figure 2.

1. The bathtub is modern and safe. It has a seat-type rim and is fully enclosed to serve the dual purpose of a shower.

2. Safe grab bars have been provided.

3. The water closet is noiseless and sanitary.

4. The sliding window is glazed with attractive translucent glass.

5. The space can be converted into two areas by means of a folding curtain.

6. The vanity-type lavatory provides storage drawers and counter space.

7. A dressing table adds to the convenience of the remodeled area.

8. Wall storage cabinets have been provided.

9. A modern and sanitary floor has been provided.

10. The tile walls are beautiful and easy to keep clean.

11. Wall decorations add to the beauty of the area.

12. All dust-catching cracks have been avoided.

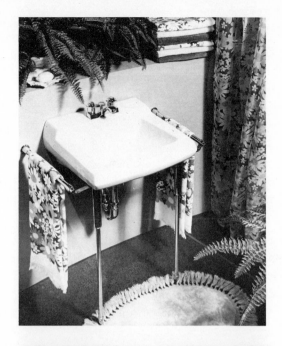

FIGURE 7. (*Courtesy American-Standard*)

MODERN FIXTURES AND ACCESSORIES

The best way to visualize and study modern fixtures and accessories is by means of the catalogues distributed by manufacturers, or by visiting their display rooms. However, a few suggestions are given in the following paragraphs.

Lavatories. As illustrated in Figures 2 and 7, lavatories are available with and without cabinets. They may be obtained in several colors and sizes, but their price range calls for careful planning. They should not be selected until the size and shape of a new or remodeled bathroom has been determined.

Water Closets. There are a great many types of water closets. They differ in shape, width, height, color, quality, and action. Some have tanks, while others are flushed by means of valves. The noiseless types are becoming more popular, although they are generally more expensive.

Bathtubs. Modern flat-bottomed bathtubs of the types shown in Figure 8 are available in all colors and to suit practically any available space.

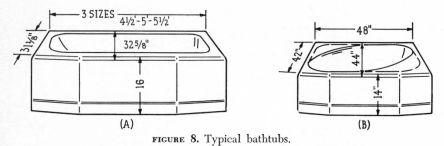

FIGURE 8. Typical bathtubs.

The type shown in the *A* part of the illustration is made to have either one, two, or three sides against partitions.

The type shown in the *B* part of the illustration is made for recesses. However, other similar types are available for corner installations.

NOTE: Removable wall panels through which the supply, waste, and vent pipes for bathtubs are accessible should be provided.

Shower Stalls. Shower stalls, entirely separate from bathtubs, can be purchased complete and ready to install in various sizes and qualities. Usually, such stalls require floor space that is 3 feet square. As indicated in the lower part of Figure 2, glass enclosures are also available for use in connection with bathtubs.

Medicine Cabinets. Figure 9 illustrates a modern medicine cabinet with mirror, sliding doors, and tubular lights. Such cabinets are made to be installed between the studs of a partition.

FIGURE 9. Modern medicine cabinet.

Water Heaters. A constant supply of hot water is an essential convenience in modern bathrooms. Automatic gas or electric heaters can be obtained in 30- to 40- or more gallon capacities.

Ventilation. Where possible, electric ventilating fans should be provided in connection with new or remodeled bathrooms. The fans should be located in the ceilings, as near to the center of the rooms as possible, or centered next to an exterior wall, or in a corner. For bathrooms of ordinary size, fans with 8-inch blades are adequate.

LOCATION OF BATHROOM ACCESSORIES

Figure 10 shows the recommended location for several bathroom accessories.

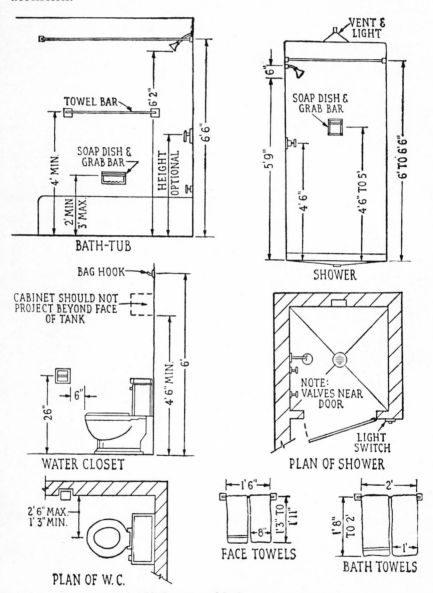

FIGURE 10. Location of bathroom accessories.

MINIMUM-SIZED BATHROOMS

Figure 11 illustrates four of the more or less basic types of bathrooms designed for small areas. With but little modification, one of these types will usually be found to fit remodeling requirements, especially where only limited space is available and when economy is important.

The *W* part of Figure 11 shows the most economical plan. Plumbing costs can be kept to a minimum because the fixtures are all on one wall,

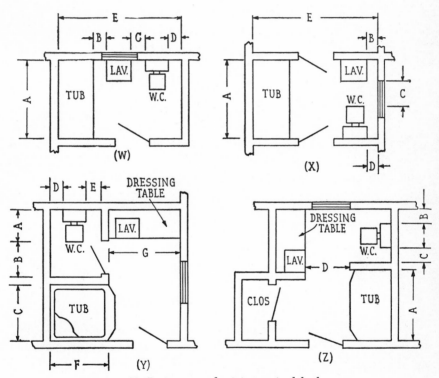

FIGURE 11. Basic types of minimum-sized bathrooms.

and a maximum of 50 square feet of floor space allows ample access between fixtures. As shown in the illustration, the *A* dimension is 5′ 6″ and the *E* dimension is 9′ 0″. These dimensions allow a 5′ 6″ by 2′ 6″ bathtub, a 20- by 18-inch lavatory, and a standard-sized water closet. The distances shown at *B, C,* and *D* are each 12 inches. This plan could be applied to an even smaller floor space by reducing the *A* dimension to 5′ 0″ and by allowing somewhat less than 12 inches at *B, C,* and *D.* However it is wise to allow at least 12 inches between fixtures and between fixtures and partitions.

The *X* part of Figure 11 shows a minimum-space plan for a bathroom between two bedrooms. A corner lavatory could be substituted for the one shown. The one weakness of this plan is that wall space for towel bars is limited. As the illustration is shown, the *A* dimension is 5′ 6″ and the *E* dimension is 9′ 0″. In this plan, the *B* and *D* dimensions should not be less than 12 inches and the *C* dimension not less than 1′ 9″.

The *Y* part of Figure 11 shows a simple, duplex bathroom. The following minimum dimensions are recommended:

A—27 inches	*C*—48 inches	*E*—12 inches
B—30 inches	*D*—12 inches	*F*—48 inches
		G—60 inches

The *Z* part of Figure 11 shows another simple, duplex bathroom in connection with a closet.

The following minimum dimensions are recommended.

A—60 inches	*C*—12 inches
B—12 inches	*D*—36 inches

DUPLEX BATHROOMS

Figure 12 illustrates three basic types of duplex bathrooms designed for large areas and for use by large families. Such bathrooms can be used in odd-shaped areas and serve a double or triple purpose, since up to three people can use them at the same time with full privacy.

The *X* part of the illustration shows a bathroom that has three separate areas all of which may be entered from a hall. All of the areas can be closed to provide complete privacy in each. Minimum dimensions are indicated.

The *Y* part of the illustration shows a three-area bathroom in which a bathtub, stall shower, and three lavatories are available. The *A* and *B*

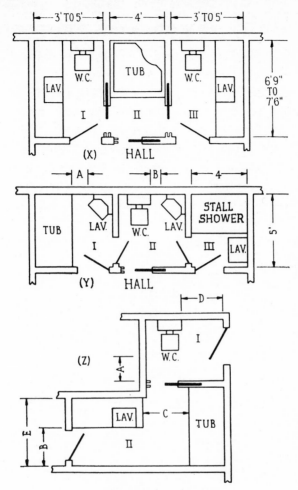

FIGURE 12. Duplex bathrooms.

dimensions should not be less than 12 inches. The 4- and 5-foot dimensions are minimums.

The Z part of the illustration shows a two-area bathroom designed for an L-shaped space. The following minimum dimensions are recommended:

A—24 inches   C—42 inches
B—30 inches   D—36 inches
E—57 inches

TYPICAL REMODELING PROJECTS

The following problems and their solutions are typical of the remodeling projects which owners of old houses are likely to be interested in:

PROBLEM 1. The X part of Figure 13 shows part of the first-floor plan in connection with a typical old house. We can assume that a kitchen, a dining room, a bedroom, and a living room are located on either side of the central portion indicated in the illustration. We can further assume that kitchen remodeling has eliminated any need for the pantry and that the owner wants to transform the pantry into a bathroom for the first-floor bedroom.

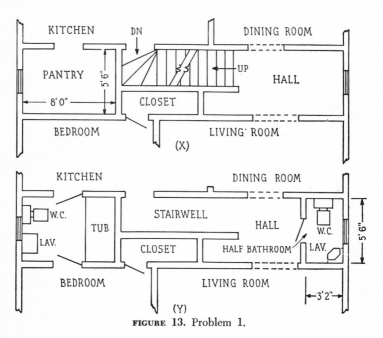

FIGURE 13. Problem 1.

SOLUTION. The first step consists of preliminary planning to determine what the requirements are. We can assume that a bathtub, a lavatory, and a water closet constitute the required fixtures and that entrance to the new bathroom must be possible from both the kitchen and bedroom. We can also assume that the brand and size of fixtures have been selected and determined.

The next step should be accomplished by means of sketches drawn to accurate scale. Draw single-line rectangles to represent the interior of the 8′ 0″ by 5′ 6″ space. Indicate the position of the necessary doors and their widths. Then draw in various arrangements of fixtures, making sure that the symbols are drawn to the same scale as the space outline.

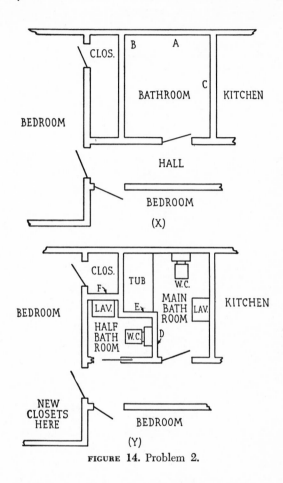

FIGURE 14. Problem 2.

We can assume that the arrangement shown in the *Y* part of the illustration is satisfactory. In this arrangement, the lavatory and water closet are located so that connections to a soil stack in the kitchen wall can be made without too much trouble or expense. The arrangement allows ample space between fixtures and between fixtures and the partitions. Also, there is ample space for the two doors and a passageway between the water closet and the bathtub.

NOTE: Half bathrooms (sometimes known as powder rooms) can be provided by use of excess hall or other space, as indicated in the Y part of Figure 13.

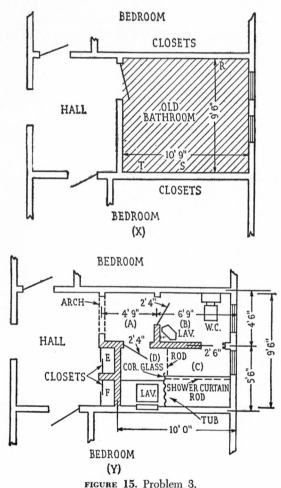

FIGURE 15. Problem 3.

PROBLEM 2. The X part of Figure 14 shows part of the floor plan for a one-story house. We can assume that the bathroom space is surrounded by a bedroom closet, a hall, and a kitchen. Also, that the letters A, B, and C indicate the positions of the old water closet, bathtub, and lavatory.

We can further assume that the owner wants to remodel the old bathroom and provide an additional half bathroom to serve the needs of a growing family.

SOLUTION. The Y part of Figure 14 indicates one solution to the problem. Note that partitions $D, E,$ and F are planned so that there is room for a water closet and lavatory in the half bathroom and that the three necessary fixtures are well arranged in the main bathroom.

The new half bathroom will require an additional soil stack, but in a one-story house such installation work can be carried on without too much trouble or expense.

PROBLEM 3. The X part of Figure 15 shows part of the floor plan for a one-story house that includes large rooms and halls. This is typical of many old houses. Note that the old bathroom occupies a space that is 9′ 6″ by 10′ 9″. The letters $R, S,$ and T indicate the positions of the old water closet, bathtub, and lavatory. The problem is to remodel the old bathroom to suit the needs of an enlarged family.

SOLUTION. The Y part of Figure 15 shows one solution to the problem in the form of a duplex bathroom.

The shaded partitions are new. They divide the space into four areas.

A. This is a small entrance hall to serve the needs of two doors.

B. This area contains a water closet and a lavatory.

C. This area contains the bathtub. Note that a curtain can be hung from the rod indicated to separate areas C and D.

D. This area contains the lavatory and dressing table.

Note that new closets have been provided at E and F and that all areas can be closed off, by means of doors or a curtain, to provide privacy and facilities for more than one person at a time.

CHAPTER ELEVEN

Storage Spaces

The concept of planned storage is an extension of the modern doctrine which states that houses are actually "machines for living," that they must provide much more than mere shelter; they must be focal points for pleasant family life. As such, houses should be planned to provide maximum convenience with a minimum amount of work required to keep the machines functioning smoothly.

A major trend in all types of houses to achieve this end is the use of more and better storage spaces. Several factors are responsible. One is the popular demands for well-organized, uncluttered living. Another is the need for more living space. This is particularly true in houses without attic and basement wherein storage space is at a premium. Even in larger houses, owners have found that such traditional catch-alls as attics and basements are at best inefficient storage spaces and are better suited to use as auxiliary living or sleeping areas. See Chapters 9 and 10.

Given enough well-planned storage spaces, not only can everything be stored neatly and out of sight, but there will be far more actual living area available. For example, note the storage space illustrated in Figure 1. Garments, bedding, and boxes are neatly and conveniently stored and the folding doors do not interfere with furniture or appliance placement in the living area.

Most old houses are so arranged that additional storage spaces may be provided without a great deal of expense. This chapter proposes to outline the items relating to storage spaces which require careful considera-

FIGURE 1. Modern storage closet with folding doors.

tion, to call attention to various types of storage spaces, and to show how they can be planned and installed.

STORAGE-SPACE SAFETY

Several important safety precautions should be carefully considered and kept in mind when new or remodeled storage spaces are being planned.

Lighting. Natural and artificial lighting of storage spaces should be sufficient to make all contents plainly visible. Many serious injuries have occurred because unseen contents fell when disturbed. If the light from adjacent living areas does not make all contents easy to distinguish, electric light fixtures should be installed inside of storage spaces.

Ventilation. Ventilation is especially important in clothes storage spaces to help keep the clothing free from odors and, in humid regions of the country, to prevent the formation of mold or mildew. Air may be kept in circulation by windows or by means of openings in the tops and bottoms of doors.

Dust Prevention. In dusty parts of the country a threshold is needed in connection with "walk-in" storage spaces to help keep contents clean. Shallow "reach-in" storage spaces need doors that are almost as wide as the interior spaces. For doorways more than 2′ 8″ wide, sliding doors are apt to be more dustproof.

Access. Many injurious falls have been the result of difficult access or of crowding in storage spaces. Many more accidents are caused by articles for which no storage space was provided.

Reaching and Climbing. Storage for articles in more or less constant use should be designed so that no reaching or climbing is necessary, to prevent falls and strains. They should be within reach of the average person standing on the floor.

Seldom Used Articles. Storage for articles in seldom or seasonal use should be on the main floor if possible, with ladder or other provision for safe access if they are stored out of reach from the floor.

Outdoor Articles. Outdoor articles such as garden tools and bicycles should be stored on the ground level.

Poisons. Insecticides and other poisons should be stored high, out of children's reach, and kept locked.

Locations. Ordinarily, storage spaces should occupy a floor area that would not be used in other ways. They should be accessible but inconspicuous. However, they should not be located where one side of a chimney forms one of their walls or sides. The reason for this is explained in the following:

During cold weather, when a furnace is in operation, the walls of a chimney will be warm. This is especially true when coal is used as fuel. If a storage space is located next to a warm chimney wall, a circulation of air is created within the storage space which tends to distribute dust over its contents.

If there is no alternative but to locate a storage space next to a chimney wall, an air space at least 6 inches wide should be provided between the chimney and the storage space. This will eliminate undesirable interior circulation.

BASIC TYPES OF STORAGE SPACES

In general, all spaces used for storage of any kind are known as *storage spaces*. This term is in keeping with modern design and construction terminology. However, the older term *closet* is much better known and understood. Therefore, we shall employ the two terms as follows.

All spaces where clothing, linen, towels, etc., are stored will be called closets.

All spaces where general household items such as games, books, sporting equipment, etc., are stored will be called *storage spaces*.

Clothes Closets. All clothes closets are basically the same, regardless of their location. No matter what shape of space is available, one of the six plans shown in Figure 2 can be adapted. Minimum dimensions marked on the plans may be increased and the arrangement then varied by adding hooks, trays, shelves, drawers, racks for shoes, etc. Clothing on hangers is indicated by the lines drawn at right angles to the rods.

For a space limited as to width but fairly deep, the narrow closet with extension rod (*U* part of Figure 2) is a good arrangement. The doorway to this closet should be at least 2 feet wide.

The shallow closet (*V* part of Figure 2) is a typical reach-in arrangement. This is an excellent closet to use when depth is limited. However,

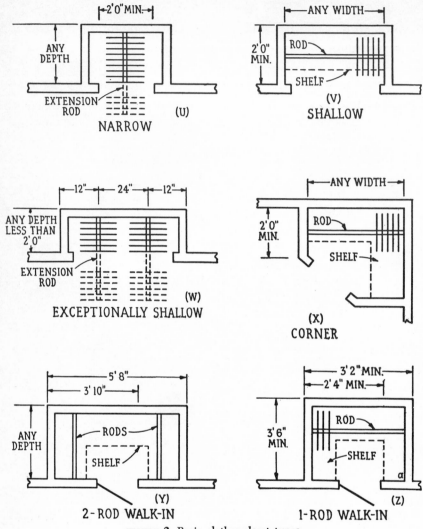

FIGURE 2. Basic clothes-closet types.

the depth should never be less than 2' 0". That much space is advisable so that clothes on hangers will not brush against the wall surfaces. This closet requires an opening practically as wide as the closet. For openings more than 2' 8" wide, two doors are recommended.

For space that is too shallow to place hangers crosswise, the plan shown in the *W* part of Figure 2 is a good arrangement. Here two extension rods provide the maximum hanging space. The doorway must be practically as wide as the closet.

The corner closet (*X* part of Figure 2) provides considerable hanging space for very little floor area. This closet has no sharp corners that project into living areas.

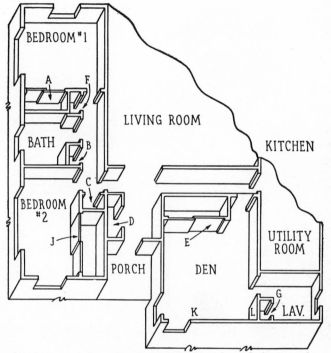

FIGURE 3. Typical floor plan showing basic and wardrobe-type closets.

A walk-in closet (*Y* part of Figure 2) may be any depth. For more shelf space and less hanger space, one side of such a closet may be fitted with shelves.

The walk-in closet shown in the *Z* part of Figure 2 is similar to the reach-in arrangement shown in the *V* part of the illustration. This closet may be any width that is wider than the door opening. If desired, place the door at *a*, making the shelf L-shaped.

Any of the closets indicated at *B, C, D, E,* or *G* in Figure 3 can be planned and erected following the plans shown at *U, V, W, Y,* or *Z* in Figure 2.

Wardrobe Closets. This type of closet is indicated at *A, E,* and *J* in Figure 3. Either sliding or swinging doors may be used. Generally, rods are installed to extend the full length of such closets, and shelves are erected above the rods. As indicated in Figure 4, storage spaces which have hinged doors are often placed above such closets.

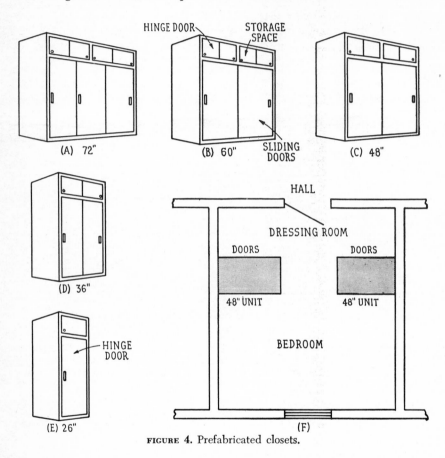

FIGURE 4. Prefabricated closets.

Prefabricated Closets. The *A, B, C, D,* and *E* parts of Figure 4 show typical prefabricated closet units which can be purchased knocked down in cartons, complete with hardware, shelves, rods, and drawers ready for installation. As indicated, the units range from 26 inches to 72 inches wide and have from one to three doors. In all but the 26-inch unit, sliding doors are provided. The units are 8′ 0″ high and 26′ 6″ thick.

They may be used as room dividers or, where no joists must be supported, as partitions between rooms.

The *F* part of Figure 4 illustrates one way in which the units may be used. Two 48-inch units provide ample closet and storage space and create a dressing room at one end of a long bedroom. The units can also be installed at such locations as *A, E,* and *J* in Figure 3. Or, they may be installed along such walls as indicated at *KL* in Figure 3. In fact, these units can be installed wherever closet or storage space is desired.

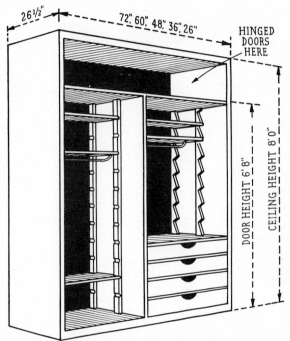

FIGURE 5. Typical storage space assembled from prefabricated units.

Storage Spaces. The prefabricated units previously mentioned may also be used as storage spaces for all manner of household articles. As indicated in Figure 5, the interiors can be fitted with shelves and drawers. No carpentry work is necessary, owing to the fact that side cleats permit shelves and drawers to be added or subtracted at 6-inch intervals. Cleats, drawers, and shelves are available at building-material dealers where the units are purchased.

CLOSET FITTINGS

It pays to plan carefully the details of closet fittings. Rods, hooks, and trays that are well located make it easier to keep clothing in good condition and to keep the closet in good order.

Rods take care of practically all clothing on hangers. Usually this will include all dresses, except for small children's, all skirts, blouses, trousers, and coats. Table 1 shows the space to allow on the rod for different types

TABLE 1. Rod allowance for garments and location of rod
with respect to wall and floor

Garment	Space on rod, inches	Wall to center of rod, inches	Floor to top of rod, inches
Adults'			
Skirts	2	12	45
Jackets	3	12	45
Shirts	1½	12	45
Suits	2	12	45
Trousers	3	12	45
Dresses	1½	12	63
Overcoats	4	12	63
Coats with fur collar	3–6	12	63
Coats without fur collar	2–5	12	63
Evening gowns	2	12	72
Garments in mothproof bags	3	12	72
Children's, 6 to 12 years		10	45
Children's, 3 to 5 years		8	30

of clothing. This table also shows how much space to allow from wall to rod and from floor to rod, depending on the width and length of garments hanging from it. If there is a shelf above the rod, a minimum of 2½ inches should be allowed between the top of the rod and the bottom of the shelf.

In deep, narrow closets there should be an extension pole so that the rod can be pulled out for greater convenience. See *U* part of Figure 2.

There should be enough hooks in a closet to accommodate nightgowns, pajamas, slips, aprons, and other garments that do not belong on hangers. Hooks should be within easy reach of the doorway but not any closer than 5 inches. There should be a minimum allowance of 4 inches between the top of a hook and the bottom of a shelf above it. It is better not to place hooks behind a rod. For the clothing of small children, hooks should not be above a child's eye level. Hooks for garments on hangers cannot safely be put on a door that is less than 30 inches wide.

The distance from hook to hook or from hook to corner will vary with the kind of garments hung on them. For clothing ordinarily kept in a

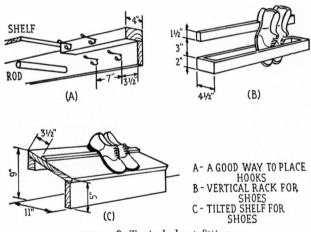

A - A GOOD WAY TO PLACE HOOKS
B - VERTICAL RACK FOR SHOES
C - TILTED SHELF FOR SHOES

FIGURE 6. Typical closet fittings.

bedroom closet there should be a minimum of 7 inches between hooks and 3½ inches from hook to corner. For children's clothing, the hooks should be spaced about 9 inches from hook to hook, and 4½ inches from hook to corner.

The *A* part of Figure 6 shows a space-saving method of placing hooks. Hooks in the upper row are on a strip that sets them out from the wall about 3 inches more than the hooks in the row below. If these hooks are placed any closer than 12 inches from a rod, they will reduce the amount of rod space that can be used. The upper hooks will reduce the amount of usable rod space about 8 inches, the lower ones about 4 inches.

The vertical shoerack shown in the *B* part of the illustration is a good one to use when wall space is not so limited as floor space. The lower bar may be covered on the inside with felt to protect the shoes.

The tilted shelf shown in the *C* part of the illustration fits in the floor space of the closet, below garments on hangers or hooks. For both rack and shelf a width of 18 inches will accommodate at least two pairs of shoes.

Other fittings should supplement the storage space provided in bureaus, chests, and dressers. For folded clothing, shelves are less expensive than trays or drawers; they provide enough protection for most articles.

The width and distance between shelves as well as the depth of trays and drawers varies according to the articles stored. They should be planned to accommodate the largest articles commonly stored in or on them. A minimum for shelves for hats, for instance, would be 12 inches from front to back, a maximum about 15 inches. The distance between shelves used for hats should be 9 inches from the top of the lower shelf to the bottom of the shelf above.

Where walk-in or reach-in closets are involved, dust may create a problem. It is practically impossible to prevent the settlement of dust on the shoulder parts of garments unless bags such as shown in Figure 1 are employed, or unless some sort of cloth or plastic covers are placed over the garments just above hanger levels.

CEDAR CLOSETS

Aromatic-red-cedar closet lining is produced in random lengths up to 8 feet. It is ⅜ inch thick and comes in a choice of widths from 2 to 4 inches. It is usually put up in bundles or cartons, each containing 40 feet board measure. A 40-foot bundle or carton will cover about 30 square feet of actual space. Table 2 shows the number of 8-foot bundles required for closets of various sizes.

Application. In remodeling work, the cedar can be applied over old plaster or plasterboard in existing closets or directly over the studding in new closets. The cedar strips should be placed horizontally on walls, beginning from the bottom. Courses are placed with the groove edges down. Face nailing is recommended. Use 4d nails and set them just below the surface. Joints need not occur over studs, as the tongue and groove "welds" the pieces together. When cedar is being placed over plaster or

TABLE 2. Number of 8-foot bundles required for various-sized closets

Closet size in feet			Bundles
Deep	Wide	High	
1½	3	7	3
1½	3	8	3
2	3	7	3
2	3	8	4
2	3½	7	4
2	3½	8	4
2	4	7	4
2	4	8	4
2	4½	7	4
2	4½	8	5
2	5	7	4
2	5	8	5
2	6	7	5
2	6	8	6
3	4	7	5
3	4	8	5
3	5	7	5

plasterboard, short pieces will remain securely in place, even if located between bearing points.

Cedar molding is available for corner treatments. Closet doors should also be lined for best results. To assure greater air tightness of a closet, a condition which increases moth repellency, the door should be weatherstripped.

The cedar lining should be left in its natural state. Application of shellac or other finish would seal in the oil fumes and prevent their functioning as a moth repellent.

CLOSET DOORS

Several types of sliding or hinged closet doors, along with the necessary hardware, are available at lumberyards. However, for simplicity and speed of installation, especially when homeowners are doing the work, prefabricated units such as shown in Figure 4 are recommended. Such units are complete with doors. Wardrobe units such as indicated at *A*, *E*, and *J* in Figure 3 are also available in various sizes with hinged or sliding doors.

Folding Doors. Hinged doors require a considerable amount of swing area. For example, note the *X* part of Figure 7. The 2' 6" door requires a swing area that is the equivalent of 5 by 2½ feet, or 12½ square feet. That much area cannot be used for any other purpose in a room.

As a further example of the floor space required for hinged doors, suppose that the closet indicated in Figure 1 has hinged doors such as shown at *A* and *B* in the *Y* part of Figure 7. Also-suppose that the door shown at the left in Figure 1 has a hinged door such as shown at *C* in the *Y* part of Figure 7. The three swing areas required would take up most of the floor space in the *FDE* corner of the room.

Folding doors, such as shown in Figure 1, can be obtained for practically any width of door opening. Following manufacturer's directions, they are easy to install and provide considerably more usable living area in any room.

Sliding Doors. Closet units such as indicated in Figure 4, and at *A*, *E*, and *J* in Figure 3, have sliding doors which slide back of one another and do not require partition space. However, in order to provide a sliding door for the closet opening shown in the *X* part of Figure 7, a length of the partition, such as indicated between *G* and *H*, would have to be torn out and rebuilt. This procedure would require plaster patching and other undesirable work.

If *new* partitions around a closet or storage space are to be erected, sliding-door pockets can be installed without difficulty, owing to the fact that they may be purchased ready for installation and because they constitute part of such partitions.

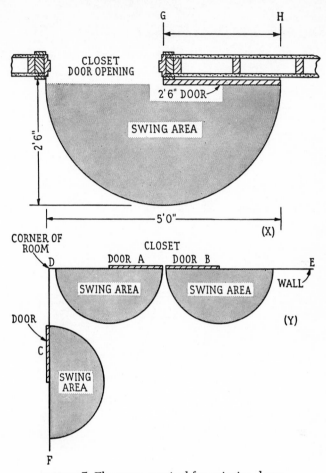

FIGURE 7. Floor area required for swinging doors.

TYPICAL PROJECTS

The following problems and their solutions are typical of the closet remodeling projects which owners of old houses are likely to be interested in:

PROBLEM 1. The X part of Figure 8 indicates parts of two bedrooms and their positions in connection with a hall. Partition AB is the dividing partition between the two rooms, both of which are large. The problem is to plan and erect a new partition so that three new closets will be created: one for each bedroom and one for the hall.

SOLUTION. The Y part of the illustration indicates the position of the new partition CD. This partition may be located from 3 to 6 feet away from partition AB. Short partitions at J and K divide the space into the required three closets.

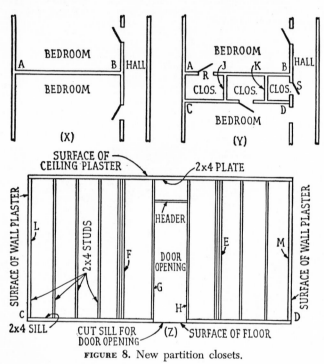

FIGURE 8. New partition closets.

Partition CD may be constructed as indicated in the Z part of the illustration. First, place a 2 by 4 sill from C to D. It should be nailed directly to the floor. Then, by means of a plumb bob, locate the position of the 2 by 4 plate directly above the sill. Use $3\frac{1}{2}$-inch nails to fasten the plate to the ceiling. The nails should go through the lath and plaster and penetrate well into joists. Toenail the 2 by 4 pieces L and M to the sill and plate.

In partition CD, two corner assemblies, shown at E and F, are required for the short partitions K and J. It is a good idea to have the frames for the doors on hand so their widths can be measured and the positions of studs *G* and *H* established accordingly. All other studs should be placed 16 inches on centers, or as near to that spacing as possible.

Erect the short partitions, *K* and *J*, using sills, plates, and studs in much the same manner as explained in connection with partition *CD* (see *Y* part of illustration).

Doors *R* and *S* will have to be cut into the old partitions. Remove the lath and plaster in areas somewhat wider than the doors and from floor

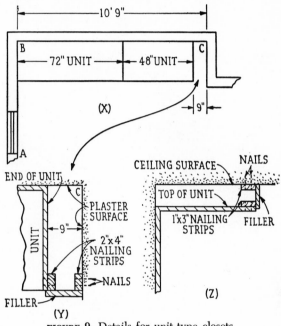

FIGURE 9. Details for unit-type closets.

to ceiling. It may be necessary to erect new studs on either side of the door openings. Also, headers will be necessary.

Partitions *CD, J,* and *K* may be covered with any of the surface materials explained in Chapter 5.

The new trim for portions *CD, K,* and *J* should closely match the old trim.

The new closets may be fitted as explained earlier in this chapter.

PROBLEM 2. The *X* part of Figure 9 shows one end of a bedroom, *ABC*, in which closet and storage space is desired. The problem is to plan and install unit-type closets of the type illustrated in Figure 4.

SOLUTION. In a space 10′ 9″ long, one of the 72-inch and one of the 48-inch units can be installed.

The units may be fastened to the floor and walls by means of nails or screws in ample quantity to make them secure. Use a carpenter's level to make sure that the units are level and plumb. Shim as may be necessary.

The two units have a combined length of 120 inches or 9 inches short of the 10′ 9″ (129 inches) space between *B* and *C*. Therefore, a filler is required. The *Y* part of Figure 9 indicates how the filler is applied.

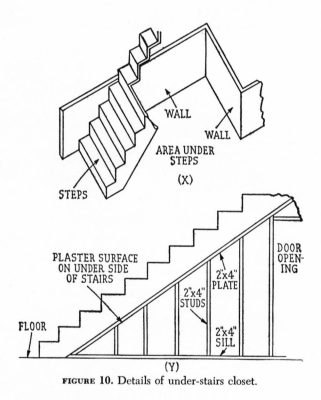

FIGURE 10. Details of under-stairs closet.

Sometimes the ceilings of old houses are more than 8′ 0″ high. In such cases, fillers must be applied between the tops of the units and the ceiling, as indicated in the *Z* part of Figure 9.

PROBLEM 3. The *X* part of Figure 10 shows a cutaway view of stairs and of the open space under the stairs. Situations of this kind are common in old houses. The problem is to provide a storage space under the stairs.

SOLUTION. The Y part of Figure 10 indicates how a partition can be framed to enclose the space. The door size will depend upon the available height. The new partition may be covered using any of the surface materials explained in Chapter 5. The new trim should closely match the old trim.

CHAPTER TWELVE

Electric Lighting

Without good lighting, the time, money, and effort in building, remodeling, furnishing, and decorating a home may well go unappreciated by occupants and guests. The nice things done may be hardly noticeable. Yet, improper lighting may attract attention to areas that should be obscure. Good lighting, in contrast, can enhance living in the home, give pleasure, and add to comfort.

During daylight hours, good lighting throughout most parts of a home can be obtained through proper placement and treatment of windows. But even in daylight hours, some parts of a house require artificial illumination for adequate visibility. After dark, electric lighting throughout the interior and usually also on the exterior is necessary.

It is not enough, however, to provide just enough light to see things. You need light of both sufficient quantity and quality to prevent eyestrain, whether working in the home or relaxing. You need light to prevent accidents. You need light to delineate the character and pattern of the various spaces in the home. And you need light to accent features that you put on display—your paintings, your sculptures, your dishes, your flowers, and your trophies.

In addition, light is an important element of interior design. Lamps and fixtures may be made part of the interior decoration. Also, light may be used to achieve predetermined emotional responses. It can affect the mood and atmosphere of each room, thus influencing the emotional responses of occupants. Recall, for example, the romance of candles on the dining room table, how the flickering candlelight creates dancing highlights on crystal and silver and catches the changing expressions on the face of your dining partner. Similarly, light can create desired moods in family rooms, play areas, studies, and bedrooms.

Planning the lighting for your home is a fascinating, exciting project. This chapter outlines the items relating to such a project that require careful consideration and shows how to go about transforming inadequately lighted spaces into well-lighted, cheerful rooms that will produce the mood and atmosphere you wish.

REMODELING FOR BETTER LIGHTING

Lighting can be improved in many ways, often at low cost. For example, you may be able to provide good lighting in some spaces with decorative table lamps and floor lamps. In some cases, you can hang from the ceiling or from a wall bracket an attractive fixture that you need merely plug into a nearby electrical outlet. Also, you can light a closet with an inexpensive light that goes on when you open the closet door. In other cases, you may wish to light rooms with more elaborate installations to obtain the effects you desire.

Because of this wide choice, you can remodel the electric lighting in your home at any time, whether or not you plan other types of remodeling. But if you are remodeling any spaces in your house, you should plan new lighting at the same time you plan the other work.

REASONS FOR REMODELING

The following purposes comprise practical reasons for providing better lighting:

1. Better visibility for work areas—kitchen, study, utility room, sewing center, reading, bathrooms, storage spaces.

2. Better visibility for play areas—game rooms, family room.

3. Safety—low-voltage lighting to reduce electrical hazards; avoiding tripping hazards, as at stairways; and for security reasons also, lighting on the house exterior.

4. Comfort—kitchen, living room, television areas.

5. Mood—dining room, family room, living room, front door, and foyer.

6. Accent—select spaces in all rooms.

7. Decoration—living room, family room, bedrooms, halls.

REMODELING PRECAUTIONS

As a first step in planning, decide what effects you would like to achieve in each space throughout your home. Then, in a preliminary way, plan means for achieving those effects, as explained later in this chapter.

Check Costs. Also decide how much money you are willing to spend for this project. Next, obtain cost estimates. If the total cost is too high, you can change your preliminary plan to bring costs into line. After that, you can make detailed plans.

Check Electrical-system Capacity. Cost is not the only important consideration in the preliminary phase of planning. The new lighting and other electrical equipment you install, such as electric range, refrigerator, or air conditioning, may require considerably more electrical power than originally provided to the home. The home power system may not be adequate to handle the new power requirements. In that case, you will have to increase the capacity of the system or reduce the power requirements of the new installations.

Capacity of a residential electrical distribution system usually is computed in amperes. For example, your system may have a total capacity of 60 amperes or 100 amperes, at 110 or 120 volts. The amperes required by electrical equipment is obtained from manufacturer's ratings usually provided on nameplates on the equipment. Power requirements for lighting is given in terms of watts noted on the light bulbs. To obtain the amperes required for lighting, add up the wattages for all the light bulbs you will need; then divide the sum by 100. The total amperes required to be carried by your system then is the sum of the amperes required for lighting and the amperes required for all the other electrical equipment in the home. If this total is less than the rated capacity of your electrical system, you will not have to make any changes in the system. If you are not certain of the system capacity or the power requirements of your new installations, you should have both checked by an electrician.

Check Circuit Breakers. In addition, the entrance, or main switch, fuses, and circuit breakers should be suitable for the new power requirements. These are additional details you should check with an electrician.

Check Outlets. Also, you should ascertain that electrical outlets for plugging in lamps will be available where you will need them. They are especially necessary if you intend to use portable lamps to meet some of your lighting objectives. If new outlets will be needed, you should include the cost of installing them in your cost estimate. Placement of new outlets in existing partitions or walls can be quite expensive. When new partitions are being erected, however, cost of new outlets may be relatively low, especially if a power line is available without much cutting into existing construction.

Check Switches. Bear in mind, too, that switches must be provided in convenient locations for all lighting fixtures. Cost considerations for these are practically the same as for new outlets and should be taken into account in the same way.

Handle with Care. Homeowners and inexperienced mechanics should use special precautions in handling electrical wiring. A "live" wire can be very dangerous. Touching one can cause death or serious injury. Furthermore, an arc or short circuit can cause a bad fire. Before you touch an uninsulated wire or a wire detached from electrical taps, be sure that the circuit is "dead." Switches and circuit breakers should be open, fuses removed.

Preferably, you should leave electric wiring to experienced electricians. The cost savings in doing the electrical work yourself is not worth the risk of death or injury, or of fire damage to your home. Furthermore, electrical installations must be in accordance with the local building code. Thus, a knowledge of the code is essential for all electrical work. This is an added reason for employing an experienced electrician.

Get Several Bids. Ask two or more electrical contractors for cost estimates early in the planning stage and when you have planned the lighting, so that costs may be reasonably close to what you expect to pay. When your plans have been completed, ask these contractors to bid on the electrical work. Make sure, preferably in writing, that it is perfectly clear to both you and the contractors what fixtures they are to supply and install, the prices of which are to be included in their bids, and what fixtures you are to provide, the installation costs of which are to be included in their bids.

SAFETY RULES

More accidents happen in homes than in autos, trains, and airplanes. These accidents usually result from carelessness or neglect. Often, they can be prevented by adequate lighting.

Outdoor Lighting. Accidents, for example, can happen right at your front door or on the walk leading to it. Someone might trip and fall in the dark over an unseen stair or bump. Hence, for safety as well as appearance, lights should be placed on the outside of the house, especially at the entrance.

Stairway Lighting. One of the most hazardous areas inside a house is a stairway. For safety, a shielded fixture at the top and bottom of all stairways is essential. These lamps should be controlled by a switch at top and bottom of the stairs, so that the lamps can be turned on and off from either floor.

Light Control. Never walk across a dark room. Provide a wall switch at the entrance and exit of each room to control at least one lamp in the room, so that you can put the light on before entering. Leave small night lights on at night in hallways, bathrooms, and bedrooms. These lamps should provide enough light for walking for dark-adapted eyes but yet not be bright enough to disturb sleepers.

Illuminate Work Areas. Provide lighting over sink, range, ironing boards, laundry equipment, workshop, and other moving equipment to ensure good visibility. Lights should be located and shielded to avoid glare and to make it unnecessary for you to work in your own shadow.

Light up Bathrooms. You undoubtedly are aware of the importance of good lighting at mirror areas in bathrooms. But you should also bear in mind the importance of good general lighting to eliminate the possibility of misreading labels on medicine bottles because of dim light. Also, provision of illumination over bathtubs in large bathrooms is a wise safety precaution. In stall showers, install a moistureproof fixture.

Switches for controlling the lights should be located where you are not likely to reach them from the bathtub or shower. Many persons have received severe shocks by operating a switch when wet. Some localities prohibit placement of switches inside bathrooms.

LIGHTING PRINCIPLES

As was pointed out previously, good lighting does more than just provide visibility. It influences mood and atmosphere. It also enables you to meet various objectives in home decoration. To obtain good lighting, you have to plan around certain important characteristics of illumination.

Quantity of Light. Many activities are carried on within a home. For any task to be done without eyestrain, sufficient light must be provided. The amount of illumination needed depends on the type of work. More light is needed with small details, with dark colors, and when there is poor contrast with the background. Nearly seven times as much light is recommended for sewing on dark cloth as for reading a book. Also, more light is needed for tasks lasting several hours than for the same tasks when completed in a few minutes. Furthermore, more light may be needed for subnormal eyes and for older people.

In addition to their effects on visibility, high levels of general lighting usually are cheerful and stimulating. Low levels tend to create an atmosphere of relaxation, intimacy, and restfulness. By controlling the level of general lighting, you can change the mood of the space to meet your objectives.

Quality of Light. Visibility, mood, comfort, and eyestrain are all influenced by the contrast of light and dark areas. When shadows are minimized, the lighting is said to be *soft* or *diffused.* Such nearly uniform lighting provides an atmosphere more relaxing and visually less compelling than contrasting lighting. When deep shadows are present, the lighting is said to be *hard.*

When soft lighting is used alone in a space, it becomes less interesting. When hard light is used artfully, it provides highlights and contrasts. It can emphasize texture, delineate form, and create a sense of life and gaiety. Often, it is advisable to have both hard and soft lighting available in a room, so that you can produce distinct changes in atmosphere and mood at will.

Contrast between light and dark areas, however, can also be a source of glare, which can cause severe discomfort. Therefore, contrast must be strictly controlled, as is explained later.

Color. At one time, fluorescent lighting was unpopular for home use because the light emitted had an unpleasant effect on colors of people and things. As a result, manufacturers of fluorescent lamps immensely improved the output color for home use. This example points up the importance of color in lighting.

Color of light influences the colors of objects observed. Usually, it is desirable that the color of light enhance the color identification of an object or area. But bright colors may not be satisfactory for a light source, because they can destroy the accepted appearance of people and things.

Incandescent lamps radiate light throughout the visible spectrum, but mostly in the yellow-to-red end. Fluorescent lamps radiate light with much blue, green, and yellow and little red, unless they are color-adjusted. For home use, the color is adjusted to enhance skin tones and flatter general decor. It is possible to change the entire color atmosphere of a room by changing from incandescent to fluorescent light, or from "cool" to "warm" fluorescent lamps.

Quantity of light also affects perceived object color. Low levels tend to make colors appear grayer. High levels intensify colors.

Consequently, when planning the decoration of a home, you should select colors to be used for rooms and furnishings under the type of light source with which they will be used, and preferably at about the same illumination level. Use of brightly colored lights should be restricted to decorative effects or accent lighting.

Applications. The preceding discussion of the characteristics of lighting implies that good lighting may be achieved with different lighting arrangements, used alone or in combination. These arrangements include the following:

GENERAL LIGHTING—a low level of light throughout an area, for moving about, for most housekeeping, and for making local light more pleasing.

LOCAL, OR FUNCTIONAL, LIGHTING—a higher level of illumination applied to a relatively small area in which a task is to be performed, such as reading, sewing, or operating power tools.

ACCENT OR DECORATIVE LIGHTING—a higher level of light than that used for general lighting, with the objective of creating focal points, emphasizing displayed objects, and adding a personal and distinctive touch.

LIGHTING EQUIPMENT

Whether merely adding to or improving the existing lighting in your home or completely remodeling it, you have a wide variety of lighting equipment from which to choose. Following is a summary of the various options open to you.

Electrical Distribution Systems. In almost all cases, electricity is distributed throughout a home at 110 to 120 volts. Some equipment, such as ranges and air conditioners, must be supplied with 220 volts. Lighting generally operates on 110 to 120 volts. Also, the lights are put on and off usually by flicking switches through which electric current at the same voltage passes.

If a person is accidentally subjected to 110 volts or more, severe injury or death can result. Also, short circuits at those voltages can cause fires. The risks of these events can be eliminated by substantially reducing the voltages in the electrical distribution system.

One option available is operation of lighting at about 110 volts but use of low voltage to put the lights on and off. Initial cost of installing such a control system may be somewhat higher than for a system completely at the higher voltage, but operation costs should be slightly less. Control-system voltages generally range from 6 to 24 volts.

For special purposes, especially outdoor applications, to reduce hazards from electrical shock, you can use low-voltage lamps in low-voltage circuits to advantage. Swimming pools and fountains are good examples. Accidental breakage of a low-voltage lamp or failure in the low-voltage wiring system is less hazardous to people in swimming pools or shoveling in gardens than would be the case if 110 volts were used.

Lighting Distribution. Illumination specialists usually refer to a light source and its enclosure or housing as a *luminaire.* We will find it convenient in future discussions to use this general term to avoid confusion in terminology with lamps, bulbs, and fixtures and other light sources.

The importance of quantity of light has previously been discussed. Thus, one factor in the selection of a luminaire is the quantity of light you wish to obtain from it. Some luminaires are designed for lamps with wattage no larger than 40 watts. Other types of luminaires may permit 150 watts or more. Still other types may permit use of several lamps. Considering cost and appearance, choose the luminaire that will give the amount of light you want.

Another factor in selecting a luminaire is the type of light distribution it provides. Luminaires may supply *direct* or *indirect lighting.* Direct lighting travels in a straight line from light source to observed objects. Indirect lighting is reflected from room enclosures—walls, floor, and ceiling—in traveling from light source to observed objects. Some luminaires supply a combination of direct and indirect lighting. For example, a table lamp may throw some light directly on objects below it, such as a book, while projecting some light upward to be reflected from the ceiling onto the objects below. Such luminaires often are used to provide a combination of general lighting and local lighting in a room.

Luminaires may also provide light *symmetrically distributed* or *asymmetrically distributed*. With symmetrical distribution, the quantity of light in a small or large area directly under the luminaire is nearly uniform. With asymmetrical distribution, light is concentrated in a specific direction.

Most luminaires used for home lighting have a symmetrical distribution. Sometimes, however, an asymmetrical distribution is desirable. Suppose, for example, you wanted to illuminate a mural on a wall. In that case, you could use a luminaire called a *wall washer,* recessed in the ceiling. It directs a broad spread of light at a nearby vertical surface to produce nearly uniform lighting on it.

Incandescent Lamps. Luminaires should also be selected in accordance with the type of light source preferred. The types that are designed for incandescent lamps differ from those designed for fluorescent lamps, and they are not interchangeable.

Incandescent lamps develop light by heating very small-diameter wires or filaments. Most of the light produced is in the yellow-to-red portion of the spectrum. The higher the wattage of the lamp, the whiter the color. Reduced wattage or voltage causes a yellower light.

You must consider physical size and wattage in selecting lamps, to be sure they are compatible with luminaires in which they are to be used. If the lamps give off excessive heat, they may cause socket and wiring damage.

If a luminaire produces lighting with harsh shadows and veiled reflections, you can diminish the effect by selecting the proper lamp. The degree of harshness is influenced by the finish on the bulb. Inside-frosted lamps produce softer illumination than clear bulbs. Silica-coated (white) lamps yield softer lighting than the inside-frosted.

Fluorescent Lamps. As mentioned previously, if you decide on fluorescent lighting, you must use a luminaire designed for fluorescent lamps. These lamps generally are tubular and vary in length and diameter, depending on the wattage. Because the length varies with wattage, a luminaire designed for one wattage will not accept lamps of a different wattage.

Fluorescent lamps produce light by using an electric current to excite a coating on the inner surface. The color of light produced depends on the coating material used. Some fluorescent lamps approximate daylight in their effect on colors. Other types produce light ranging from bluish white to nearly the same as incandescent light. Choice of type depends on personal preference. You have to take into account your color scheme, the atmosphere you wish to create, and the influence of adjacent areas.

Fluorescent lamps offer more light for power consumed than do incandescent lamps. Therefore, they cost less to operate. Initial cost of luminaires, however, may be greater for fluorescent lamps. Not only are larger fixtures required, because of the length of the tubes, but extra equipment is needed. Fluorescent lamps cannot be operated directly from a power supply. They need a ballast, a current-limiting device. Also, different types of circuits are needed, depending on the method of starting the lamp. Such circuits include preheat, trigger start, and rapid start.

One factor to consider in deciding between incandescent and fluorescent lighting is that all ballasts make some noise. Where the ambient noise level is very low, for example, in a living room or a study, ballast hum can be objectionable. When selecting a fluorescent fixture for use where ballast noise may be of concern, find out what noise rating has been assigned the ballasts in the fixtures of interest. An *A* sound rating is best, *B* is not so good, etc.

Colored Lighting. Color effects can be obtained by using colored light sources or ordinary lamps with colored luminaires. Incandescent lamps are available with colored coatings that make the light emitted colored. If such lamps are not suitable for your purpose, you can use a luminaire with colored glass or filter.

Other Special Lamps. When planning improved lighting for your home, you will also find it worthwhile to consider installing some special types of lamps. For example, heat lamps in the bathroom ceiling can provide comfort at times when you do not wish to use the house heating system to heat the whole house. Also, ultraviolet lamps in bathrooms or bedrooms can be used for health reasons during long periods of inclement weather or when, for other reasons, a member of the family cannot get outdoors. In addition, you should consider the use of germicidal lamps in playrooms and nurseries.

Recessed Luminaires. When you wish to illuminate a room without table or floor lamps and without projections below the ceiling, you can do it with recessed luminaires. Installed in the ceiling, they send all their light downward. Thus, they provide only direct lighting. Figure 1 shows several types of recessed luminaires.

Part *A* of Figure 1 illustrates a wide-profile type of fixture, with an incandescent lamp. Shielding may be a flat diffuser or dropped opal glass. A similar type may be equipped with fluorescent lamps, shielded with a domed diffuser, plastic louver, or formed diffuser. By placing several recessed luminaires in the ceiling, you can provide general lighting in basement, recreation rooms, kitchen, laundry, and service halls. Such luminaires can also be used singly or in small groups for small areas, such as in walk-in closets, in the garage, at entry doors, and under porch overhangs. Because of the brightness of the diffuser, however, the wide-profile type is seldom used in living or social areas.

Part *B* of Figure 1 shows a medium-profile recessed luminaire. The lamp may be shielded with various shapes of a Fresnel lens, which spreads the light. This is suitable for specific task lighting where the task area is large. The luminaire may be placed over the kitchen sink, island counter and range, laundry equipment, ironing area, game table, workbench, and hobby area. When shielded with a metal bottom plate with a relatively small opening, the luminaire has sufficiently low brightness so that it can be used in living and dining rooms. A similar effect can be obtained with a silver-bowled incandescent lamp with circular shielding island.

Part *C* of Figure 1 shows a narrow-profile recessed luminaire (high hat). It may come equipped with an ellipsoidal, polished metal reflector, or an annular baffle cylinder, or a concentric-ring, spiral, or egg-crate louver. It is suitable for a variety of accent and decorative applications.

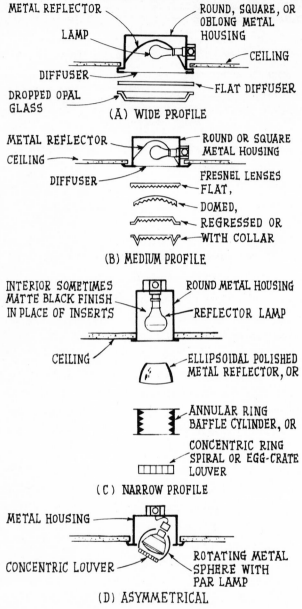

METAL REFLECTOR

LAMP

DIFFUSER

DROPPED OPAL
GLASS

ROUND, SQUARE, OR
OBLONG METAL
HOUSING

CEILING

FLAT DIFFUSER

(A) WIDE PROFILE

METAL REFLECTOR

CEILING

DIFFUSER

ROUND OR SQUARE
METAL HOUSING

FRESNEL LENSES
FLAT,

DOMED,

REGRESSED OR

WITH COLLAR

(B) MEDIUM PROFILE

INTERIOR SOMETIMES
MATTE BLACK FINISH
IN PLACE OF INSERTS

ROUND METAL HOUSING

REFLECTOR LAMP

CEILING

ELLIPSOIDAL POLISHED
METAL REFLECTOR, OR

ANNULAR RING
BAFFLE CYLINDER, OR

CONCENTRIC RING
SPIRAL OR EGG-CRATE
LOUVER

(C) NARROW PROFILE

METAL HOUSING

CONCENTRIC LOUVER

ROTATING METAL
SPHERE WITH
PAR LAMP

(D) ASYMMETRICAL

FIGURE 1. Recessed luminaires.

It can provide accent lighting to displays, flower arrangements, or cocktail table. Effective when used near the perimeter of a room so that some light spills onto the wall, the luminaire can provide dramatic effects in family rooms, recreation rooms, and formal living areas. It can also be used for supplementary stair lighting, so that shadow patterns more clearly define treads and risers. Still another use is provision of functional lighting on a dining table to supplement a decorative hanging luminaire.

Part *D* of Figure 1 shows a recessed luminaire for providing light with an asymmetrical distribution. It can be used to illuminate paintings, sculpture, maps, and niches. It may also be used for lighting sewing machines or piano music. The type shown (eyeball) projects slightly below the ceiling. Other types with asymmetrical distribution that are completely recessed are available.

Ceiling-mounted Luminaires. When projections below the ceiling are not objectionable, or when other than direct lighting is desired, you can use ceiling-mounted luminaires. They may be of the general-diffusing, diffuse-downlighting, or downlighting type. Figure 2 shows several types of ceiling-mounted luminaires.

Part *A* of Figure 2 shows a small general-diffusing type and Part *B*, a large general-diffusing type. They direct their light in a very wide pattern. Because they illuminate walls and ceiling, they are usually used for general lighting. In selecting this type of luminaire, carefully consider its brightness in relation to the presence of shiny surfaces in the room. Be sure that light sources, whether incandescent or fluorescent, are not visible either through or over the luminaire. No part of the diffusing element should be more than twice as bright as the average brightness of this element. For this reason, lamps within the luminaire should be neither too widely spaced nor too close to the diffuser.

Part *C* of Figure 2 shows two of the many variations of the diffuse-downlighting type of luminaire. This type usually has opaque or nearly opaque sides. Consequently, it does not throw light on the ceiling, and it has to be placed close to walls if it is to illuminate them. If diffuse-downlighting is to be used for general lighting, there should be at least one luminaire for each 100 square feet of floor area. Also, the room finishes should be very light in color.

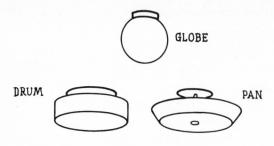

GLOBE

DRUM

PAN

(A) SMALL GENERAL-DIFFUSING TYPE

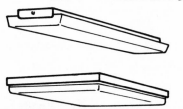

LINEAR FLUORESCENT DIFFUSER

SQUARE OR RECTANGULAR FLUORESCENT DIFFUSER

(B) LARGE GENERAL-DIFFUSING TYPE

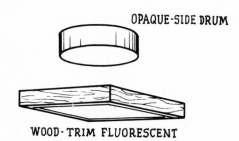

OPAQUE-SIDE DRUM

WOOD-TRIM FLUORESCENT

(C) DIFFUSE-DOWNLIGHTING TYPE

CAN

BULLET

(D) DOWNLIGHTING TYPE

FIGURE 2. Ceiling-mounted luminaires.

Part *D* shows downlighting types of luminaires. They are intended for accent lighting or supplementary illumination of critical visual tasks, such as sewing. The resulting lighting is hard; that is, shadows are sharp.

Pendant Luminaires. As an alternative to ceiling-mounted luminaires, fixtures hung from the ceiling may be used. They may be of the general-diffusing, direct-indirect, downlighting, or exposed-lamp type. Figure 3 shows several types of pendant luminaires.

Part *A* of Figure 3 shows two of the many variations of the general-diffusing type, which are used for both functional and decorative purposes. For decorative purposes, the light emitted is kept at low level. Hence, the lamps in the luminaire may be of low wattage, or tinted, or controlled by a dimmer. The lamps are treated as ornaments. When selecting a pendant luminaire for functional purposes, though, you should ascertain that it meets the brightness limitations given previously for general-diffusing, ceiling-mounted luminaires. But if the pendant luminaire is to be hung low enough to be in the line of sight, its brightness should be much lower.

Part *B* of Figure 3 shows two of the many variations of the direct-indirect type of pendant luminaire. These provide upward lighting, which, reflected from the ceiling, serves as general lighting. They simultaneously provide downlighting, which can be used for functional lighting. This type of luminaire has opaque or nearly opaque sides. As a result, it is often suitable for low hanging. Bottom shields or louvers are required when the luminaire can be viewed from below, and top shields are necessary when it is hung very low. Diffusers, however, should not be visible below or above the sides of the luminaire. For added flexibility, the luminaire may be mounted on a pulley, for height adjustment when desired, and suspended from a track, for horizontal adjustment. The direct-indirect luminaire is suitable for lighting dining tables, snack bars, game tables, coffee tables, and planters.

Part *C* of Figure 3 shows the downlighting type of pendant luminaire. Its main purpose is to provide accent lighting. It is usually hung at or below eye level. If set above eye level—for example, in halls or above stairways—it should have bottom shielding. The light emitted is hard; that is, it produces sharp shadows. But usually the larger the luminaire the less sharp the shadows.

Part *D* shows the exposed-lamp type. It is mainly decorative. The lighting contributes highlights, sparkle, and accent but is kept at low level. Hence, the lamps may be of low wattage, or tinted, or they may be dimmer-controlled. Nevertheless, the lamps are apt to be bright enough to make it necessary for the luminaire to be mounted above the normal line of sight.

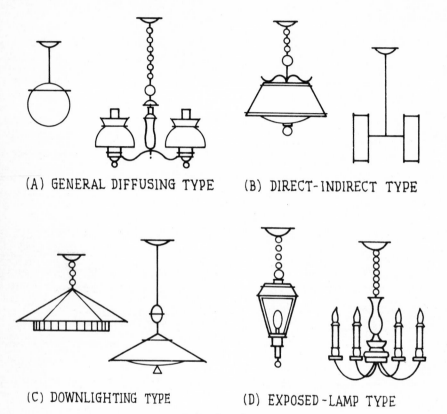

(A) GENERAL DIFFUSING TYPE   (B) DIRECT-INDIRECT TYPE

(C) DOWNLIGHTING TYPE   (D) EXPOSED-LAMP TYPE

FIGURE 3. Pendant luminaires.

Wall-mounted Luminaires. In some cases, you might find it advantageous to set luminaires on a wall. A common instance is the installation on the outside wall of a house of a luminaire or two at the entrance door. The characteristics of wall-mounted luminaires are about the same as those described previously for ceiling-mounted luminaires. Figure 4 shows several types of wall-mounted luminaires.

· The exposed-lamp type, illustrated in the *A* part of Figure 4, is often

used for decorative purposes. The small diffuser type, shown in the
B part, is sometimes used in pairs, in groups, or in lines for illuminating
halls, stairs, doorways, and mirrors. If this type is used in living or family
rooms where the luminaires will be in view for a long time, their brightness should be very low.

The linear type, shown in the *C* part, often is mounted over mirrors,
under cabinets, and where functional lighting is required for close-up

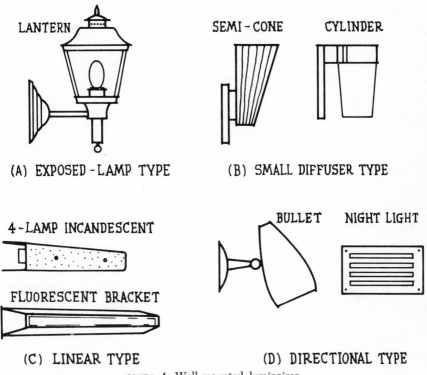

FIGURE 4. Wall-mounted luminaires.

tasks. The luminaire usually is equipped with high-output lamps. Hence,
the light sources should have an opaque shield or be enclosed in a good
diffuser.

Part *D* of Figure 4 shows two of the many variations of the directional
type of wall-mounted luminaire. The bullet type provides downlighting
and is suitable for accent and display illumination. Other types provide
uplighting and can be used in groups for general lighting. In either case,
opaque shielding should be used so that the light source is not visible.

Structural Lighting Elements. In addition to the basic types of luminaires previously described, you may also have lighting built in as part
of the structure of your home or built to use structural elements, such
as spaces between joists, as parts of luminaires. Figure 5 shows some
commonly used types. But you can also utilize such devices as bookshelves
with integral concealed lighting, illuminated fish tanks, luminous wall
panels, lighted niches, artificial skylights, and concealed lighting in china
closets, to mention a few.

Structural lighting has the advantage of conforming to the architecture
or interior decoration of a room. The luminaire may be designed to
provide light in an unobtrusive manner.

The basic considerations of lamp concealment, diffused brightness,
light distribution, and light-source color apply equally as well to structural lighting as to the other types of luminaires previously discussed.
Structural lighting, however, generally is designed as a linear type and
consequently is often designed for fluorescent lamps.

Part *A* of Figure 5 shows a lighted cornice. All the light is directed
downward to accent wall coverings, draperies, or murals. This type may
also be used above windows where there is insufficient space for valance
lighting. It is suitable for use in low-ceilinged rooms.

Part *B* of Figure 5 shows a lighted valance. It provides both uplighting
and downlighting. The uplighting, reflected from the ceiling, serves as
part of the general lighting. Valances are usually used over windows,
where the downlighting accents the draperies. If the lamp must be closer
than 10 inches from the ceiling, the top should be shielded to prevent
ceiling brightness that would be annoying.

Part *C* shows a lighted cove. All light is directed to the ceiling. Hence,
this type is suitable for use in high-ceilinged rooms and for spaces where
ceiling heights change abruptly. Because of the soft lighting produced,
cove lighting is best used as a supplement for other lighting.

Part *D* shows a lighted wall bracket. Mounted high, usually at window
or door height, this type provides both up and down light for general
illumination. It is used on interior walls to balance window valances
both architecturally and in light distribution. Mounted low, at about
eye height, a lighted wall bracket may be used for accenting wall displays
or for illuminating work areas—for kitchen duties, reading, and other

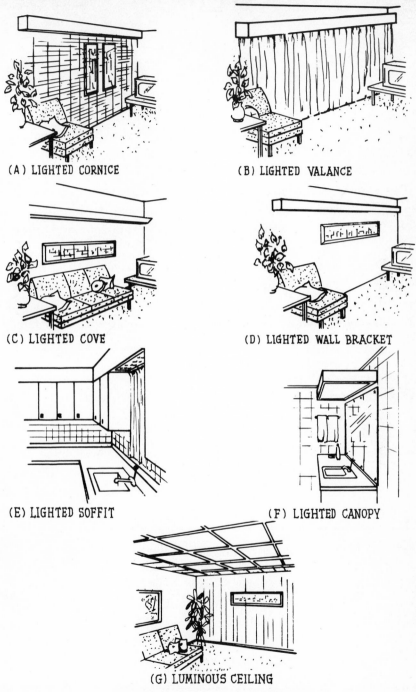

(A) LIGHTED CORNICE

(B) LIGHTED VALANCE

(C) LIGHTED COVE

(D) LIGHTED WALL BRACKET

(E) LIGHTED SOFFIT

(F) LIGHTED CANOPY

(G) LUMINOUS CEILING

FIGURE 5. Types of structural lighting.

close-up tasks. Length of brackets depends on nearby furniture group, room scale, and length of display.

Part *E* shows a lighted soffit. The light may be placed over a work area to provide a high level of light directly below. One may usually be easily installed in the furred-down ceiling above the sink in a kitchen, as indicated in *E*. A lighted soffit also is convenient in bathrooms and dressing rooms for face lighting, and it is decorative as well. It generally is mounted over a long mirror and counter-top lavatory, normally being made about as long as the mirror.

Part *F* shows a lighted canopy. Projecting from a wall over a counter top or other work area, it can throw light up and down and thus is useful for general illumination. It is often used in bathrooms and dressing rooms.

Part *G* illustrates a luminous ceiling. It has a skylight effect suitable for interior rooms or utility spaces, such as kitchens, bathrooms, and laundries. When used with decorative supports, attractive diffuser patterns, and color accents, a luminous ceiling becomes acceptable for family rooms and playrooms.

Portable Lamps. Your lighting objectives often can be met, at least partly, with portable lamps. For the purpose, you can select from a wide variety of table lamps and various types of floor lamps, such as torch lamps, pole lights, and tree lights. They may be merely decorative or both decorative and functional. They may supply downlighting on a task area or uplighting to add to general lighting, or both. But care must be taken that they are correctly placed relative to the task and the user's eyes.

Use care also in selecting table lamps with shades. Avoid deep, narrow shades for lamps intended to supply useful illumination. The inner surface of the shade should be highly reflective. The shade material should transmit adequate light yet should have good diffusing quality. Light-colored shades should be used in front of light-colored walls and darker shades in front of darker walls, for pleasing appearance. If an opaque shade is used, the room should also have supplementary lighting from other sources, such as lighted valances or brackets, to illuminate areas, such as walls, not lighted by the portable lamp. The proper height for a shade for reading places the bottom of the shade at about eye level. For a dressing-table lamp used for makeup, the useful light must pass through the shade onto the face. Hence, the center of the shade should be at cheek level.

HOW TO PLAN NEW LIGHTING

A first step in planning a lighting project is to take a critical look at each room with lighting as your main consideration. Pay special attention to the furnishings. Decide what should be accented and what should be played down. If the room is to be remodeled, plan the lighting around the proposed layout.

Draw a floor plan to a scale of $\frac{1}{4}'' = 1' \, 0''$. Also, draw the furniture to scale on it in planned locations. Decide for each room how you will provide general lighting. Indicate the luminaire locations by small circles for incandescent luminaires and rectangles for fluorescent luminaires. Indicate the locations of the switches that are to control them with an S. Connect each switch to the light it is to control with a light dashed line. If a light is to be controlled by two switches, write a 3 after the S for each of those switches, to indicate a three-way switch is needed. If a light is to be controlled by a dimmer, write *DIM.* under the S.

Next, decide where you are likely to use table or floor lamps in each room. Indicate on the floor plan the locations of outlets that will be needed. Each outlet can be represented by a tiny circle with two lines through it perpendicular to the wall. An outlet should be located on a wall within 5 feet of each lamp. If this is not feasible, either rearrange the furniture layout or choose some other means of providing desired illumination.

After that, consider special-effects lighting. What displays do you want to accent? What moods do you wish to create? What work areas need higher lighting? Where are lights needed for safety and security reasons? Where do you want decorative effects? What play areas need special lighting? In each case, indicate the luminaires on the floor plan with a circle or rectangle and a brief identification, such as *valance, cove, high hat,* or *eyeball.* Also note on the plan with an S and a dashed line the location of the controlling switch.

Take the plan with you when you look for lighting fixtures and obtain cost estimates. Make changes in the plan, as necessary, as you obtain costs or develop new ideas for decorating. Get preliminary cost estimates for the entire electrical installation for remodeling from at least two electrical contractors. Change the plan again to bring costs in line with what you are willing to spend. Then, request bids from the contractors for the electrical work.

TYPICAL PROJECTS

In the following, some of the conditions that you are likely to encounter in your home will be examined with the objective of providing a lighting solution. In many cases, many other excellent solutions are possible. The choice depends largely on personal preferences, actual furnishings, room sizes and shapes, and costs.

Kitchen. For general lighting, a kitchen with a floor area of between 75 and 120 square feet should have lamps with the following minimum wattages: in ceiling-mounted luminaires, 150- to 200-watt incandescent, or 60- to 80-watt fluorescent; in recessed luminaires, preferably 10 to 14 inches in size, four 100-watt incandescent, or two 40-watt fluorescent.

For general lighting, a kitchen with larger floor area should have lamps with the following minimum wattages: in ceiling-mounted luminaires, 2 watts per square foot incandescent, or ¾ to 1 watt per square foot fluorescent; in recessed luminaires, preferably 10 to 14 inches in size with incandescent, one 100-watt per 30 square feet or one 150-watt per 40 square feet; or with fluorescent, two 40-watt per 60 square feet.

We will assume that you have a large kitchen, with a sink and dishwasher along one wall and a range and cabinets along two other walls. We will also assume that the kitchen has a floor area of about 180 square feet and that fluorescent lighting is acceptable and may be ceiling-mounted.

In accordance with the recommendations above for general lighting, 1 watt or slightly less is required for each square foot. Hence, for the floor area of 180 square feet, about 180 watts should be provided. This indicates that at least four 40-watt fluorescent lamps are needed, providing a total of 160 watts. Their light will be supplemented by a spillover of the light from lamps used for local, or functional, lighting.

Since general lighting is to be provided, select two luminaires of the linear fluorescent diffuser, ceiling-mounted type (see the *B* part of Figure 2), each to hold two 40-watt tubes. Mount the fixtures about 4 feet apart, equally spaced from the center of the kitchen. Place them with their long dimension parallel to the long direction of the room, as indicated in the *C* part of Figure 6. Use deluxe cool-white fluorescent tubes if you want a daylight atmosphere, or else, deluxe warm-white.

For local lighting over the sink, recess in the soffit above the sink two 75-watt R-30 floodlights (incandescent) in louvered high hats. (See the *A* part of Figure 6 and the *C* part of Figure 1.) Set the fixtures with 15 inches between their centers, as shown in the *B* part of Figure 6.

For illuminating the counter top along the long wall, use one 40-watt fluorescent tube which is 48 inches long (see the *C* part of Figure 6). At either side of the sink use one 20-watt fluorescent tube which is 24 inches long (see the *A* part of the figure). Place another such tube along the wall perpendicular to the sink. In each case, use deluxe warm-white lamps in downlighting-type luminaires mounted under the upper cabinets. A simple arrangement with an opaque shielding faceboard, finished to match the cabinets, is shown in the *D* part of Figure 6.

The range, which has a ventilating hood over it, can be illuminated with a 100-watt soft-white or 75-watt R-30 flood lamp mounted above it.

Dining Room. Light is needed for mood effects as well as for seeing in a dining room. A chandelier, when used, is chosen for decorative purposes as well as for illumination.

We will assume a large formal dining room, as illustrated in the *A* part of Figure 7. Along one wall is a server, above which is an attractive mural. Along an intersecting wall is a recessed china cabinet and a fireplace. Two beautiful pictures hang above the fireplace.

The decision whether to use a chandelier at all and, if one is to be used, which type to select is very much a matter of personal preference.

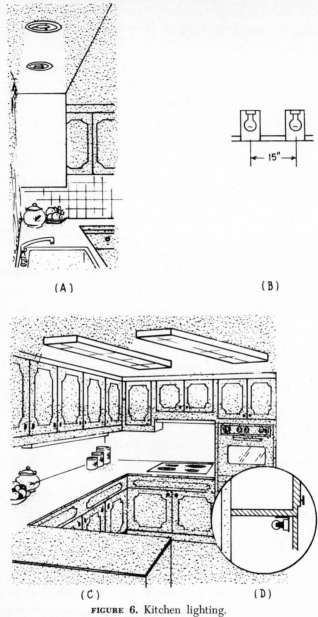

(A)

(B)

(C)

(D)

FIGURE 6. Kitchen lighting.

For example, if you want a dramatic effect, with lighting that adds spar-kle to your china and silverware, you might pick an exposed-lamp type, supplemented by recessed downlights. In this case, we will assume that a general-diffusing type, as shown in the *A* part of Figure 7, is desired.

WOOD
BLOCKING

7"

FLUOR
TUBE

PAINT INSIDE
MATTE WHITE

7"

(A)   (B)

FIGURE 7. Dining room lighting.

It will be centered over the table, with its bottom from 30 to 36 inches above the table. It will be provided with six 60-watt, soft-white incan-descent lamps. The lighting level will be controlled by a dimmer. The fixture should have a spread of at least 20 inches and the shades should be at least 5 inches in diameter.

Over the mural, a lighted cornice should be mounted, just below the ceiling. Cornice and mural should have the same length. Use the longest fluorescent tubes that will fit in the cornice. (See the *B* part of Figure 7.)

In front of the pictures above the fireplace, recess in the ceiling two 75-watt PAR-38 lamps in eyeball luminaires (see the *D* part of Figure 1). Directed at the pictures, they should be set about 2 feet from the wall and centered on the pictures (about 24 inches apart).

The recessed china cabinet can be dramatically illuminated in several ways. A general rule is that several small incandescent bulbs are usually better than one or two higher-wattage lamps. In any event, the lamps must be hidden from view so as not to distract attention from the objects on display. Furthermore, because the display is at eye level, a low level of illumination would be much more pleasant than a high level.

In this case, use lumiline lamps or show-case tubes, concealed behind a shallow lip on each shelf. (You might instead attach shielded, tiny, low-voltage incandescent strips to the bottom front edge of each shelf. If the cabinet had vertical framing, you could hide clear Christmas tree bulbs behind the frame.)

Living Room. You have a very wide freedom of choice in designing the lighting treatment of a living room. This occurs because you can use both portable and built-in light sources to obtain good, balanced lighting. But you should exert special care in selecting the illumination for this room. It is here where you will entertain friends and visitors and where they will gain their main impressions of the character of your home.

We will assume that you have a large living room. The focal point will be assumed to be along a long wall that extends into the dining room. Strategically placed along the wall are a coffee table, long sofa, and planter (see the *A* part of Figure 8).

Above the sofa, mount a low, lighted wall bracket. It will provide uplighting, for general illumination, and downlighting on the sofa, for functional purposes. Use fluorescent tubes, one 40-watt (48 inches long) or two 40-watt (about 100 inches long, end to end), depending on the length of the sofa. See the *B* part of Figure 8 for placement of lamp and shield. The bracket may be set about 2 feet above the sofa.

Over the planter, suspend four decorative luminaires that provide downlighting, for accent.

Additional general illumination for the room can be provided by perimeter wall lighting, such as valances above the windows, and floor and table lamps. These lamps can also be used for reading and other activities. Displays can be treated as in the dining room.

Bedrooms. A bedroom can be a space just for dressing or sleeping, or it may also be used for relaxing away from the family and guests,

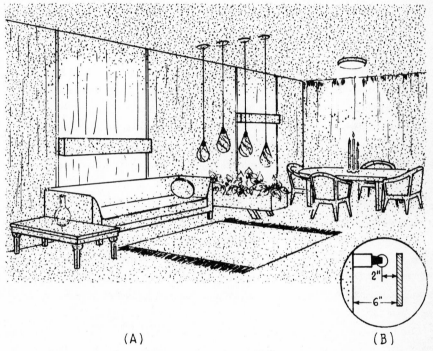

(A)   (B)

FIGURE 8. Living room lighting.

or it can be a place for study. In any event, it is a very personal room. It must suit the needs and moods of the persons who occupy it. And it must look attractive, although the room may be small and the furniture large. By keeping the room uncluttered and providing proper lighting, you can get the feelings of spaciousness, serenity, and beauty that are desired. In the following, we will consider a master bedroom and a child's room that also can be used as a guest room.

We will assume a large master bedroom. Twin beds with a night table between them are set along one wall (see the *A* part of Figure 9). A dresser-desk is placed under draperied windows in an intersecting wall.

For both general and functional lighting, place a low, lighted wall bracket on the bed wall. Continuous over both beds, this luminaire throws light upward to the ceiling to be reflected and downward to permit reading in bed (see the *A* part of Figure 9). The bracket may be similar to the one shown in the *B* part of Figure 8. Place in the bracket two 40-watt, deluxe cool-white, fluorescent lamps, end to end. For general lighting, mount in the center of the ceiling a drum luminaire of the general-diffusing type. It should provide 120 to 150 watts of incandescent light.

Above the dresser-desk, mount a lighted canopy just above the windows. It should be as long as the dresser-desk. Equip the canopy with two pairs of 40-watt, deluxe warm-white, fluorescent lamps (see the *B* part of Figure 9). Additional lighting can be provided elsewhere in the room by portable table and floor lamps as desired.

In the child's room, for general lighting mount in the center of the ceiling an opaque-side drum (see the *C* part of Figure 2). It should provide at least 120 watts of incandescent light. About 2 feet above the small table, place a wall-mounted luminaire with opaque shade and adjustable arm (see the *C* part of Figure 9). In the bookcase on the opposite wall, use concealed fluorescent lamps for display lighting. About 2 feet above the dresser-desk, place a lighted wall bracket with a 40-watt, deluxe cool-white fluorescent lamp, as indicated in the *D* part of Figure 9.

Bathroom. Your bathrooms can and should be just as charming as the other rooms in your house, and good lighting can help make them so. Like the other rooms, a bathroom needs both general and local lighting. The latter is especially necessary in mirror and vanity areas and should be of the highest quality. A simple rule is always to light from both sides and from above. Basins and counter tops should be light in color to reflect light up under the chin for shaving.

When incandescent lighting is used, soft-white bulbs are good because they give a soft light. When fluorescent lighting is used, the tubes should be natural-white or deluxe warm-white or similar, because these flatter the skin tones, giving a warm, vibrant appearance. All lamps should

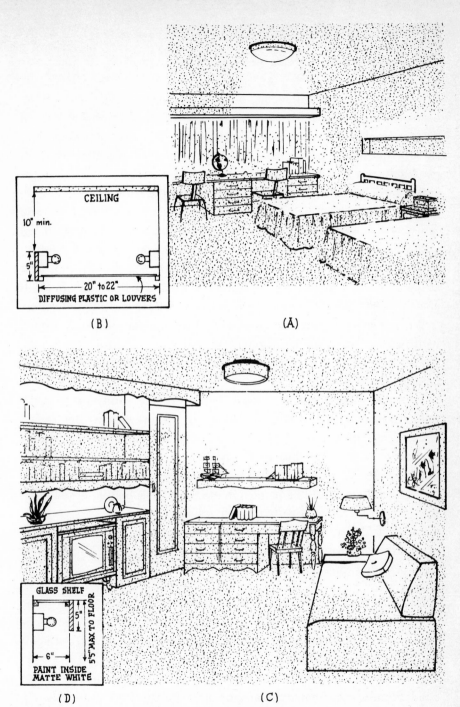

CEILING

10" min.

5"

20" to 22"

DIFFUSING PLASTIC OR LOUVERS

(B)

(A)

GLASS SHELF

5"

5'5" MAX TO FLOOR

6"

PAINT INSIDE
MATTE WHITE

(D)

(C)

FIGURE 9. Bedroom lighting.

be concealed with a translucent material that effectively conceals their image.

Except for very small rooms, a bathroom needs a light in addition to the mirror lights. If the room is compartmented, lighting is needed in each section. Over enclosed bathtubs and showers, use watertight, vaporproof luminaires that provide at least 60 watts of incandescent light, preferably recessed in the ceiling. For safety, the light should be controlled by a switch outside and out of reach of the bathing area.

In addition, night lights should be provided. For the purpose, you can plug a 7-watt incandescent lamp into an outlet. Or you can recess a 25-watt louvered luminaire into the wall. Or you can use an electroluminescent light source that provides a low level of light day and night at low cost for electricity. Switch plates with such a light source are available and serve as both a night light and a device for locating the switch.

We will assume that you have a medium-size bathroom. A vanity, with two lavatories in the counter top and with a mirror above, lines one wall (see Figure 10). Along the opposite wall are a partly enclosed bathtub and shower.

For both general and functional lighting of the vanity area, install soffit lighting. The luminaire should be at least as long as the vanity. Use at least three rows of 40-watt (48-inch-long), deluxe, warm-white fluorescent tubes, extending as nearly as possible the full length of the soffit. The soffit should be at least 12 inches deep and about 22 inches wide. The inside should be painted matte white. The bottom of the luminaire should be enclosed with a plastic diffuser.

Install a 75-watt incandescent lamp in a recessed, watertight, vaporproof fixture above the bathtub. Provide a high hat with 75-watt R-30 lamp over the water closet area.

Entrance Hall. A visitor gains his or her first impression of your home on entering the front door. Consequently, the entrance hall should be attractive and impart a sense of graciousness and hospitality. Good lighting can contribute considerably to this effect.

Since an entrance hall usually offers a revealing glimpse into the home, select fixtures coordinated in design and lighting effect with those in surrounding areas visible from the hall. If a stairway serves the hall, the tops of the entrance-hall luminaires should be shielded to protect persons descending the stairs from glare.

For a low-ceilinged entrance hall with an area of more than 75 square feet, a single ceiling-mounted luminaire at least 12 inches in diameter can be used with about 150 watts of incandescent light. If, however, this size of hall is high-ceilinged, and especially if a stairway leads into

FIGURE 10. Bathroom lighting.

it, a pendant luminaire may be more suitable. If the luminaire is multi-armed, it should have a spread of 18 to 28 inches and carry three to six shielded incandescent lamps with a total of about 200 watts. If the entrance hall is less than 75 square feet in area, you can use a recessed high hat with a 150-watt R-40 flood lamp or a ceiling-mounted fixture with about 100 watts of soft-white incandescent light.

We will assume the entrance hall shown in Figure 11. For main lighting, provide a decorative pendant luminaire. Since the top is not visible from the stairs, it can provide both uplighting and downlighting. Use incandescent bulbs supplying a total of 150 watts. Also, recess an eyeball

FIGURE 11. Entrance hall lighting.

in the ceiling about 2 feet from the wall and direct it at the picture. Equip it with a 75-watt PAR-38 lamp. In addition, place a wall-mounted luminaire above the stairs about 3 feet from the corner of the wall. Set 6′ 6″ above the stairs at that point, the luminaire should be opaque-shielded to provide both uplighting and downlighting. One or more similar wall-mounted luminaires should be installed in the upper part of the stairway.

CHAPTER THIRTEEN

Air Conditioning

Air conditioning provides a means for controlling the indoor climate in a home. It maintains conditions under which people can live, work, and relax in comfort regardless of outdoor temperature and humidity.

In its general concept, air conditioning encompasses heating, cooling, and ventilation. Nearly everyone, however, has heating in his home, unless he lives in a tropical climate and can easily provide ventilation by opening a window. So in many cases air conditioning has come to mean cooling. In this chapter, we will assume that your home has a heating system and that you wish to add a cooling system. The purpose of this chapter is to describe the kinds of systems generally used in homes, to explain several important aspects of air conditioning, and to guide you in the installation of a system suitable to your needs and available funds.

HOW MUCH AIR CONDITIONING?

An air-conditioning installation for a home can range from the relatively simple and inexpensive installation of a window cooling unit in one room to the extensive and sometimes expensive installation of complete and automatic climate control all year round for a whole house. The choice depends mainly on how much money you are willing to spend.

Cost of a year-round system would be less if your home had a warm-air heating system with ductwork that was also adequate for cooling. If the house does not have such a system, you have to either replace the existing heating plant with a year-round system or add a cooling system

365

that is independent of the heating system. Thus, if there is not to be a complete replacement of the existing system, you can choose a cooling installation from among systems that are independent of the heating system or from among systems that can be used in conjunction with the heating plant. And if you pick an independent system, you have a choice of several types of installations, ranging from placement of individual cooling units in all rooms to central systems.

HOW AIR CONDITIONING WORKS

Before you can decide on a type of air-conditioning installation, you should have some understanding of how a system works and what parts are needed.

To begin with, you should know that cooling of a room is accomplished by mixing cool air with the warm room air. The purpose of an air-conditioning system is to supply the cool air in required quantities at desired temperature and relative humidity.

At a minimum, a cooling system requires the following:

Refrigeration cycle—a source of cold
Air handler—a means for transferring the cold to the air supply
Air distribution—a means for spreading the chilled air over the spaces to be cooled

These items may be concentrated in a single piece of equipment, called a *package unit,* or they may require several pieces of equipment. A package unit may provide all three items, or it may provide only the refrigeration cycle and air handler, and ductwork may be used for air distribution. In addition, an air-conditioning system usually includes a *filter* for cleaning the air, *fans* or *blowers* for moving the air, *registers* for diffusion of the air, and *louvers* for fresh-air intake. Also, provision normally is made for exhausting a small amount of indoor air from points of odor, heat, or moisture generation, such as kitchens, toilets, and bathrooms.

The refrigeration cycle, which is a source of cold, contains a liquid, called a *refrigerant,* which is kept cold by several operations performed on it. This liquid is used to absorb heat from the *supply air,* the air to be used in cooling the house.

To explain the refrigeration cycle, let us start with the refrigerant after it has cooled the supply air. This cooling has been accomplished by a transfer of heat from the supply air to the refrigerant, which becomes so warm that it is transformed into a gas. The first step in the cycle is to compress the gas. This makes it even warmer and puts it in under

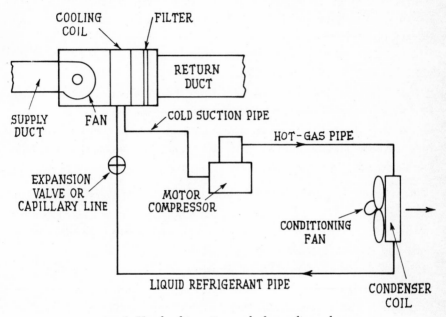

FIGURE 1. Usual refrigeration cycle for cooling a home.

high pressure. The second step is to cool the gas, to transform it back to a liquid, still under high pressure. The third step relieves the pressure on the liquid, cooling it even more. And in the fourth and final step, the liquid, now cold, cools the supply air by extracting heat from it, completing the cycle.

The following items of equipment are needed to accomplish the refrigeration cycle (see Figure 1):

Compressor—for compressing the gas. Compressor and motor drive are manufactured as a single, sealed unit, complete with safety controls.

Condenser—for transforming the high-pressure, hot gas to a high-pressure, cooler liquid. Condenser cooling may be accomplished by immersing the hot-gas pipe in flowing water or by blowing outdoor air over that pipe. Water is more efficient and may be used if an inexpensive, inexhaustible cold supply is available. Outdoor air is not so efficient, because its efficiency decreases as its temperature increases, a condition that can be expected on a hot day. Nevertheless, outdoor air is generally used in condenser cooling for home air conditioning. Besides a cooling source, a condenser also requires a fan and motor, a condenser coil in which the gas-liquid conversion of the refrigerant takes place, and sometimes a liquid receiver or accumulator.

Expansion valve or capillary line—for converting the high-pressure liquid to colder, low-pressure liquid.

Cooling coils—for extracting heat from the supply air. The coils may be located in an air handler, which also incorporates a fan or blower for moving the supply air over the coils and into ductwork or directly into a room. The air handler may also contain the expansion valve or capillary, plus a drip pan and filter.

An important consideration in the use of the refrigeration cycle in air conditioning is that it accomplishes not only cooling but also lowering of the humidity of the supply air. When this air passes over the cooling coils and its temperature drops, it cannot hold as much moisture as it did when it was warmer. (The moisture is deposited on the cooling coils and drips into the drip pan. Provision must be made for draining the drip pan.) The drier air delivered to the rooms contributes to comfort conditions. Normally, you will feel just as comfortable at a specific indoor temperature and relatively low humidity as at a lower temperature and higher humidity. In some cases, when a cooling system is incapable of lowering indoor temperature to a desired level, you will nevertheless be comfortable because of the low humidity.

Another important consideration in air conditioning is that the air is filtered in the air handler. Dust and dirt can be removed there.

AIR DISTRIBUTION

Depending on the type of installation, the supply air, after passing over the cooling coils, may be blown directly into a room or it may be distributed throughout a home by ductwork. Ducts may be constructed of galvanized sheet metal or plastic-impregnated glass fiber. They may be round, square, or rectangular in cross section.

Dampers often are necessary in the ducts to control air flow, balance the system, and adjust it to the desires of the building's occupants.

From the ducts, the supply air is delivered to each room through one or more registers. Because cool air tends to flow to the floor, the best location for registers is near the ceiling. Generally, also, they should be arranged to throw the air across sources of heat, such as windows. Registers are equipped with dampers and have vanes arranged to disperse the air into the room.

While cool supply air is being dispersed in a room, warm air is taken from the room and returned to the cooling coils. This return air may be removed directly by a cooling unit in the room or drawn back to the cooling unit through ducts. In either case, a return grill must be provided at the point where the return air enters the room unit or return duct.

Sometimes, it is desirable to augment the supply air with fresh air or to use outdoor air for condenser cooling. In such cases, louvers, backed by a screen, usually are installed at the point of entry where the fresh air is drawn from outdoors.

TEMPERATURE CONTROL

An essential part of every air-conditioning system, not previously mentioned, is a means for turning the system on and off and for controlling temperatures in the spaces being cooled. Thermostatic controls are available for this purpose.

If ductwork is to be used for both heating and cooling, some means must be provided for switching the system from heating to cooling and back again, when desired. Also, dampers are needed in the ducts to prevent the air from passing through the heating plant or the cooling unit, whichever is not being used. These dampers may be motor-operated, as explained later.

KINDS OF AIR-CONDITIONING SYSTEMS

As was pointed out previously, your choice of a type of air-conditioning system will be considerably influenced by whether or not your home already has a warm-air heating system with ducts that can also be used for cooling. If, for example, your home has a hot-water heating system, the cost of replacing it with year-round air conditioning is likely to be quite high. If you are not willing to pay for such an installation but wish cooling for warm weather, you can install an independent cooling system. Thus, for convenience, we can classify the kinds of air-conditioning installation as either systems independent of the heating plant or systems that can be used in conjunction with the heating plant.

SYSTEMS INDEPENDENT OF HEATING PLANT

A wide variety of separate cooling systems are available. Following are brief descriptions of the more important types for home use:

Window Unit. The simplest and least expensive installation is a package unit that is set in a window opening. This unit incorporates the refrigeration cycle, air handler, air distribution, and necessary controls. It is designed to take care of the cooling requirements of the room in which it is installed. Despite the low cost, window units offer the advantage of separate temperature control in each room. Disadvantages include a higher noise level in the room, an obstructed window opening, and appearance that may be objectionable from an architectural or interior decoration viewpoint.

Through-the-wall Unit. As an alternative to the window unit, you might consider a type of package unit that is basically the same but instead of being set into a window opening is installed in and secured to an exterior wall. The through-the-wall unit will be more expensive, however, if a hole has to be cut into an existing wall for the purpose.

Single-package Unit with Ductwork. The disadvantages of individual room units can be reduced or eliminated by installing a central cooling plant and distributing the air through ducts to the various rooms. For this purpose, you can use a package unit that is like a large window unit but equipped for supply- and return-duct connection. The package unit may be installed in an attic or a basement. When an attic is used, an opening will have to be provided in the wall so that the condensing section of the unit is set outdoors while the cooling section remains inside the attic. A basement installation requires duct connections for outside air. Therefore, the basement can be used only when the level of the outside ground surface is low enough so that the air intake and discharge can be placed above ground level. This air is needed for condenser cooling.

Split Systems. For a quieter air-conditioning system, still using duct-work, you can place the noisier portion of the system, the compressor-condenser part, outdoors and install the air handler with cooling coils inside the house. This arrangement eliminates the need for a wall opening for the condenser or for louvers for intake and exhaust air for condenser cooling. But new concerns are introduced. These include finding a location for the compressor-condenser part and providing refrigerant piping and electric wiring from that section to the cooling coils and air handler.

When a suitable outdoor location is not available, the compressor-condenser part can be placed indoors. The arrangement is similar to that for a package unit installed in a basement. The major difference is the separation of the compressor-condenser part from the cooling coils and the provision of interconnecting refrigerant piping and wiring.

SYSTEMS IN CONJUNCTION WITH HEATING PLANT

If your home is heated by a warm-air furnace with a duct system, you may be able to adapt it for central air conditioning at relatively low cost. If you wish, however, you can install any of the separate cooling systems previously described.

Use of Existing Furnace and Ducts. One option is to install a cooling coil in the supply duct at the furnace. The compressor-condenser unit to which the cooling coil is to be connected could be placed in a convenient location, usually outdoors. The arrangement is like that of the split system, previously described, except that the blower and ducts used for heating can also be used for cooling. Some changes, however, may have to be made in some duct sizes, and register locations may have to be changed, requiring additional ducts.

Use of Existing Ducts Only. Sometimes, installation of the preceding system is not feasible. For example, it may be that the existing warm-air furnace cannot be fitted with a cooling coil. Or perhaps the existing blower, although adequate for heating, cannot be made to deliver the required amount of air needed for cooling. Nevertheless, if the existing ductwork is adequately sized or can readily be enlarged for cooling, the option of a central air-conditioning system is still open to you. You may be able to connect to the main supply and return ducts near the furnace a short length of duct containing a separate air handler and the cooling coils, bypassing the furnace (see Figure 8). Dampers are required in existing and new main supply ducts to prevent air from bypassing the heating or cooling unit, whichever is in use. The rest of the arrangement is like that of the preceding system.

HOW TO PLAN AIR CONDITIONING

If you have decided that you want to add a cooling system to your home, your first step in implementing this decision should be to decide whether you will air-condition the whole house or specific parts and about how much money you wish to invest in the installation. Next, make a tentative selection of the kind of system that would be suitable and convenient. Take into account your desires with respect to noise levels and esthetics. Also, consider the space problems that the selected system might pose. With this selection in mind, obtain a preliminary cost estimate to determine whether the cost of the installation would be within your budget. If it is financially feasible you can proceed with more detailed planning. Otherwise, you should investigate a less expensive installation.

When costs appear favorable, the next step is to draw floor plans of the house to the scale of $\frac{1}{4}'' = 1'\ 0''$ (see Figure 2). Lay out on these plans to scale the equipment in the selected locations and ductwork, registers, and louvers, if required (see Figure 3). Indicate needed dampers. Show the desired location of thermostats that are to be used.

The following steps, up to the requesting of cost estimates and bids, are explained in detail later: Select a condensing unit of adequate capacity. Estimate sizes of ductwork, registers, and louvers. Obtain cost estimates. If cost is acceptable, request bids for equipment and installation from at least two air-conditioning contractors. Don't forget to include associated electrical work when you compute costs and arrange for the installation.

ZONING

In planning the layout for air conditioning, you might find it necessary to install more than one system to provide nearly equal comfort conditions throughout your home. A house containing portions with considerably different cooling requirements should be zoned so that each portion with about the same requirements can be served by its own system. The importance of proper zoning cannot be overemphasized.

As an example, consider the main level of a ranch-type house, the floor plan of which is shown in Figure 2. Cooling requirements of all the rooms are about the same. As a result, air conditioning can be accomplished with a single system.

Assume now that this house has a basement with finished rooms that also are to be air-conditioned. Because a large portion of the basement is below grade, it requires much less cooling than the main level. If a single system were to be used for the whole house, the basement would be too cold when comfort conditions were maintained on the main level. Also, the main level would be too warm when the basement was made comfortable. Therefore, it is advisable to use a separate system for each level.

Similarly, a two-story house should be air-conditioned with two separate systems, one for the first story and one for the second. Here is why: At midafternoon on a mild, sunny day, the sun beating down on the roof will heat the second story, despite insulation. This level will require cooling. Yet, the first story will be comfortable without cooling. If a single system is used, an attempt to cool the second story will make the

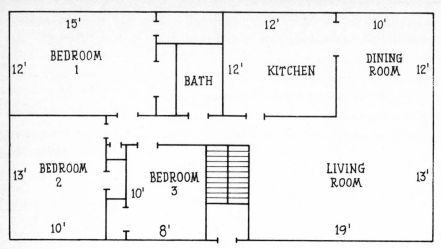

FIGURE 2. Plan of one-story house.

first level too cold. If the system were designed to maintain comfort conditions in the first story, the system would not operate, and the second story would remain too warm. So use of two systems is advisable.

WHAT SIZE OF COOLING UNIT TO INSTALL

The heart of any air-conditioning system is the cooling unit—the portion that produces the chilled air that cools the spaces in the home. In planning the system, you have determined the location of the unit or its components. You also must estimate its cooling capacity, or size. Before you can do this, however, you must first determine the cooling requirements of the spaces to be air-conditioned.

Table 1 provides an approximate but reasonably accurate means of doing this, as will be explained later. To be able to use the table, however, you must first become familiar with some terms and concepts used by air-conditioning manufacturers and installers.

Bear in mind that cooling is accomplished when the cool supply air mixes with the warm room air. The supply air extracts heat from the room air. The return air transports this heat to the cooling coils, where the heat is transmitted to the refrigerant and ultimately removed from the house. Thus, the cooling requirements of the home are met by providing cool supply air in adequate quantities. These quantities are measured in *cubic feet per minute,* abbreviated *cfm.*

Total supply air needed for an air-conditioning system, in cfm, is one way of expressing the required capacity of a cooling unit. The unit must be able to cool that much air if comfort conditions are to be maintained. Also, the fan or blower must be able to move that much air.

The heat that has to be removed from each room or from the zone to be cooled is measured in *British thermal units,* abbreviated *Btu.* Because heat removal is a continuous process, we must deal with the rate of heat removal, or the number of *Btu per hour.*

The total number of Btu per hour that a system is capable of handling is another way of expressing the capacity of a cooling unit. Sometimes, however, capacity is given in *tons.* One ton of refrigeration is the cooling effect obtained when 2,000 pounds of ice melts to water in 24 hours. One ton is equivalent to 12,000 Btu per hour.

For a typical home installation, you can convert the air requirements in cfm to Btu per hour or to tons, to obtain the capacity needed in a cooling unit. To obtain the tonnage capacity of a condenser, divide the number of cfm needed by 400. To obtain the capacity in Btu per hour, multiply the number of cfm required by 30.

Many manufacturers of residential air-conditioning equipment have standardized on air handlers capable of providing 400 cfm of supply air per ton of refrigeration capacity. Thus, a 2-ton system is equipped with an air handler rated at $2 \times 400 = 800$ cfm. A 3-ton system is provided with an air handler rated at $3 \times 400 = 1,200$ cfm, etc.

An exact calculation of the cooling requirements for your home most likely would indicate that more than 400 cfm per ton is necessary. In that case, if you installed a condensing unit that exactly matched your cooling requirements in tons, the associated air handler would not be capable of meeting air-delivery requirements. (This may not have a serious adverse effect on comfort conditions, because the relative humidity would be kept low even if room temperature cannot be lowered to the thermostat setting.) On the other hand, if you install an air handler capable of satisfying air requirements, the condensing unit will have excess cooling capacity. The system will not only be able to maintain desired room temperature but will also provide a lower relative humidity. Thus, when air requirements exceed 400 cfm per ton, as is likely to be the case, you should preferably select a unit that can meet supply-air requirements in cfm.

As an example, suppose a residence requires 3 tons of cooling and 1,600 cfm of air. The air handler usually matched with a 3-ton con-

TABLE 1. **Quantity of supply air, in cubic feet per minute (cfm), for cooling rooms of an average home**
(Based on 8-foot ceiling height and usual window areas)

| Room size, feet | With insulated walls and roof | | | | With uninsulated walls and roof | | | |
| | Space over ceiling air-conditioned | | Warm attic over ceiling | | Space over ceiling air-conditioned | | Warm attic over ceiling | |
	One wall exposed	Two walls exposed	One wall exposed	Two walls exposed	One wall exposed	Two walls exposed	One wall exposed	Two walls exposed
8 × 8	66	82	78	94	79	95	108	122
8 × 10	77	92	90	107	93	122	130	155
8 × 12	87	103	103	120	107	137	160	178
8 × 14	98	114	117	134	122	152	190	208
10 × 10	87	106	106	124	100	122	141	163
10 × 12	102	120	124	142	120	150	169	200
10 × 14	116	132	142	157	138	173	198	233
10 × 16	130	144	160	172	156	198	226	265
12 × 12	115	134	140	160	135	175	196	237
12 × 14	131	150	161	180	154	193	226	265
12 × 16	145	165	180	200	173	212	256	295
12 × 18	160	180	198	219	190	230	282	322
12 × 20	176	197	220	240	210	250	312	352
12 × 22	192	213	241	260	229	270	341	381

densing unit is rated at 1,200 cfm. A 1,600-cfm air handler, which would satisfy the air requirements of the residence, usually comes with a 4-ton condensing unit. This combination would be the better selection.

To aid you in selecting cooling-unit size, Table 1 gives the cfm of air required for some usual room dimensions. You can use the table even if a room does not have exactly the same size given in the table. If the dimensions are close, just pick the nearest larger room size given in the table. If the actual room size is considerably larger than those in the table, consider the room divided into two parts and treat each part as a separate room in using the table. For example, if you have a 22 by 16-foot room exposed to the outside on two sides, break it up into a 10 by 16 exposed on one side and a 12 by 16 exposed on two sides. Then, find the air, in cfm, required for each component from Table 1 and add the two tabulated values.

To illustrate the method of selecting a cooling unit, let us calculate the cooling requirements of the ranch-type house shown in Figure 2.

TABLE 2. Calculation of supply air needed for home in Figure 2

Room	Actual size, feet	Nearest size given in Table 1, feet	Number of exposed walls	Supply air required, cfm
Living	19 × 13	20 × 12	2	240
Dining	10 × 12	10 × 12	2	142
Kitchen	12 × 12	12 × 12	1	140
Bedroom 1	12 × 15	12 × 16	2	200
Bedroom 2	10 × 13	10 × 14	2	157
Bedroom 3	8 × 10	8 × 10	1	91
Total				970

We will assume that the house has been insulated. Therefore, in using Table 1, we will pick values from the left half. We will also assume that there is an attic above the ceiling that is not air-conditioned.

Calculations of the required air, in cfm, are tabulated in Table 2, using values obtained from Table 1. These indicate that a total of 970 cfm of air is required for the main level. The minimum capacity in tons of the condensing unit is found by dividing 970 by 400, to obtain 2.43 tons. The minimum capacity of a unit rated in Btu per hour is found by multiplying 970 by 30, to obtain 29,100 Btu per hour. These results provide a basis for selecting a unit.

If much cooking is to be done or if large groups are to be entertained, a 3-ton condensing unit, with a 1,200-cfm air handler, would be suitable.

But a 4-ton unit should not be selected for this residence. It would have too much capacity. Temperatures called for by the thermostat would be quickly met and the unit would shut down. This short cycling is not only inefficient but could result in periods of discomfort when the unit is not operating.

HOW TO DETERMINE DUCT SIZE

When your system requires the movement of air through ducts, you must determine not only the location of the ducts but also their sizes. The size of each duct is determined by the maximum quantity of air, in cfm, that must be discharged at its outlet. Thus, the size of a duct discharging air into a room depends on the amount of air dispersed by the room register at the end of the duct. If you proceed back along the duct toward the air handler, you will come to a point where another duct joins it. From there on back toward the air handler, a larger duct must be used. Its size is determined by the sum of the maximum quantities of air to be handled by each of the branch ducts. As each additional branch duct joins the main supply, the size of the supply duct must be increased to accommodate the air required by that branch. Finally, to obtain the size of the main duct, you must add the quantities of air discharged by every supply-air register.

Table 3 lists the maximum air quantities, in cfm, that different-size ducts are usually capable of carrying for air conditioning. This table is based on the assumption that the usual fans supplied by manufacturers of residential and heating equipment will be used.

To illustrate the use of the table, let us determine the duct sizes that would be required for the residence shown in Figure 2. We will assume that the air-conditioning system will include an outdoor condenser, an air handler hung in the attic, ducts for air distribution located in the attic, and ceiling diffusers to supply air to each room.

Figure 3 shows the floor plan of Figure 2 with the supply-duct runs imposed on it. The branches terminate in diffusers in the various rooms, and the amount of air, in cfm, discharged by each diffuser is also shown in Figure 3. These quantities were obtained from Table 2, previously

TABLE 3. Air delivery capacity of round and rectangular ducts

Round duct diameter, inches	Air quantities, cfm	Equivalent sizes of rectangular ducts, inches						
3	15	2 × 4	2½ × 3					
4	35	2 × 7	2½ × 6	3 × 5	4 × 4			
5	65	2½ × 9	3 × 7	4 × 5				
6	114	3 × 12	4 × 8	5 × 6				
7	160	3 × 15	4 × 11	5 × 9				
8	240	4 × 14	5 × 12	6 × 9	7 × 8			
10	420	4 × 24	5 × 18	6 × 19	7 × 12	8 × 10	9 × 9	
12	700	5 × 28	6 × 22	7 × 18	8 × 15	9 × 13	10 × 12	
14	1,050	6 × 30	7 × 25	8 × 21	9 × 16	10 × 13		
16	1,500	7 × 34	8 × 29	9 × 25	10 × 22	12 × 17	14 × 15	
18	2,000	8 × 38	9 × 32	10 × 28	12 × 22	14 × 19	16 × 17	
20	2,600	9 × 41	10 × 36	12 × 29	14 × 24	16 × 21	18 × 18	
22	3,400	10 × 44	12 × 36	14 × 29	16 × 25	18 × 22	20 × 20	
24	4,300	12 × 42	14 × 35	16 × 31	18 × 26	20 × 24	22 × 22	

calculated. Note, however, that the 240 cfm required for the living room is split up into two 120-cfm discharges. One of these is assigned to the dining-room diffuser to obtain better air distribution.

Table 4 lists the air quantities that each duct has to carry. For example,

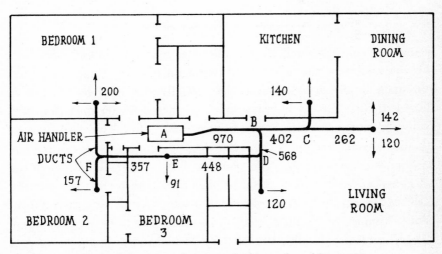

FIGURE 3. Duct runs drawn on the house plan of Figure 2.

the duct from F to Bedroom 1 should be able to carry at least 200 cfm, and that from F to Bedroom 2 at least 157 cfm. The duct from E to F then should have a capacity equal to the sum of these quantities: $200 + 157 = 357$ cfm. Similarly, with 91 cfm being discharged at E, the duct from D to E should be sized for $91 + 357 = 448$ cfm. And the main duct at the air handler must be capable of carrying all the air required, 970 cfm, as indicated in Tables 2 and 4.

With the air quantities to be handled by each duct known, we can now pick the required duct sizes from Table 3. If you plan on using

TABLE 4. Calculation of duct sizes for house in Figure 2

Duct section	Air quantity, cfm	Round duct diameter, inches	Rectangular duct size, inches
A-B	970	14	8 × 21
B-C	402	10	8 × 10
C-DR/LR	262	10	8 × 10
B-D	568	12	8 × 15
D-LR	120	7	8 × 6
D-E	448	12	8 × 15
E-F	357	10	8 × 10
F-BR 2	157	7	8 × 6
F-BR 1	200	8	8 × 7

round stovepipe or prefabricated, flexible, glass-fiber ducts, sizes may be obtained from the column for round ducts. For example, consider the main supply duct at the air handler. It must be able to carry at least 970 cfm. Table 3 indicates that a 12-inch-diameter duct can carry 700 cfm, and a 14-inch-diameter duct 1,050 cfm. The 14-inch duct should be used, because its capacity exceeds 970 cfm.

Suppose, however, that you plan on using rectangular ducts, made of either galvanized sheet metal or glass-fiber boards. In this case, you can use the equivalent-size columns of Table 3 for picking duct dimensions. Assume, for example, that all the ducts are to be 8 inches deep. Then, Table 3 indicates that an 8 by 21-inch duct should be used to carry the 970 cfm from the air handler.

Table 4 lists the duct sizes to be used for supply air distributed in accordance with Figure 3. These duct sizes are minimums. You may increase the size of small ducts if it will be easier for you to work with larger ducts.

Sizes of return-air ducts can be determined in the same way. These ducts must be sized to return to the cooling coils quantities of air equal to those supplied to the conditioned spaces.

Table 3 also can be used in the same way to determine if existing heating ducts will be adequate for cooling. Suppose, for example, you have an 8 by 16-inch heating duct (see Figure 4). For cooling, this

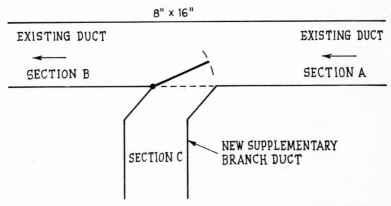

FIGURE 4. Connection of a new branch duct to an existing heating duct.

duct would have to carry 700 cfm. Table 3 shows that the minimum size that could be used is an 8 by 15. So the 8 by 16 is O.K. Now, suppose branch C, to carry 200 cfm, is to be installed for cooling purposes. Then, branch B will have to carry $700 - 200 = 500$ cfm. Table 3 shows that this duct also should be at least 8 by 15 inches. Again, the 8 by 16-inch heating duct is O.K.

DIFFUSERS, REGISTERS, GRILLS, AND LOUVERS

Diffusers and registers are used to disperse air into a space to be conditioned. For the purpose, they are equipped with dampers for adjusting air flow. Some are also provided with adjustable vanes for changing the flow direction.

Table 5 lists recommended maximum quantities of air, in cfm, to be discharged by supply-air registers and diffusers.

Return grills should be amply sized, for quiet operation. Table 6 gives recommended maximum quantities of air, in cfm, for various sizes of return grills.

TABLE 5. Air capacity of supply registers and diffusers, in cfm

One outlet dimension, inches	Second outlet dimension, inches (register or diffuser)							
	4	5	6	8	10	12	15	18
4	45	55						
6	65	85	100					
8	90	110	135	180				
10	110	140	165	220	275			
12	135	165	200	265	330	400		
14	155	195	230	310	390		625	
16	180	220	265	350	440			
18	200	250	300	400	500			900
20	220	275	330	445	550			
24	260	335	400	530	665			
30			500	665	830			

Screened louvers are used to discharge air to or withdraw air from outdoors (see Figures 5 and 6). Table 7 lists recommended maximum quantities of air, in cfm, for various sizes of louvers.

When louvers are used for air for a condenser, size is determined by the quantities of air to be handled by the condenser blower. Blower capacity, however, has not been standardized. It should be obtained from the condenser manufacturer. (A condenser designed for ductwork is equipped with a squirrel-cage-type centrifugal blower. A condenser with a propeller-type fan usually cannot be used with ductwork and must be located outdoors.)

Louver vanes usually are set at a 45-degree angle to keep out rain.

TABLE 6. Air capacity of return grills, in cfm

Grill size, inches	Air capacity, cfm
6 × 6	75
6 × 12	150
12 × 12	300
12 × 18	450
12 × 24	600
18 × 18	675
18 × 24	900
18 × 30	1,125
24 × 24	1,200
24 × 30	1,500
24 × 36	1,800

TABLE 7. Air capacity of discharge and intake air louvers, in cfm

Louver size, inches	Air capacity, cfm
6 × 6	200
6 × 12	400
6 × 18	600
12 × 12	800
12 × 18	1,200
12 × 24	1,600
12 × 30	2,000
18 × 18	1,800
18 × 24	2,400
18 × 30	3,000
18 × 36	3,600
24 × 24	3,200
24 × 30	4,000
24 × 36	4,800

When, however, a discharge louver (Figure 6) is placed above the intake louver (Figure 5), there is danger that the hot discharge air may be recirculated back to the intake louver. In such cases, the discharge vanes should be pitched only slightly toward the outside, so that the hot discharge air is blown away from the intake louver.

As may be seen from Figure 5, the effective opening of the louver is less than the cross-sectional area of the duct. If the intake louver has two vanes, the effective opening area is ½ the duct area. If the louver has three vanes, the effective opening area is ⅔, and with four vanes, ¾ the duct area. As an example, suppose a condenser requires 1,600

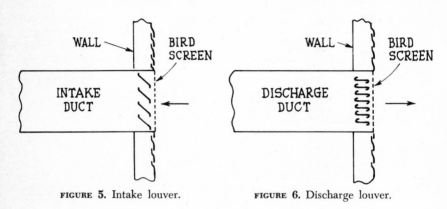

FIGURE 5. Intake louver. FIGURE 6. Discharge louver.

cfm of air. According to Table 7, a 12 by 24-inch louver could be used for discharge air. The size of the intake louver, however, would be influenced by the number of vanes it had. If that louver has three vanes, the 12 by 24-inch size could handle ⅔ of 1,600, or only 1,065 cfm. An 18 by 24-inch size, probably made with four vanes, would have a capacity of ¾ of 2,400, or 1,800 cfm. This size of louver would be satisfactory.

REFRIGERANT PIPING

When a package cooling unit is not used for your air-conditioning system, but instead the cooling coils are remote from the condenser, refrigerant piping must be run between these units. One pipe is needed to feed liquid refrigerant to the cooling coils; the other, called the *cold suction pipe,* returns the refrigerant to the compressor (see Figure 1).

Table 8 lists recommended sizes of copper pipe for various distances between cooling coils and compressor condenser for Freon-22.

You can use ordinary tubing or tubing prefilled with refrigerant. If you use ordinary tubing, the system, after being soldered, should be isolated from the compressor and expansion valves and then pressure-tested at about 300 pounds per square inch. If the system is perfectly tight, it is ready for the refrigerant, usually Freon-22. The system should be

TABLE 8. **Diameters of copper refrigerant tubing, in inches**

Cooling capacity, tons	Distances between cooling coils and condenser, feet					
	Up to 50		50–100		100–150	
	Liquid	Suction	Liquid	Suction	Liquid	Suction
2	$\frac{1}{2}$	$\frac{7}{8}$	$\frac{1}{2}$	$\frac{7}{8}$	$\frac{1}{2}$	$\frac{7}{8}$
2½	$\frac{1}{2}$	$\frac{7}{8}$	$\frac{1}{2}$	$1\frac{1}{8}$	$\frac{5}{8}$	$1\frac{1}{8}$
3	$\frac{1}{2}$	$\frac{7}{8}$	$\frac{5}{8}$	$1\frac{1}{8}$	$\frac{5}{8}$	$1\frac{1}{8}$
4	$\frac{5}{8}$	$1\frac{1}{8}$	$\frac{5}{8}$	$1\frac{1}{8}$	$\frac{5}{8}$	$1\frac{3}{8}$
5	$\frac{5}{8}$	$1\frac{1}{8}$	$\frac{5}{8}$	$1\frac{3}{8}$	$\frac{7}{8}$	$1\frac{3}{8}$

first evacuated of air with a remote vacuum pump, then charged with refrigerant. The manufacturer's instructions for charging should be followed in detail. When you use prefilled tubing, it should come with special couplings to fit the cooling coils and condenser for a "quick connect." Use of this tubing eliminates soldering, pressure testing, and evacuating.

SYSTEM INSULATION

In Chapter 3, the need for and benefits of insulation for the home were discussed. The same need and benefits apply also to some of the components of the air-conditioning system.

To prevent sweating and loss of cooling effect, all sheet-metal ducts that run through spaces not air-conditioned must be insulated. Glass-fiber ducts, however, are inherently insulated and generally will not require additional insulation. Any metal collars, though, if in nonconditioned spaces, must be insulated. For insulating sheet-metal ducts, standard 1-inch-thick glass-fiber blankets are usually satisfactory when securely wired after they have been wrapped around the ducts.

In addition, for the same reasons, refrigerant suction pipe must be insulated. Preformed sponge-rubber, composition, jacket insulation is available for all tubing sized for use as refrigerant suction pipe. The warm-liquid pipe need not be insulated. For an improved refrigeration cycle, however, you may run the liquid pipe in contact with the suction pipe and wrap the two pipes together in a single insulating jacket.

ELECTRIC WIRING

Most likely, your home will require additional electric wiring to accommodate the air-conditioning system. Most municipalities have laws that require that licensed electricians do all the wiring. Where no such law exists, it still is advisable to have the wiring done by a qualified electrician. In any event, whoever does the job should study carefully the instructions of the manufacturers of the equipment being installed. The following discussion is intended mainly to call your attention to some special electrical considerations..

Low-voltage Systems. One is the use of low voltage for controlling the operation of the system. Most manufacturers of residential air-conditioning equipment have standardized on 24 volts. Figure 7 is a schematic drawing of the usual wiring for a split system, where the cooling coils and the air handler are remote from the condenser.

Fan Controls. When you wish to use the existing fan in your heating system for cooling also, fan controls must be interconnected with those for the cooling units. The manufacturer of those units usually provides

a wiring diagram showing how they and the heater fan should be interconnected. An additional fan relay is usually required. It is generally
included in the wiring kit for the cooling units.

If you desire, you can have the present heating thermostat replaced
with a new cooling-heating thermostat and switch base. The wiring

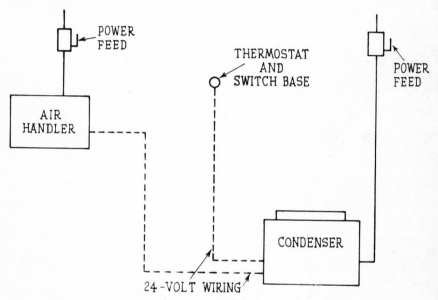

FIGURE 7. Electric wiring diagram for a split system.

hookup is a little more intricate, but diagrams and instructions are available with such thermostats when the thermostats are purchased.

Heating-cooling Damper Controls. Special wiring also is required if
dampers are to be automatically controlled when a heating plant and
cooling unit are connected to a single duct system, as shown in Figure
8. In the previous discussion, "Systems in Conjunction with a Heating
Plant," the need for dampers was pointed out. These dampers must be
positioned to prevent air from passing through the cooling coils when
heating is required. When cooling is required, they must be positioned
to prevent air from passing through the furnace. To operate automatically, the dampers can be motorized and controlled with a single toggle

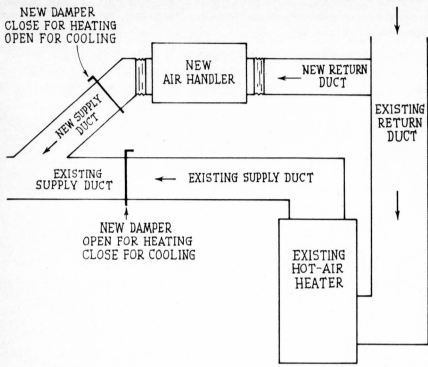

FIGURE 8. Addition of an air handler and new ducts to an existing heating plant.

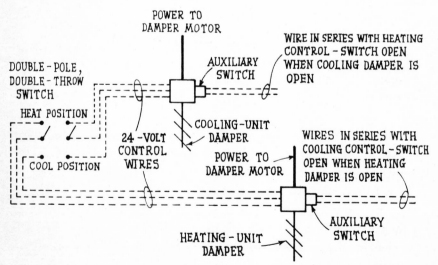

FIGURE 9. Wiring diagram for opening and closing dampers automatically for the swingover from heating to cooling, or the reverse.

switch. As shown in Figure 9, the controls can be wired so that only one damper is open, whereas the other is closed. Furthermore, the cooling system cannot operate when this double-throw, double-pole switch is in the heating position; nor can the heating plant operate when the switch is in the cooling position.

TYPICAL PROJECTS

In the following, some recommendations are made that you should consider when you air-condition your home.

Window Units. There are a number of reasons why you may choose window units, in addition to that of low cost. One important reason may be that you can install one or two units at a time as money becomes available for air conditioning. But remember that a window unit is intended to cool only the room in which it is installed.

If you air-condition only one or two rooms, the doors to them should be kept closed. Otherwise, the cooling effect will be lost to the nonconditioned spaces.

If the whole house is to be done with window units, there is a tendency to select oversize units. This may sometimes be done because a room is small and requires less cooling than the capacity of the smallest available window unit. Or a larger unit may be chosen because "it costs so little more." Or, for economy, three or four oversized units may be installed to air-condition a six-room house, with all doors left open. These oversize installations will result in short cycling of the units, with attendant inefficient operation and discomfort. Oversized units will quickly produce required temperatures in the rooms in which they are installed, and the thermostats will stop the cooling. Cooling will not start again until temperatures in those rooms rise again. Meanwhile, rooms without units, although getting some secondary cooling, will always be much warmer than the rooms with units. Attempts at cooling large, open spaces such as living room-dining room areas, with one unit also results in "too cold" complaints near the unit and "too warm" complaints away from the unit.

Following are a few general rules to keep in mind when attempting to cool a residence with window units:

1. Try to cool no more than about 300 square feet with one unit.
2. Try to reach no more than 18 feet with the unit fan.
3. For quieter sleep, make sure that bedrooms are provided with units with a two-speed fan, so that the lower speed can be used during sleeping hours.
4. Each unit should have its own thermostat.
5. Size of electric wiring should not be less than number 12. Provide individual grounded outlets. Note that larger units that require 220 volts must be provided with 220-volt outlets and plugs.
6. Carry out installation instructions supplied with each unit in detail. Pay particular attention to:
    a. Leveling
    b. Securing the unit to the surrounding structure
    c. Sealing the unit to the sash and having seals between the sash

Through-the-wall Units. Since through-the-wall units are basically window units, the preceding recommendations apply also to them.

The best location for a through-the-wall unit is 6 to 7 feet above the floor. Then, the cold air, which is heavier than warm air, is discharged high and cools the room as the air drops to the floor. Because many people object, for esthetic reasons, to units set high in a room wall, the units usually are placed under windows (see Figure 10), with the vanes of the supply-air grill set to blow the air above the horizontal.

When a through-the-wall unit is to be installed in a new wall, an opening to exactly fit the unit can be formed in the wall when it is constructed. For an installation in an existing wall, however, the opening must be cut out.

If the house has wood framing, chances are that, after the interior plaster or wallboard and exterior facing and sheathing have been cut away from the opening area, the exposed framing will look like that shown in Figure 1 of Chapter 4. If the unit is to be installed under a window, the studs under the window sill must be removed from the opening for the new unit. Then, the opening should be framed out with 2 by 4's, much as shown in the *A* part of Figure 10. The *B* part of Figure 10 shows how the unit would look in place in a cutaway view through the wall. Note the use of sealing material and flashing to keep out rain and outside air.

If a through-the-wall unit is set high in a wall, the procedure for cutting and framing the opening is much the same if the ends of joists are not supported on the wall plate above the opening. If they are supported on the wall plate above the opening, the joist ends must be supported temporarily while the new framing is being installed.

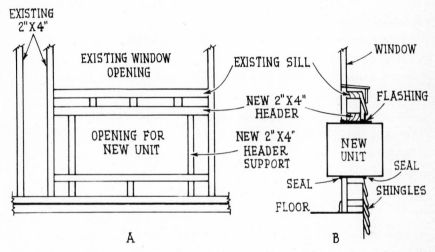

FIGURE 10. Installation of a through-the-wall unit under a window, with wood framing.

If the house has masonry bearing walls, the masonry above the through-the-wall unit will have to be supported on a lintel, as indicated in Figure 11. Steel angles can be used for the purpose. Before the lintel can be installed, the masonry above the opening will have to be supported temporarily or removed. In the latter case, if structural framing is carried by the masonry, the framing will have to be supported temporarily until the lintel has been installed and the masonry above the opening replaced.

The opening for the unit should be formed so that the sleeve into which the unit is set and that secures the unit to the wall pitches slightly to the outdoors. This will reduce the chance that rain running down the wall will seep under the flashing and into the interior. Be sure that the sleeve is properly secured to the wall.

Single-package Unit with Ductwork. A package unit used with ductwork is basically a large window unit but with connections for ducts. A low-voltage thermostat and switch base should be provided for control of the system from the living area.

ATTIC INSTALLATION. The package unit is set in the wall with the condensing section outdoors and the cooling section inside the house. For the purpose, an opening must be cut and framed out in the attic wall. The procedure is much like that for a through-the-wall unit (see Figures 10 and 11).

Access must be provided to the unit for periodic inspection, lubrication, and filter changing. Duct connections for supply and return air should be made so that they can be detached to enable a serviceman to slide the unit into the attic for servicing.

The condenser section is placed outdoors because outdoor air is needed to cool the hot refrigerant gas. To avoid such complications as the need to have duct sections removable and wiring connections flexible for ser-

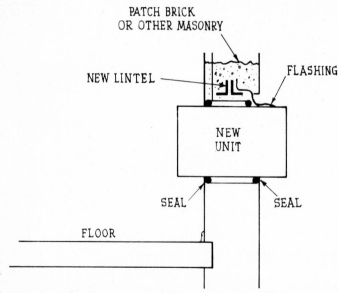

FIGURE 11. Installation of a through-the-wall unit in a masonry bearing wall.

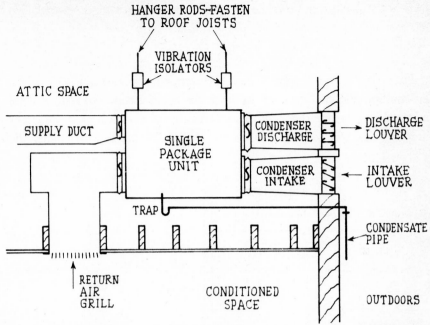

FIGURE 12. Installation of a single-package unit with ductwork in an attic.

vicing, however, it may be desirable to install the whole unit in the attic. In that case, duct connections are required for condenser-air intake and discharge, and louvers are needed in the attic wall (see Figure 12). Bear in mind the following recommendations:

1. Do not rest the package unit on the ceiling joists. Preferably, hang the unit from the roof rafters. Use hangers with rubber-in-shear or spring vibration isolators.

2. If ducts are made of sheet metal, isolate them from the package unit with canvas connections to prevent the ducts from transmitting vibrations and noise. Such connections are not necessary when glass-fiber ducts are used.

BASEMENT INSTALLATION. The procedure for a package unit in the basement is similar to that for a unit completely in an attic. The ducts carrying supply air for cooling the house can be run at or above the basement ceiling and up through the floor. They may terminate at floor level with grills that blow air upward. Or the ducts may extend into a closet or other dead space and terminate at a wall with a register that discharges the air into a room.

Split Systems. In a split system, the compressor-condenser part of the air-conditioning system is remote from the cooling coils. To reduce noise in the house when the compressor operates, the compressor-condenser unit may be placed outdoors on an elevated concrete pad, while the

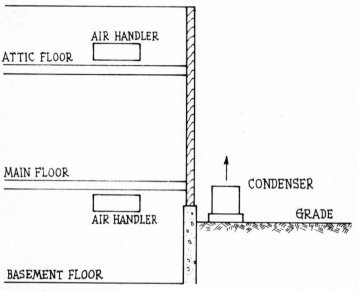

FIGURE 13. Split system, with compressor-condenser outdoors and air handler with cooling coils inside the house.

air handler with cooling coils remains indoors (see Figure 13). The separated units must be interconnected with refrigerant piping and electric wiring.

Systems Using Existing Furnace and Ducts. There are a number of precautions to be observed when existing fans, ducts, and registers are to be utilized for cooling:

When the amount of cooling required and quantities of air to be distributed are estimated, you should ascertain that the main duct and every branch duct is adequately sized to carry the required air.

Make sure that the fan or blower is capable of distributing this amount of air despite the added resistance of the cooling coil. (Many fans used for warm-air heating are belt-driven. They can be speeded up to overcome the coil resistance and also to take care of any additional air that may be required for cooling above that needed for heating. Usually, a large fan motor and motor pulley will suffice. Should the heating plant have a direct-driven fan, mounted on a motor shaft, the motor may be of multispeed design. If the motor is operating below top speed, arrange to increase the speed, if necessary. Check the motor nameplate for directions. If the motor already is at top speed and more capacity is needed, you may have to install a separate air handler.)

If the existing heating registers are set in the lower part of walls and air blows across the floor, the cold air, when these registers are used for cooling, will tend to stay near the floor. The upper part of the room may remain uncomfortably warm. For a satisfactory cooling system, the low wall registers may be replaced by a type that blows air upward. If feasible, additional ducts can be installed—in closets, for example—to provide registers up high for cooling. Registers set in the floor near exterior walls usually provide enough air velocity to mix the cold air with the room air at a higher level.

Systems Using Existing Ducts Only. Figure 8 shows an arrangement for using existing ductwork for heating and cooling, with a new duct and an air handler. The following precautions should be observed:

Do not attempt to heat the house with the furnace dampers closed, and do not attempt to cool the house with the air-handler damper closed. These dampers can be controlled automatically, as explained previously.

Systems with Supplemental Ductwork. When adding ducts for cooling purposes to existing warm-air ductwork, make sure that the main or branch duct to which the connection is being made can carry the additional air. In Figure 4, section *A* of the existing duct must be able to carry the air required of section *B* of the existing duct plus the air required of section *C* of the new branch duct. An adjustable splitter at the new connection is a necessity, to scoop in from the main duct the air needed in the new branch.

Index

A

Adhesives, 41, 125, 145, 146
  (*See also* Mastic)
Air conditioning:
  air handler for, 366, 368, 375, 376,
    394
  Btu of cooling, 375, 377
  capacity needed, 374–378
  capacity selection, 375–378
  cfm of cooling, 375–377
    tables, 376, 377
  components of, 366
  compressors for, 367, 394
  condensers for, 367, 368, 382, 392–394
  cooling coils for, 367, 368
  with cooling only, 366, 370, 371
  diffusers for, 381, 382
  distribution of, 366, 368–371, 378–384
    tables, 379, 380
  dust removal with, 368
  electric wiring for, 386–390
  fresh air for, 369
  grills for, 369, 382, 383
    table, 383
  with heating and cooling, 365,
    370–372, 394, 395
    damper controls for, 387–389, 395
  humidity control with, 368
  louvers for, 369, 382–384
    table, 383
  with package units, 366, 370, 371,
    389–394
  planning of, 372, 373
  purposes of, 365, 366, 368
  refrigerant for, 366, 367, 385
  refrigerant piping for, 367, 384–386
    table, 385
  refrigeration cycle for, 366–368
  registers for, 369, 381, 382, 395
    table, 382
  split systems, 371, 386, 387, 394

Air conditioning (*Cont.*):
  temperature controls for, 369, 387, 392
  tons of cooling, 375–378
  with wall units, 370, 390–392
  with window units, 370, 389, 390
  zoning of, 373, 374
Ash:
  classification of, 2
  grain of (figure), 10
  nailability, 29
  shrinkage, 5
  stiffness, 9
  uses for, 18–20
  warping, 7, 18, 19
  workability, 7
  (*See also* Lumber; Wood)
Attics:
  bathrooms in, 279, 286, 287
  ceilings for, 108, 109, 269, 270
  floor construction, 175–177, 270, 271,
    278
  floor resurfacing, 155–157, 173–175
  framing for, 269–271, 281, 283–285,
    287–289
  heating of, 275, 276
  insulation of, 57–59, 70–74
  remodeling: areas needed, 269
    around chimneys, 276–278
    heights needed, 269, 270
    planning of, 280–288
    purposes of, 262–266
  stairs to, 274, 275, 280–283, 285, 286
  ventilation of, 55, 56, 72, 74, 77, 267
  walls for, 127
  windows for, 267, 268

B

Bars, serving, 260
Baseboards, 33
Basements:
  ceilings for, 105–108, 195, 217, 218

397

HOUSE PLANS
Plates I to VI

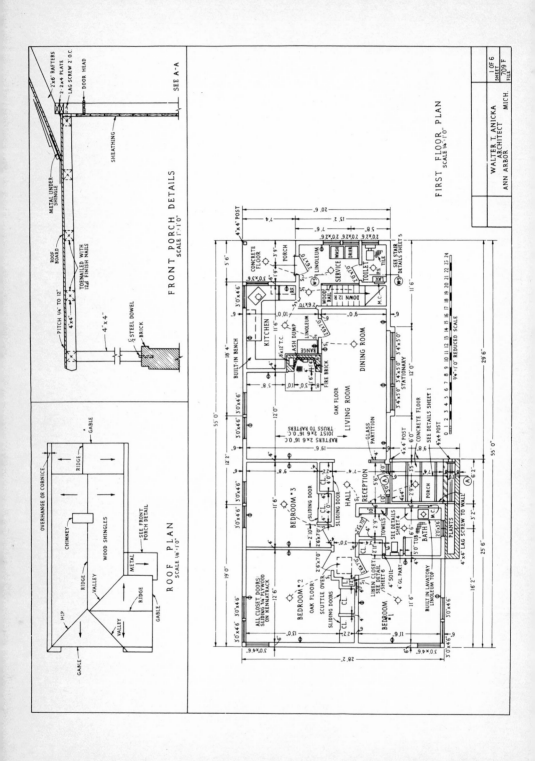

FRONT PORCH DETAILS
SCALE 1"=1'-0"

2x6 RAFTERS
2-2x4 PLATE
LAG SCREW 2' O.C.
DOOR HEAD

SEE A-A

METAL UNDER SHINGLE

SHEATHING

ROOF BOARD

TOENAILED WITH
12d FINISH NAILS

PITCH ¼" TO 12"

4"x4"

½ STEEL DOWEL

4" x 4"

BRICK

ROOF PLAN
SCALE 1/8"=1'-0"

OVERHANG OR CORNICE

RIDGE

GABLE

CHIMNEY

WOOD SHINGLES

SEE FRONT
PORCH DETAIL

METAL

RIDGE

HIP

RIDGE

VALLEY

VALLEY

RIDGE

GABLE

GABLE

VALLEY

GABLE

FIRST FLOOR PLAN
SCALE ¼"=1'-0"

WALTER T. ANICKA
ARCHITECT
ANN ARBOR   MICH.

1 OF 6
SHEET
709 F
FILE

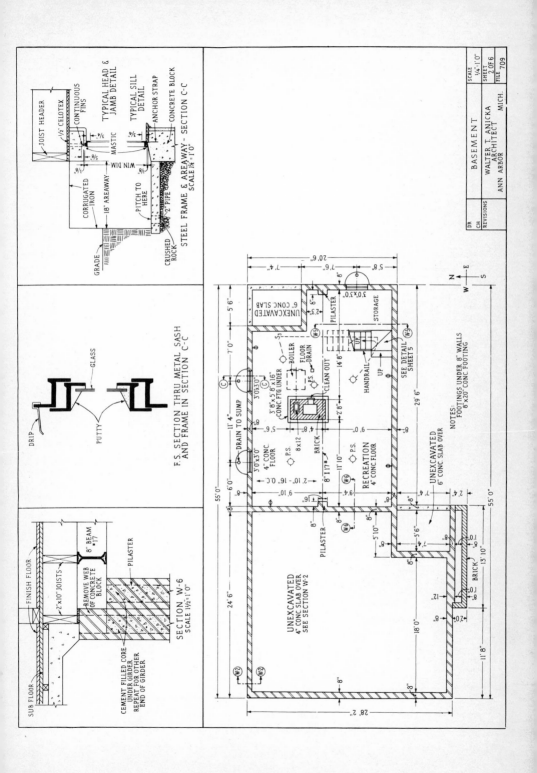

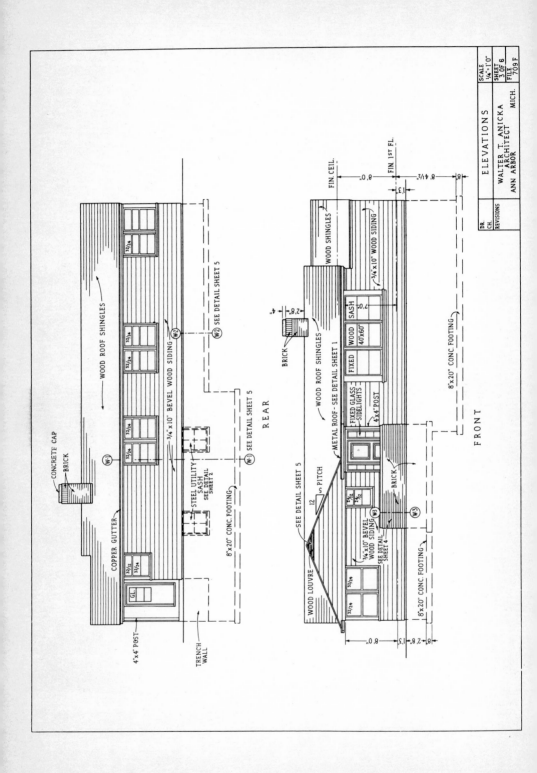

REAR

FRONT

ELEVATIONS

WALTER T. ANICKA
ARCHITECT
ANN ARBOR   MICH.

SCALE
¼"=1'0"
SHEET
3 OF 6
FILE
709 F

DR.
CH.
REVISIONS

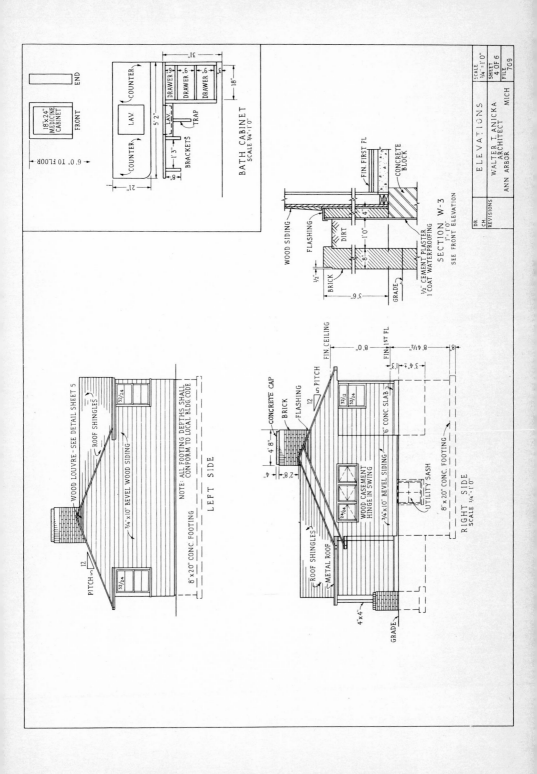

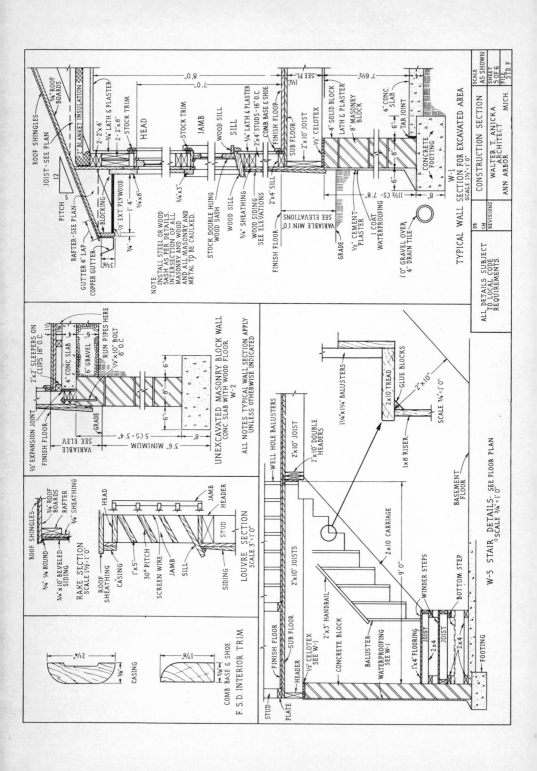

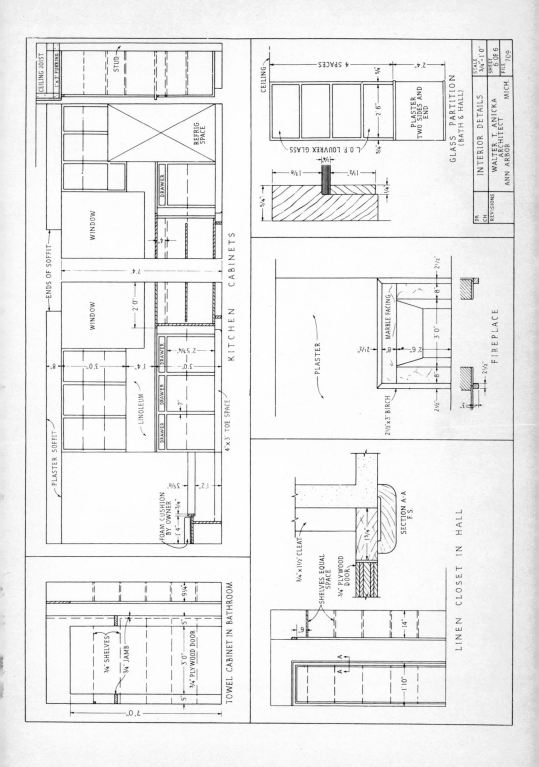